ANTICIRISE

Analysis for Strategic Warning

Cynthia M. Grabo

Edited by Jan Goldman

University Press of America,® Inc.

Lanham · Boulder · New York · Toronto · Oxford

University Press of America,® Inc.
4501 Forbes Boulevard
Suite 200
Lanham, Maryland 20706
UPA Acquisitions Department (301) 459-3366

PO Box 317
Oxford
OX2 9RU, UK

Library of Congress Control Number: 2004107091
ISBN 0-7618-2952-0 (paperback : alk. ppr.)

ISBN: 978-0-7618-2952-2

Contents

FOREWORD

At his confirmation hearing the present Director of Central Intelligence, George Tenet, defined his job by saying he was hired "not to observe and comment but to warn and protect." Unfortunately, few members of the Intelligence Community remain from among the corps of experts developed during the Cold War to provide warning. Warning is a skill unto itself, requiring an understanding of the attitudes and disciplines of potential adversaries as well as their capabilities, their history, their culture and their biases.

In an era of asymmetric warfare in which our national security and well being can be seriously threatened by hostile groups as well as nations, it is imperative that lessons from the past not be forgotten but be brought up to date and the discipline of warning reinvigorated. Warning intelligence differs significantly from current intelligence and the preparation of long-range estimates. It accepts the presumption of surprise and incomplete intelligence and requires exhaustive research upon which to build the case for specific warning. Relationships among events or involving the players may not be readily evident at first and initial signs often consist of fragmentary evidence, conflicting reports, or an absence of something. It is not merely a compilation of facts. It is an abstraction, an intangible, a perception or a belief.

While a specific methodology for developing warning may have been tailored to the needs of the Cold War, the same principles apply even to asymmetric conflict. This updated and revised edition of an earlier, classified publication is an excellent primer for both intelligence analysts and policymakers. Events have shown that accurate and timely warning has most often been produced by a minority viewpoint brought to the attention of decisionmakers in some way; it is not the product of a majority consensus.

In the rush to build new intelligence mechanisms to combat terrorist attacks and to provide warning for the homeland as well as for forces deployed, the nation and the Intelligence Community would be well served by reviewing this book to gain an understanding of what constitutes warning and how it is arrived at. As the author points out, "warning does not exist until it has been conveyed to the policymaker, and ...he must know that he has been warned."

All intelligence professionals and key policymakers must understand the principles outlined in this very relevant publication.

James Williams

LTG James Williams (Ret.)
Former Director,
Defense Intelligence Agency

EDITOR'S PREFACE

This book has a long history. It took over three years to write and over 30 years before it could be released to the public. During that time it was a classified government document distributed within the United States Intelligence Community. It has been recognized as one of the first government publications to focus specifically on the relationship between warning and intelligence analysis. In the aftermath of the 2001 surprise attacks on this country, this book is as relevant today as when it was first written.

Soon after the Japanese attack on Pearl Harbor on 7 December 1941, Cynthia Grabo, then a graduate student at the University of Chicago, was recruited as an intelligence analyst for the U.S. Army. Over the next 38 years, Ms. Grabo continued working as an intelligence analyst for the United States government. She observed from the inside such conflicts as the Korean War (in the early 1950s), the Cuban Missile Crisis (in 1962) and finally the Soviet invasion of Afghanistan (in 1979). Assigned to the interagency staff known as the National Indications Center, she was a senior researcher and writer for the U.S. Watch Committee throughout its existence from 1950 to 1975.

During this period Ms. Grabo became frustrated by what she perceived as several failures by the Intelligence Community to produce clear warnings for policymakers of impending hostile actions. She decided to do something about it. Using her observations, experiences and knowledge of warning intelligence, she wrote a chapter a month for over three years.

The result was the publication of a classified document that was circulated within the U.S. Intelligence Community. The first volume was released in June 1972, and it ultimately became three volumes and 800 pages. A second volume was published in 1972 and the final volume in 1974. The trilogy was given the title, *A Handbook of Warning Intelligence*.

The books became mandatory reading for intelligence analysts whose job it was to forecast threats to the United States. Soon other analysts within the U.S. Intelligence Community wanted a copy for their classified bookshelf. Unfortunately, except for the initial printing of a few hundred copies of the book, no other copies were published by the Defense Intelligence Agency. With the passing of the years, the book soon became forgotten.

In mid-2003 the Joint Military Intelligence College sponsored the re-issue of an unclassified text of this classic publication. However, with the fall of the Soviet Union, and to keep the book relevant to today's generation of intelligence analysts, the work was abridged and given a new title, *Anticipating Surprise: Analysis for Strategic Warning*. The book quickly regained acceptance by the U.S. Intelligence Community, its agencies and schools.

To generations of intelligence analysts, Cynthia Grabo has become synonymous with warning intelligence. After an almost 40 year career, she retired from government service in 1980. During that time she was awarded the National Intelligence Medal of Achievement, the Defense Intelligence Agency's Exceptional Civilian Service Medal, and The Central Intelligence Agency's Sherman Kent Award for outstanding contribution to the literature of intelligence.

The world is much different since this book was first written. Nevertheless, the fundamental principles of basic intelligence analysis and the ability to interpret information to policymakers in an expedient manner will never change. Regardless of the threat, it is the job of the Intelligence Community to warn and be heard. Although this book has a long history, unfortunately some of the same problems remain for a new generation of intelligence analysts.

Jan Goldman
Professor of Strategic Warning and Analysis
Joint Military Intelligence College
Washington, DC

INTRODUCTION

Some years ago, a group from several intelligence agencies was discussing the question of indications analysis and strategic warning. Reminded by an individual present that analysts who used indications methodology had correctly forecast both the North Korean attack on South Korea in 1950 and the Chinese intervention, a relative newcomer to the intelligence business said, "Yes, but you couldn't have done a very good job, because no one believed you." This bit of unintentional humor aptly describes much of the problem of warning intelligence. Why is it that "no one"—a slight but not great exaggeration—believes in the indications method, despite its demonstrably good record in these and other crises which have threatened our security interests? Can the reluctance to believe be in part from the lack of understanding of the nature of indications analysis or the lack of experience with "real" warning problems?

This work was originally written in the early 1970s as a classified textbook for intelligence analysts and their supervisors and for use in intelligence courses. It was the product of some twenty-five years experience with indications and warning intelligence from the analytic standpoint. So far as I know, it was the first and perhaps still the only effort by an intelligence analyst to bring together a body of experience on the warning problem and to set forth some guidelines to assist analysts and others involved in the warning process. The examples used in the text were drawn largely from World War II and the Cold War.

Within little more than the past decade, major and dramatic developments have significantly altered the nature of the warning problem. The first was the collapse of communism in the Soviet Union and the countries of Eastern Europe, the areas that had been the primary focus of collection and indications analysis for over forty years. The second was the emergence of terrorism—dramatically brought home on 11 September 2001—as a major, if not *the* major threat to our security. Obviously, these great developments have significantly altered the targets of collection and focus of analysis in the Intelligence Community.

A casual observer might conclude that these changes would render irrelevant the lessons of history, and particularly of the Cold War. But a more perceptive view will allow that the analytic problems of warning, and the nature of errors, are really little changed. Thus we continue to see the same types of problems:

- Inadequate perception of emerging threats, particularly those of low probability but potential great danger;
- A consequent inadequate collection against such threats;
- Breakdown of communication between collectors, analysts and agencies;
- Failure to heed the views of the minority;
- Vulnerability to deception.

Thus, it is my hope that the discussion of real examples will make some contribution to an understanding of warning intelligence, both within and outside the Intelligence Community.

I wish to express thanks to the Defense Intelligence Agency for printing and distributing the original and much longer version of this work; to the Joint Military Intelligence College for sponsoring this shorter unclassified version; and above all to Jan Goldman, professor in strategic warning and threat management at the JMIC, for his enthusiastic support and hours of voluntary work in preparing this text. Without his efforts, this work would never have seen the light of day.

Cynthia M. Grabo

Cynthia M. Grabo
January 2002

Chapter 1

THE ROLE OF WARNING INTELLIGENCE

GENERAL NATURE OF THE PROBLEM

Function of Warning Intelligence

Warning intelligence at the strategic level, or as it is sometimes called "indications intelligence," is largely a post-World War II development. More specifically, it was a product of the early days of the Cold War, when we began to perceive that the Soviet Union and other communist states were embarked on courses inimical to the interests and security of the Free World and which could lead to surprise actions or open aggression. Enemy actions in World War II, such as the Japanese attack on Pearl Harbor in 1941, had dispelled many of the conventional or historical concepts of how wars begin. The fear that America's enemies once again might undertake devastating, surprise military action—and without prior declaration of war or other conventional warning—had become very real. The advent of modern weapons and long-range delivery systems further increased the need for warning to avoid surprise attack.

Surprise military actions and undeclared initiation of wars are not, of course, exclusively a modern phenomenon. History has recorded many such actions, going back at least to the introduction of the wooden horse into the ancient city of Troy. The military intelligence services of all major powers during World War II devoted much of their time to collection and analysis of information concerning the military plans and intentions of their enemies in an effort to anticipate future enemy actions. Many of the problems and techniques associated with warning or indications analysis were recognized and practiced during World War II. The history of the war records some brilliant intelligence successes in anticipating enemy actions as well as such conspicuous failures as the attack on Pearl Harbor and the Battle of the Bulge.[1]

A coup in Bolivia, the outbreak of civil war in Lebanon, the kidnapping of a diplomat or member of the Embassy staff in Iran, terrorist attacks on U.S. installations in Guatemala, conflict between Pakistan and India, or the assassination of a chief of state anywhere—all these and other military and political develop-

---

[1]Editor's note: Although strategic warning is not a new concept, it has only recently become recognized as a *distinct function* of intelligence, in war and in peace, rather than a *definable type* of intelligence. Warning intelligence—although sometimes expressed in current, estimative or even basic (database-related) intelligence production—is distinguished by its purpose or function. Its function is to anticipate, insofar as collection and analysis will permit, what potentially hostile entities are likely to do, and particularly whether they are preparing to initiate adverse action. Generally, the consumer of strategic warning is a national-level policymaker. The warning function at the operational level typically centers around two individuals—a commander and his senior intelligence officer; at the tactical level, a "warfighter" is the consumer. Warning intelligence responsibilities are more diffused among intelligence producers and consumers at the strategic level, creating a challenging environment for the successful performance of this most important function.

ments are of strategic concern to the U.S. and it is a function of intelligence, insofar as possible, to anticipate such developments and to alert the policymaker to them. In this sense, "warning" could be said to be an almost unlimited responsibility of the intelligence system and to involve potentially almost any development anywhere in the world. The current intelligence process is involved daily with this kind of problem. At both the national level and overseas, operational centers, alert centers and watch offices are concerned with problems and potential crises of this type.

The term "warning intelligence" as it has been used since World War II, and as it will be used throughout this book, generally is restricted to: (a) direct action by hostile states against the U.S. or its allies, involving the commitment of their regular or irregular armed forces; (b) other developments, particularly conflicts, affecting U.S. security interests in which such hostile states are or might become involved; (c) significant military action between other nations not allied with the U.S., and (d) the threat of terrorist action.

Obviously, no absolute guidelines or directives can be laid down in advance as to when, or under what circumstances, any particular situation or area properly becomes a subject for warning analysis or judgments. Some events are demonstrably warning problems that gravely threaten U.S. forces or security interests, such as the Chinese intervention in Korea or the Cuban missile crisis. Other situations, although not involving such direct threats of confrontation for the U.S., pose grave risks of escalation or the involvement of other powers, such as a series of Middle East conflicts and crises. For many years Berlin and Southeast Asia were considered long-term, almost chronic, warning problems; while others, such as the Taiwan Strait, have occasionally become critical subjects for warning intelligence. Conflicts or potential conflicts between communist states—such as the Soviet suppression of the Hungarian revolt (1956), the threat of possible Soviet military actions against Poland, and the invasion of Czechoslovakia (1968)—also have been subjects for warning analysis and judgments.

Whether or not an immediate crisis or threat exists, however, the function of warning intelligence also is to examine continually—and to report periodically, or daily if necessary—any developments which could indicate that a hostile state or group is preparing, or could be preparing, some new action which could endanger U.S. security interests. It examines developments, actions, or reports of military, political or economic events or plans by our adversaries throughout the world which could provide a clue to possible changes in policy or preparations for some future hostile action. It renders a judgment—positive, negative or qualified—that *there is* or *is not* a threat of new military action, or an impending change in the nature of ongoing military actions, of which the policymaker should be warned. This will usually include some analytical discussion of the evidence to support the conclusion or warning judgment.

Thus warning intelligence serves both a continuing routine function and an exceptional crisis function. A daily or weekly routine report may say little and its final judgment may be negative. Yet it serves as a kind of insurance that all indications or possible indications are being examined, discussed and evaluated, and that significant potential indications have not been overlooked. In time of crisis or potential crisis, it serves (or should serve) the function for which it really exists—to provide warning, as clear and unequivocally as possible, of what the adversary is probably preparing to do.

Indicators and Indications

Dictionary definitions of the word "indicate" refer to something less than certainty; an "indication" could be a sign, a symptom, a suggestion, or grounds for inferring or a basis for believing. Thus, the choice of this term in warning intelligence is a realistic recognition that warning is likely to be less than certain and to be based on information which is incomplete, of uncertain evaluation or difficult to interpret.

An *indication* can be a development of almost any kind. Specifically, it may be a confirmed fact, a possible fact, an absence of something, a fragment of information, an observation, a photograph, a propaganda broadcast, a diplomatic note, a call-up of reservists, a deployment of forces, a military alert, an agent report, or anything else. The sole provision is that it provide some insight, or seem to provide some insight, into the enemy's likely course of action. An indication can be positive, negative or ambiguous (uncertain). Uncertainty concerning the meaning of a confirmed development is usually conveyed by such phrases as: "it is a possible indication," "it may indicate" or "it suggests." Uncertainty as to the validity of the information itself may also be phrased this way, or more accurately as: "if true, this indicates."

An *indicator* is a known or theoretical step which the adversary should or may take in preparation for hostilities. It is something which we anticipate may occur, and which we therefore usually incorporate into a list of things to be watched which is known as an "indicator list." Information that any step is actually being implemented constitutes an indication. The distinction between expectation and actuality, or between theory and a current development, is a useful one, and those in the warning trade have tried to insure that this distinction between indicators and indications is maintained. Many non-specialists fail to make this careful distinction.

Strategic versus Tactical Warning

The term *strategic warning* somewhat regrettably has no single, accepted definition. To those in the field of warning intelligence, strategic warning is generally viewed as relatively long-term, or synonymous with the "earliest possible warning" which the warning system is supposed to provide. Thus, strategic warning can be issued weeks or even months in advance, if a large-scale deployment of forces is under way, or the adversary has made known his political commitment to some course of action entailing the use of force. This judgment—of the probability of military action at some time in the future—is unrelated to the imminence of action. The judgment may be possible only when enemy action is imminent, but it may also be possible long before that.

Tactical warning is much more easily defined, although there is some shading in meaning. Strictly defined, tactical warning is not a function of intelligence (at least not at the national level) but is an operational concern. It is warning that would be available to the commander on the front line, or through the radar system or other sensors, which would indicate that the attacking forces were already in motion toward the target. In practice, the line between strategic and tactical warning may not be so precise. Many observers would consider that the Intelligence Community had issued tactical warning if it were to issue a judgment that an attack was imminent, particularly if this followed a series of earlier judgments that an attack was likely. When would warning of the Tet Offensive of 1968 have become tactical? Would a warning issued in the early afternoon of 20 August 1968 of a Soviet invasion of Czechoslovakia have been strategic or tactical?

WHAT IS WARNING?

Warning Is Not a Commodity

> *"Warning is an intangible, an abstraction, a theory, a deduction, a perception, a belief. It is the product of reasoning or of logic, a hypothesis whose validity can be neither confirmed nor refuted until it is too late."*

Warning is not something which the analyst, the Intelligence Community, the policymaker or the nation has or does not have. This frequent misconception is expressed in casual questions such as, "Did we have warning of the Soviet invasion of Czechoslovakia?" Particularly when taken out of context, this misconception has also appeared in high-level official documents, in such statements as "it cannot be concluded that the U.S. surely will, or surely will not, have strategic warning."

Warning is not a fact, a tangible substance, a certainty, or a provable hypothesis. It is not something which the finest collection system should be expected to produce full-blown or something which can be delivered to the policymaker with the statement, "Here it is. We have it now."

Warning is an intangible, an abstraction, a theory, a deduction, a perception, and a belief. It is the product of reasoning or of logic, a hypothesis whose validity can be neither confirmed nor refuted until it is too late. Like other ideas, particularly new or complex ideas, it will be perceived with varying degrees of understanding or certitude by each individual, depending on a host of variable factors to include: knowledge of the facts behind the hypothesis, a willingness to listen or to try to understand, preconceptions of what is a likely course of action by the adversary, cognizance of that state's objectives and its military and political doctrine, knowledge of history or precedent, objectivity, imagination, a willingness to take risks, time constraints, confidence in the person giving the briefing, or even the individual's health or what he had for breakfast. These and other factors may influence the receptivity to the message or idea.

There are times, of course, when the volume of evidence, the sheer number of facts pointing to the likelihood of war is so overwhelming and so widely recognized that the conclusion is almost inescapable. This was the situation which prevailed before the outbreak of World War II and particularly in the week immediately preceding it, when the man on the street if he had read the newspapers probably was as qualified to judge that war was imminent as were the heads of state. In such a case, everybody, in the strategic if not the tactical sense, "has warning."

On the other hand, it is readily apparent that virtually no one—and particularly not the people who mattered—"had warning" of the Japanese attack on Pearl Harbor, although the buildup of Japanese military power and Tokyo's aggressive designs in the Pacific were almost as well recognized as were Hitler's designs in Europe. In a series of lesser conflicts and crises since World War II warning rarely has been as evident as in August 1939. The odds therefore are that warning will remain an uncertainty in the years to come.

Warning Intelligence Is Not the Same As Current Intelligence

This opinion will no doubt surprise a lot of people who have come to look on warning as a natural byproduct or handmaiden of current analysis. Who is better qualified to detect and report indications of possible impending hostilities than the military and political analysts whose function is to keep on top of each new development and fast-breaking event? Is it not the latest information that is most needed to "have warning"?

The answer is both "yes" and "no." It is imperative that the analyst receive and track timely information which may be an indication of hostilities. The analysts who are to produce the intelligence needed for warning cannot afford to fall behind the flood of incoming information lest they miss some critically important item. Both the collection and the processing of information must be as current as possible. There have been instances in which even a brief delay in the receipt of information contributed to the failure to draw correct conclusions.

Nonetheless, the best warning analysis does not flow inevitably or even usually from the most methodical and diligent review of current information. The best warning analysis is the product of a detailed and continuing review of all information, going back for weeks and months which may be relevant to the current situation, and a solid basic understanding of the potential enemy's objectives, doctrines, practices and organization.

The latest information, however necessary it may be to examine it, will often not be the most useful or pertinent to the warning assessment. Or, if it is, it may only be because it can be related to a piece of information received weeks before, or because it may serve to confirm a hitherto uncertain but vital fragment of intelligence which the analyst has been holding for months. Only in rare instances where events erupt very suddenly (such as the Hungarian revolt in 1956) can indications or warning analysis be considered more or less synonymous with current analysis. Most crises have roots going deep into the past, much farther than we usually realize until after they erupt. Preparation for war or possible war often can be traced back for months once it becomes clear that a real threat exists, and pieces of information which appeared questionable, unreliable or even ridiculous when received will suddenly have great relevance to the present situation, provided the analyst has saved them and can fit them into the current pattern. Further, information which is months old when it is received (and therefore scarcely current intelligence) may be immensely valuable. An indication is not useless or invalid because it occurred months ago but you just found out about it today; it may help to demonstrate that the preparations for conflict have been far more extensive and significant than you had believed.

In normal times, the current analyst must cope with a large volume of material. In times of crisis, he may be overwhelmed, not only with lots of information but with increased demands from his superiors for briefings, analyses, estimates and the like. It is no wonder in these circumstances that he can rarely focus his attention on the information which he received last month or find the time to reexamine a host of half-forgotten items which might be useful to his current assessment. The night duty officer who may be the most "current" of all, will likely as not never even have seen many of the items from the preceding months which might be important now.

In addition, it may be noted that the weeks or days immediately preceding the deliberate or "surprise" initiation of hostilities may be marked by fewer indications of such action than was the earlier period. Or, as it is sometimes expressed, "warning ran out for us" ten days or two weeks before the attack occurred. Given this circumstance, the strictly current intelligence approach to the problem can be misleading or even dangerous. Since there are not many new indications to report, the current intelligence publication may convey the impression (and the analyst may actually come to believe) that the threat is somehow lessened, when in fact it is being maintained and may be increasing.

In time of approaching crisis when many abnormal developments are likely to be occurring, the current intelligence analysts more than ever will need the assistance of those with detailed expertise in basic military subjects, such as mobilization, unit histories, logistics, doctrine, a variety of technical subjects and other topics. Even such things as the understanding of terminology rarely if ever noted before may be of vital importance. It is a time when current and basic intelligence must be closely integrated lest some significant information be overlooked or incorrectly evaluated.

There is still another difference to be noted between the current intelligence and warning processes, and that is the nature and content of the reporting. Since the primary function of the current analyst is not to write warning intelligence but to produce good current items, he will necessarily have to omit from his daily reporting a large number of indications or potential indications. There may be a variety of reasons for this, such as: the indications are individually too tenuous or contradictory, some of them are not current, there are just too many to report them all, they don't make a good current story, and a number of them (sometimes the most important), are too highly classified for the usual current intelligence publication or the analyst is otherwise restricted from using them. Some persons looking into the warning process or attempting to reconstruct what happened in a crisis have initially believed that the best place to look is in current intelligence publications. While there is nothing wrong with this approach to a point, and providing the situation which prevailed at the time is understood, no one should expect to find the whole story or the real story of what was happening in these publications. To pick an extreme example, in the week between the discovery of Soviet strategic missiles in Cuba on 15 October 1962 and President Kennedy's speech announcing their discovery on 22 October, the Intelligence Community was precluded in all its usual publications from alluding to the discovery at all, and for obvious reasons.

The foregoing are some of the ways in which warning and current analysis and reporting are distinguished from one another or should be. It is in part for these reasons that it has been deemed prudent and desirable to have indications or warning specialists who, hopefully, will not be burdened or distracted by the competing demands placed on current analysts and will be able to focus their attention solely on potential indications and their analysis in depth. To accomplish this, these analysts must also recognize the value of basic intelligence and the importance of understanding how the adversary goes about preparing for action.

Warning Does Not Emerge from a Compilation of "Facts"

Warning does not arise from a compilation of possible or potential facts or indications, however useful these may be. It is not the intention of this study to downplay the importance of a diligent and imaginative pursuit of indications. They are the foundation on which warning is built. The more hard evidence available, the more valid and significant the indications, the more likely it is—at least in theory—that there will be warning or that we shall come to the right conclusions. It all sounds so simple, until we are confronted with a condition and not a theory. In retrospect, it all looks so clear.

In actuality, the compilation and presentation of facts and indications is only one step in the warning process, occupying somewhat the same place that the presentation of testimony in the courtroom does to the decision of the jury and ruling of the judge. Just as the seemingly most solid cases that are backed by the most evidence do not necessarily lead to convictions, neither do the most voluminous and best documented lists of indications necessarily lead to warning. On the other hand, a few facts or indications in some cases have been sufficient to convince enough people (or more importantly the right people) of impending hostilities or other critical actions. Some facts obviously will carry a lot more weight than other facts. The total number of different facts or possible facts will not be as important as the interpretations attached to them. Too many facts or indications may even be suspect—why should it be so obvious? There must be something more (or less) than meets the eye. A major portion of this treatise is devoted to a discussion of the relationship of facts and indications to warning, so these problems will not be elaborated here. Using the analogy with the courtroom case, however, there are several possible reasons why the mere presentation of facts or evidence or statements of eyewitnesses may not produce a convincing case for the jury or the presiding judge:

- The statements of the prosecution's key witness are disputed by other witnesses.

- An eyewitness is demonstrated to be of uncertain reliability or an otherwise questionable reporter of the "facts."

- Several other important witnesses have not been located and therefore cannot be interrogated.

- The evidence, although considerable, is largely circumstantial.

- The defendant has a pretty good reputation, particularly in recent years, and has not done such a thing before.

- There appears to be no clear motive for the crime.

- The jury, despite careful screening, has been influenced by prior coverage of the case in the newspapers.

- The judge, a strict constructionist, rules that certain important material is inadmissible as evidence.

Warning Does Not Flow from a Majority Consensus

Both because of the importance of warning and because the process will usually involve analysts (and their supervisors) in a variety of fields, a large number of people are likely to participate in some aspect of the production of warning intelligence. Insofar as various specialists are called upon to present their expert opinions or knowledge on various problems of fact and interpretation (such as "what is the maximum capacity of this railroad?" or "what is the estimated TO&E of the Soviet tank division?") this is obviously all to the good.

The Intelligence Community and the policymaker need every bit of expert advice, since no one would get along without such assistance. It does not necessarily follow, however, that the more people introduced into the warning process the better the judgment will be. Experience has shown that consensus of all the individuals who contribute to the analysis of the problem, together with their supervisors, those responsible for making estimates, and others who may have an interest is not more likely to be correct than the judgments of analysts who have had experience with other warning problems and are knowledgeable of all the available current information on the situation. Quite often the effect of bringing more people into the process is to dilute a judgment in the interests of compromise and unanimity.

Lamentable as it may be, the fact is that the most nearly correct judgments in crisis situations over a period of years often have been reached by a minority of individuals. This does not usually mean that one agency is right and others are wrong—it is not that political analysts will come to right conclusions and military analysts to wrong conclusions, or vice versa. What usually happens is that a majority in all agencies will likely be wrong. Thus the situation is not taken care of by the usual device of a dissenting agency footnote, since it will be a minority in each agency (not a majority in one) which will be in dissent.

Obviously, no one should say that because this situation has prevailed in so many cases that it will always be so. (It is the hope that this treatise in some small measure will help to remedy this and bring more persons in the Intelligence Community to an understanding of the warning process and the problems of analysis and interpretation.) It is important that those involved (and particularly policymakers) understand that this has been the case in the past. It is enormously important to the warning process that the views of the qualified and experienced minority be given an adequate hearing.

Warning Depends on an Exhaustive Research Effort

It is imperative to the process that the facts, including potential or possible facts, and other indications be most diligently and meticulously compiled and analyzed. *It is impossible to overemphasize the importance of exhaustive research for warning.* It is the history of every great warning crisis that the post-mortems have turned up numerous relevant facts or pieces of information which were available but which, for one reason or another, were not considered in making assessments at the time. This is separate and apart from the information in nearly every crisis which arrives just a little too late and which in some cases could have been available in time provided the substantive analysts, their supervisors, or their counterparts in the collection system had recognized a little earlier the importance of following up certain facts or leads.

All those associated with the warning business—from the lowest ranking analyst to the policymaker—should beware first and foremost of the individual who reaches judgments on a likely enemy action based on something less than the most detailed review of the available evidence which may be directly or indirectly related. Although this advice may seem so elementary that it may be taken for granted, the fact is that it cannot be taken for granted in crisis situations. Experience has shown that a large number of individuals—and often including those whose judgments or statements will carry the most weight—are rendering opinions in critical situations either in ignorance of important facts or without recognizing the relevance or significance of certain information which they may know. Indications and current analysts have been simply appalled, usually after the start of a crisis, to discover how many persons only slightly higher in the intelligence hierarchy were totally unaware of some of the most critical information from a warning standpoint. Intelligence analysts have been almost equally chagrined and remorseful to look back at the information which they themselves had available or could have obtained but which they just did not make use of or fit into the picture correctly.

How does this happen? How can the great machinery of U.S. intelligence, which is capable of spectacular collection and comprehensive analysis on many subjects, fail to carry out the necessary research in a warning situation? The answers are complex and some of the factors which contribute to this problem are dealt with in succeeding chapters. However, there are two obvious difficulties which arise and which may impede the research effort and the surfacing of the relevant facts.

The intelligence research system is set up primarily to analyze certain types of information known as intelligence "disciplines" and on which there is a more or less continuing flow of material, to include order-of-battle, economic production, weapons developments, and foreign policy to name a few. In crisis situations, great volumes of new material may suddenly be poured into the system. In order to cope, agencies often set up special task forces, and analysts work overtime in an attempt to cover every aspect of the problem. Nevertheless, it is very difficult in such circumstances to insure that some items are not overlooked, even when their relevance or significance is readily recognizable. It is not surprising that some items of potential interest may be set aside. As a developing crisis progresses, a geared-up collection system produces volumes of material for the analyst. A tenfold increase in items which the analyst should do something with, and that might be important, is by no means unusual. Analysts, often close to exhaustion, may recall items which they know are related to their current work, or they may be acutely aware of some urgent research, or papers which should be written, but they literally cannot find the time or energy to do it. Even worse, the analyst may not have the time to contact or even learn of the existence of other analysts or collectors who might have some additional information or who might already have done some research which would assist him. When it is most needed, communication may break down for sheer lack of time.

Even more insidious may be the less obvious impending crisis, where the interrelationship of developments is not readily apparent, and particularly where two or more major geographic areas may be involved. In such cases, the difficulties of conducting research are greatly compounded when items from two different areas, particularly if they seem relatively obscure or questionable at the time, may not be brought together at all. Their interrelationship is not detected until well along in the crisis, if at all, and only retrospective analyses will bring out the relevant information.

The foregoing generalities are well demonstrated in two major crises, the Soviet invasion of Czechoslovakia in 1968 and the Cuban missile crisis in 1962.

In the Czechoslovak situation, the Intelligence Community had a tremendous wealth of information, much of it highly reliable and valid, on both the political and military developments which led up to the invasion. Yet a number of important pieces of information that were extremely relevant to assessing Soviet intentions apparently were never reported to the higher officials of the Intelligence Community, let alone the policymaker. One reason for this (although fundamental errors in judgment were probably a more important reason) was the sheer volume of material which was received. It was impossible to report everything, and in the selection process some critical indications did not make the grade.

In the Cuban missile crisis, on the other hand, the Intelligence Community was confronted with a series of anomalies in Soviet behavior beginning in early 1962 which raised tantalizing questions in the minds of perceptive analysts but whose relationship to Cuba was only to become apparent months later. Almost to the time that the strategic missiles were finally detected in Cuba, two separate groups of analysts (a Soviet-Berlin group and a Latin American group) were conducting largely independent analysis, which for the most part failed to recognize that the apparent Soviet expectation of a settlement of the Berlin problem that year might in some way be related to forthcoming developments in Cuba. Thus much of the basic research which might have connected these developments was not done until after the resolution of the crisis. Only in retrospect was it apparent that the USSR's announcement of the extraordinary raising of combat readiness of Soviet forces in September probably was timed with the arrival of the first strategic missiles in Cuba. Much of the research on the likely areas and possible nature of Soviet military activity in Cuba was done by the Latin American group on a crash basis in the week between the discovery of the missiles and the President's announcement of their discovery.

It is impossible, in a brief discussion such as this, to develop examples that sufficiently stress the importance of research to the warning process. There are many reasons why warning fails, or is inadequate, and it would be unfair to single out the failure by analysts to initiate and produce the requisite research as the major cause. In many cases, it may not be the analyst but rather his superior or the system itself which is primarily at fault. Nonetheless, whatever the basic causes or extenuating circumstances, insufficient research or the failure to bring together into a meaningful and coherent pattern all the relevant intelligence must rate as a major cause of inadequate warning. The indications analyst, and others associated with the warning procedure, should never take it for granted that others know all the information available or have truly understood the facts and their implications.

The greatest single justification for the existence of separate indications offices or the employment of warning analysts is that they are devoting their full time to research in depth without the distraction of having to fulfill a number of other duties. The warning analyst should never lose sight of the fact that this is his raison d'être. It is difficult enough to come to a sound warning judgment when all the facts have been considered; it may be impossible without it.

Warning Is an Assessment of Probabilities

Rarely are impending hostilities so evident, or the intentions of an aggressor so unmistakable, that timely warning is a virtual certainty or that everyone "has warning." It is likely that there will be some degree of uncertainty concerning the plans or intentions of the adversary even when a great amount of information is available and the collection effort has functioned extremely well. The amount of uncertainty will be considerably increased when information is limited, questionable (as to its validity or interpretation), or if there are significant delays in the receipt of material. At worst, there may be insufficient factual data even to raise serious questions about whether some aggressive action may be planned.

Although the foregoing is probably generally accepted in theory—and papers on the warning problem have repeatedly cautioned intelligence officials and policymakers alike not to expect certainty in warning—there is often a tendency to forget this important point when the situation arises. Particularly because it is so important to make the right decision or right response in the face of threatened aggression, the military commander or policy level official more than ever wishes a judgment of certainty from the intelligence system—yes, the adversary is, or no, he is not planning to attack. The official may press the intelligence system to come to a positive judgment despite the inherent uncertainties in the situation, or on the other hand, demand a degree of "proof" which is absolutely unobtainable.

Now it is, of course, impossible to prove in advance that something is going to happen, when that something is dependent on the decisions and actions of people rather than the laws of nature. It could not have been "proved" in the last week of August 1939 that war was imminent in Europe, even though nearly everyone recognized this to be so, but it could be described as a development with a very high probability, or near certainty.

In contrast, what was the probability that the Japanese would attack Pearl Harbor, that North Korea would attack South Korea in June 1950, that the East Germans would close the Berlin sector borders (and subsequently erect the Berlin wall) in August 1961? The probability of course was actually very high; it was just that we did not know this. History shows that these occurrences in effect were considered by us to be relatively low probabilities at the time—that is, as evidenced by the lack of preparation against these contingencies, neither the intelligence system nor the policymakers considered it very likely that these would occur. We were "surprised," and, at least in the first instance, disastrously so. Yet, in retrospect, it can be demonstrated at least to the satisfaction of some that none of these events was all that improbable; they were at least good possibilities, or contingencies which should have been given more consideration than they were.

Some of the factors in assessing probabilities and the related problem of intentions versus capabilities are discussed in this book. Here are some guidelines for this important problem:

- In any potential warning or crisis situation, it is desirable, if not essential, that the intelligence system attempt to come to as realistic an assessment as possible of the probabilities of hostile action. Not only is the end assessment of value but the mere exercise of attempting to judge probabilities will bring out many useful facts, possibilities, precedents and viewpoints which might otherwise be ignored or overlooked.

- A knowledge of history, precedent and doctrine is extremely useful in assessing probabilities; and the citing of such precedents not only may bolster a case but also may tend to make the timid more willing to come to positive judgments. It is very important in reaching judgments to recognize the limits of our knowledge and collection capabilities and not to expect the impossible.

- Policymakers must recognize that warning cannot be issued with absolute certainty, even under the best of circumstances, but will always be an assessment of probabilities. They must realize that they

> "Policymakers must recognize that warning cannot be issued with absolute certainty, even under the best of circumstances."

will usually have to accept judgments that are less firm, or based on less hard evidence than they would wish, but that such types of assessments should be encouraged rather than discouraged.

Warning Reaches a Judgment for the Policymaker

"Warning does not exist until it has been con-
veyed to the policymaker, and he must know
that he has been warned."

It is an axiom of warning that *warning does not exist until it has been conveyed to the policymaker, and that he must know that he has been warned.* Warning that exists only in the mind of the analyst is useless. He must find the means to convey what he believes to those who need to know it. From the policy level, it is this factor probably more than any other that distinguishes warning intelligence from all other intelligence. The policymaker can and does get along without a vast amount of information which is compiled by the Intelligence Community. Some officials more than others will be receptive to intelligence information and will seek to learn details on such subjects as order-of-battle, weapons, internal political developments, economic plans and so forth. By and large, considering their numerous responsibilities, most policy officials are surprisingly well informed on the details of many subjects. For the most part, however, that which they are shown will be fairly carefully screened and condensed to the essentials which they most need to know, unless there is some particularly critical subject of national priority.

Not so in the event of an impending crisis which may involve the security interests of the country or our allies or which could entail a commitment of U.S. forces. It is essential that the possibility of such a development be clearly, and often repeatedly, brought to the attention of the policy official as the situation develops and that he be left in no doubt as to the potential gravity of the situation or what it might entail for national policy. In these circumstances, more rather than fewer facts, specific rather than generalized assessments, clear and realistic descriptions of the various alternatives rather than vague possibilities, and firm and unequivocal statements of the adversary's capabilities and possible or probable intentions are required.

Intelligence writers and briefers must remember that policy officials are extremely busy, and that assessments which carry no clear or explicit warning of what the adversary is likely to do may fail to convey the writer's beliefs. Assessments which state that the adversary can do such-and-such if he chooses or decides to do so, can convey a sense of uncertainty or even reassurance that no decisions have yet been reached, when in fact the bulk of evidence is that the adversary probably has already decided to do it. Phrases suggesting ominous possibilities which are buried in the texts of long factual discussions do not provide much warning to the policymaker who may have had time only to read the first paragraph. It is not unusual for an agency seeking to demonstrate in retrospect what a fine job of reporting it did on some subject to cull such phrases from its publications for a period of weeks. Taken in isolation or out of context, they may indeed present an ominous picture, but their impact will have been lost unless they were singled out and repeatedly emphasized at the time so that policy officials could not have failed to get the message.

A distinguished supervisor in the field of political intelligence observed many years ago that, no matter what went wrong, it was always the fault of intelligence. When disaster struck, the analyst might remind the policy official that he had been warned of the possibility or that it had been mentioned this might happen in several briefings in the past month. And he would reply, "Well, you did not say it often enough, or loud enough."

Where warning is concerned, intelligence must be sure that it is saying it often enough and loud enough. It cannot assume that, because it issued a qualified warning last week, it is unnecessary to repeat it this week. Warning has failed more than once simply because what the analysts really thought, and were saying to one another, never was put into print. Or, if it was, it was so caveated in "coordination" or by a series of editors that what the analyst meant to convey was lost. When military action is threatened, it is not time to mince words. If the policymaker has not gotten the message, it is quite likely not his fault that it was never made clear in the first place.

Warning Produces a Conviction That Results in Action

We will assume now that the intelligence system has performed commendably; it has collected the data, it has done the exhaustive research required, it has come to a judgment that a military attack is probable, and it has conveyed this judgment to the policymaker in both its estimative and warning publications. And what is the purpose of all this? The purpose is to enable the policymaker to make the best possible decisions in the light of the facts and judgments sent to him, and if needed to take military and political actions to counter the threatened attack. If he is not convinced, or for some reason cannot or does not take the necessary action, the intelligence effort will have been in vain. Troops caught in an offensive which was predicted by intelligence but ignored by the commander are just as dead as if the warning had never been issued. In these circumstances, no matter how brilliant the intelligence performance, the nation will have failed if no action has been taken. This is the ultimate function of warning.

It would be rare, although perhaps not unheard of, for intelligence to issue an unequivocal warning which would go totally unheeded by a commander or policy official. A more likely circumstance is that the warning is not explicit or clear enough (see preceding sections) or that there is a serious misjudgment of either the timing, location or nature of the attack. In any case, assuming action could have been taken to avert disaster and was not, there has been a combined failure of intelligence and command or policy. A more frequent situation in recent years has been that the policymaker makes his own intelligence, perhaps because he is dissatisfied with or distrustful of the impersonal machinery of intelligence, or perhaps simply because intellectual curiosity drives him to want to know more first-hand. This self-generated intelligence may have its advantages, in that it is immediately responsive to policy needs, although it is clear that there could also be dangers in this. It does appear that actions have been taken at the policy level to which intelligence contributed little directly, or that policymakers have run ahead of the formal processes of intelligence in taking action to forestall possible threatened actions of adversary or potentially hostile states.

Now, not all threatened military actions are a potential threat to U.S. security interests. Neither the Soviet suppression of the Hungarian revolt in 1956 nor the invasion of Czechoslovakia in 1968 posed any military threat to the U.S. or NATO, and no military actions were required or even desirable on our part. Politically, however, it would have been nice to have had a little wider understanding of the likelihood of these actions, particularly the invasion of Czechoslovakia, which caused a fair amount of concern in NATO.

Regardless of how intelligence and policy function in relation to one another, or how dependent or independent the policy level may be, the important thing in the end is that appropriate action is taken, when needed, to protect the interests of national security and the security of our allies. Without this, the warning function of intelligence will have failed no matter how brilliant the collection and analytical effort may have been.

Illustration of the Foregoing Principles

Some of the foregoing principles may be illustrated by the Chinese intervention in Korea in October-November 1950. This event is a classic example of the nature of the warning problem. Chinese Communist forces were first detected in Korea on about 26 October. They launched their massive offensive on 26 November.

American military officers and analysts in Korea in the fateful month of November have said, "Why of course we had warning. Our forces were in contact with the Chinese. We had prisoners. We had identified the units." The military analyst will look back at the voluminous reporting on the buildup of Chinese forces in Manchuria and on the numerous reports and indications of preparations for war throughout the Chinese mainland. The analyst will recognize that the Intelligence Community was slow in accepting the buildup and that the total Chinese strength was underestimated. Nonetheless, a substantial buildup was accepted both in Washington and by General MacArthur's headquarters. He would likely say, "Of course we had military warning." Political analysts will recall that Chinese officials summoned the Indian Ambassador in Beijing on 3 October and told him that Chinese forces would enter Korea if U.S. and UN forces crossed the 38th Parallel in Korea. The analyst will look at the sharp change in the Chinese and international Communist propaganda line in early November to an all-out support of the North Korean cause. And the analyst will say, "What more political warning could we have expected?"

The warning analyst will note that President Truman and General MacArthur at their meeting on Wake Island on 15 October both brought incorrect assessments (that is, that Chinese intervention in Korea was unlikely.) But the analyst also will reexamine the judgment reached on 15 November by the interagency intelligence committee then responsible for reaching an assessment of enemy intentions. And the analyst will conclude that the judgment reached by that time (or 10 days before the Chinese onslaught) did provide substantial warning of the likelihood of major Chinese intervention—a warning perhaps not as clear or loud or unequivocal as it might have been but still a substantial warning.

The analyst will ask, "What happened to this? Who read it? Who believed it? Was most of the Intelligence Community in accord with this judgment? Were the Joint Chiefs of Staff and the President convinced?" No one, then or now, can really be able to say who read it, how many believed it, or what weight it carried. But they will concur that "a warning" at least was issued.

Why then, is the Chinese intervention in Korea universally regarded as a great intelligence failure which contributed to a near military disaster? It is because *no action was taken* on any of this intelligence or judgments, because no orders were issued to halt the precipitate advance of U.S. and Allied forces toward the Yalu. No measures were initiated to prepare military defenses against even the possibility of a major Chinese onslaught. It did not matter, it must be emphasized, how much intelligence was available or who issued a warning judgment unless it resulted in such positive action. A single staff officer, if his warning had carried conviction at the right time and to the right person (in this case, to General MacArthur), could have significantly changed the course of events regardless of any other judgments which might have been made by the Intelligence Community in Washington.

INTENTIONS VERSUS CAPABILITIES

A time-honored military precept, still quoted with some frequency, holds that intelligence should not estimate the intentions of the adversary, but only his capabilities. Sometimes this has been extended to mean that we can judge his capabilities but that we *cannot* judge his intentions.

The precept that intelligence properly deals only with, or should only assess, capabilities derives, of course, from the requirements of the field commander. Confronted with military forces which may attack him or which he is preparing to attack, it is essential that the commander have the most accurate possible assessment of the capabilities of enemy forces and that he prepare his defenses or plan his offense against what the enemy is capable of doing rather than attempting to guess what he might do. There is no doubt that battles and probably even wars have been lost for failure to have followed this principle and that the commander who permits his judgment of what the adversary intends to do override an assessment of what he can do is on a path to potential disaster. (The near disaster to U.S. and Allied forces in the Chinese Communist offensive in Korea in November 1950 was directly attributable to the failure to follow this principle. The Allied campaign proceeded without regard to the capability of the Chinese to intervene and there were no defensive preparations against this contingency, since it was presumed, erroneously, that the Chinese did not intend to intervene.)

The validity of this concept, however, does not mean that intelligence at the national and strategic level should be confined to the assessment of capabilities. For the fact is that intelligence at all levels, but particularly that which is prepared for the guidance of policy officials, is expected also to deal with the question of intentions. Not only the executive branch of the government, but also the Congress and the public at large, believe that the function of intelligence is to ascertain what our enemies and even our friends are going to do, not only what they can do or might do. And, considering the cost of intelligence today in money and personnel and the potential consequences of misjudgment of intentions, it is hard to argue that the nation is not entitled to expect this.

Nearly all inquiries into the presumed failures of intelligence or criticisms of its competence are focused on why forewarning was not provided that something was going to happen. Rarely does the policymaker or the congressional committee complain that intelligence failed to make an adequate assessment of enemy capabilities, even when this in fact may have been the case. The criticism almost invariably is: "You did not tell me this was going to happen. We were not led to expect this and were surprised." Or, "You mean for all the millions that were spent on collection, you were not able to tell us that this was likely to occur?" Protests that officials had been warned of the possibility or that the capability had been recognized are not likely to be very satisfactory in these circumstances. Like it or not, intelligence is seized with the problem of intentions. However brilliant its successes may be in other ways, the Intelligence Community's competence often will be judged in the end by the accuracy of its forecasts of what is likely to happen. And indeed this is what the warning business is all about.

Let us now examine the validity of the idea that we can judge military capabilities with a high degree of accuracy, but that intentions can never be forecast with any degree of certainty and that it is therefore unreasonable to expect the intelligence process to come to judgments of intent. How can the analyst tell that something is going to occur before it happens? Is this not demanding the impossible? On the other hand, the analyst can easily tell how many troops there are deployed in a specific area and what they are capable of doing against the opposition.

Just how such concepts have gained prevalence or are seemingly so widely believed is a mystery. For in practice, as most experienced military analysts can testify, it may be very difficult to come to accurate assessments of the military capabilities of any state, even when information is readily obtainable. And when the analyst is dealing with denied areas, where elementary military facts are never publicly revealed and the most rigid military security is maintained, it is often extraordinarily difficult to come to accurate estimates of such basic factors as order-of-battle or the strength of the armed forces. Given enough time—and this often has been measured in years, not months or weeks—intelligence has usually been able to come to fairly accurate assessments of the order-of-battle of most foreign countries. Total strength figures have proved extremely elusive, and the seeming certainty on such matters reflected in estimates over a period of years is of course no guarantee whatever that the estimate was accurate. And we are speaking here of situations where military strengths and dispositions have remained relatively static. Given a situation where changes are occurring, and particularly when mobilization of several units is occurring or large deployments are under way in secrecy, estimates of capabilities as measured in terms of total force available may be very wide of the mark.

As a general rule, although not always, intelligence will underestimate the strength of forces, particularly ground forces, involved in a buildup and sometimes will greatly underestimate the scale of mobilization and deployments. In nearly all cases of recent years where subsequent proof was obtainable, this has been the case. The scale of the North Korean buildup for the attack on South Korea in June 1950, although recognized as formidable, was underestimated. Chinese Communist deployments to Manchuria prior to the offensive in Korea in late November 1950 were probably at least double that of most estimates at the time. The extent of North Vietnamese mobilization in 1965-66 was considerably underestimated. The Soviet response to the Hungarian revolt in late October 1956 was a precipitate deployment of units into that country which defied order-of-battle or numerical analysis at the time, and even today the total Soviet force employed never has been completely established. Similarly, we do not know how many Soviet troops were moved into Czechoslovakia in June 1968, ostensibly for Warsaw Pact exercise "Sumava," but it is highly likely that estimates are too low. Despite good order-of-battle information on the buildup for the invasion of Czechoslovakia, several units were not identified until afterward.

Logistic capabilities, as measured in terms of ammunition, petroleum and other supplies immediately available for the offensive, are even more difficult to establish. In fact, many logistic estimates are based not on any reliable evidence concerning the scale of the supply buildup but on an assumption that the requisite supplies will be moved forward with the units. Since the availability of supplies of course is vital to the conduct of warfare and indeed may constitute the difference between a high capability and no capability whatever, the movement of one or two items of supply may be absolutely critical. Yet it is unlikely that the collection system will provide much specific information on the movement of numerous important items. Few estimates have proved to be more slippery than assessing when a logistic buildup may be completed and hence when the adversary's forces may actually have the capability given them on paper.

Consider further the problem of assessing the presence or absence of specific weapons, and particularly new or advanced weapons, capable of inflicting enormous damage. As everyone now knows, the so-called "missile gap" of the 1950s was an intelligence gap; the U.S. was unable to make an accurate estimate of the strength of Soviet missile forces and in fact considerably overestimated Soviet capabilities in this field. It may be certain that Japanese assessments of U.S. capabilities were revolutionized with the dropping of the first atomic bomb on Hiroshima. Did the USSR have nuclear weapons in Cuba in October 1962? At the time, we thought so but could not be sure.

Add to these supposedly measurable factors the intangible factors so critical to the performance of armies and nations—such as the quality of training, leadership and morale—and it is still more apparent why estimates of capabilities may be so wrong. Nearly all Western countries at some time or another have been victims of gross misjudgment not only of the intentions but of the capabilities of other powers. In short, it is not a simple problem.

If capabilities may thus be so difficult to establish, does it follow that ascertainment of intentions is virtually impossible? I have sometimes asked those wedded to this belief to put themselves in the position of the German High Command in the spring of 1944 as it looked across the English Channel to the enormous buildup of Allied combat power in the United Kingdom. Would their assessment have been, "Yes, there is a tremendous capability here, but can we really judge their intent? Perhaps this is only a bluff and they will launch the real invasion through southern France, or perhaps they have not yet made up their minds what they will do." Merely to pose the question reveals the fallacy of presuming that it is not possible to come to reasonable judgments of intentions. Of course the Nazis could tell that the invasion was coming and that it would be made across the Channel. It is ridiculous to presume that such a buildup of military force would have been undertaken with no intention of using it or that no decisions had yet been made.

Now this is an extreme example and one should not make generalizations from this. In other cases it has not been that easy or clear-cut, and the problem of assessing intentions rarely is this simple. But neither is it necessarily as difficult as many believe, particularly if one tries to look at it in terms of probabilities, precedents, national objectives and the options available rather than absolute either-or terms. As this treatise has already noted and will emphasize again, in warning we are dealing with probabilities, not certainties, and judgments should be made and worded accordingly. Nothing involving human behavior is absolutely certain before it occurs, and even a nation which has firmly decided on a given action may change its mind. But judgments can be made that certain courses of action are more or less probable in given circumstances, or that it appears that the adversary now plans (or intends) to do such and such. Although predictions of the behavior of individuals and states may be difficult, it is not impossible to make reasonable assessments and often with a quite high percentage of accuracy.

Although some analysts may not recognize it, the intelligence process every day is making judgments concerning the intentions of others, not only our adversaries but many other states as well. Nor are these judgments confined to the national estimative or warning process. All analysts are making judgments all the time about the information they receive and are assessing whether or not it suggests that a particular actor may be getting ready to do something unusual or different from what it has been doing. Now most of the time countries are pursuing and will continue to pursue the same general courses of action which they have been following for some time; that is, their attitudes and intentions will not have changed significantly and there is no requirement to be coming to continually new assessments or to be constantly reiterating what is widely recognized or accepted. Even though judgments about intentions are continually reviewed, the judgments are generally implicit rather than explicit. To cite an example, there may be no need for months or even years to reaffirm in print that it is unlikely that China will attack the offshore islands in the Taiwan Strait when there are no indications that it is getting ready to do so. The Intelligence Community's judgment of intentions on this, as on many other subjects or areas, has been right and quite likely will continue to be right unless there is some discernible change in the situation. But it is essentially a negative judgment that there is nothing new that needs to be said because nothing new is going to happen.

The idea that intelligence either cannot or should not be making judgments of intentions usually arises only when there are sudden or major changes in a situation requiring a new judgment, and particularly a positive judgment about whether aggressive action may be planned. Analysts who hitherto had been quite willing to make negative judgments that nothing was going to happen or that things will continue as they have will suddenly realize that they cannot make that judgment any more with confidence but also will be unwilling to come to any new positive judgments. They may thus take the position that intelligence cannot (or should not) make judgments of intentions, although they have in the past been doing just this, and will quite likely be willing to do so again in other circumstances. (The various factors which contribute to unwillingness to come to judgments in new situations are addressed later in this work.)

Not only is it true that the intelligence process continually comes to judgments on intentions and that its errors are the exception rather than the rule; it can also be demonstrated that in some circumstances it is actually easier to reach judgments concerning intentions than it is to assess capabilities. This was often true, for example, of the wars in both Vietnam and Laos. There was little doubt that North Vietnam for years intended to move sufficient supplies through the Laotian Panhandle to sustain the combat capabilities of its units in South Vietnam, yet it proved very difficult to estimate the actual so-called throughput to the South, let alone the supplies which might reach any given unit. Similarly, it was often possible to forecast at least several days in advance that a new Communist offensive effort was coming, that is, was intended, but the capabilities of Communist units to carry out the planned operations might be very difficult to determine and subject to considerable error. Captured documents and prisoners in both Vietnam and Laos sometimes accurately described planned operations for a whole season; the intentions of the Communists to carry them out might be relatively clear, but other factors, most notably friendly counteractions, could be so effective that the capability to carry out the action was seriously disrupted.

It would be misleading to leave the impression that the writer believes the assessment of intentions is somehow more important than capabilities or is advocating that military precepts on assessing capabilities are outmoded or should be scrapped. Nothing could be further from the truth. If there is one lesson to be learned from the history of warning intelligence—both its successes and its failures—it is that there is nothing more important to warning than the accurate and realistic description of capabilities. It is not only the field commander but also the policy official who first and foremost needs to understand the capabilities of the adversary. Assessments of intentions without due recognition first of the capability can be as dangerous, perhaps even more dangerous, at the national or strategic level as in the field. The greatest contribution that a military analyst can make to warning often may be to explain in clear and realistic language, for those who may not have his detailed knowledge, exactly how great a capability has been built up, how great the preponderance of force actually is, how much logistic effort has been required, or how unusual the military activity really is. Policymakers, and those at lower levels as well, more than once have failed to appreciate the likelihood of military action in part because no one really ever made it clear in basic English how great the capability was.

> "It is the history of warfare, and of warning, that the extraordinary buildup of military force or capability is often the single most important and valid indication of intent."

It is the history of warfare, and of warning, that the extraordinary buildup of military force or capability is often the single most important and valid indication of intent. It is not a question of intentions versus capabilities, but of coming to logical judgments of intentions in the light of capabilities. The fact is that states do not ordinarily undertake great and expensive buildups of combat power without the expectation or intention of using it. Large and sudden redeployments of forces, with accompanying mobilization of reserves and massive forward movements of logistic support, are usually pretty solid evidence of an intention to attack unless there is some really valid or convincing evidence to the contrary. The greater the buildup of offensive capability versus that of the adversary, the greater the deviation from normal military behavior, the more probable it is that military action is planned—not certain, but probable. As someone said, "The race may not be to the swift, nor the battle to the strong, but it is still the best way to place your bets."

This principle is almost universally recognized when hostilities already are in progress. Once it has been accepted that a nation is committed to the waging of war, analysts nearly always are able to come to realistic and generally correct judgments of intentions on the basis of an extraordinary buildup of military forces in some particular area. It is when war has not yet broken out or the commitment to resort to force has not become clear or generally accepted, that there may be great reluctance to draw conclusions from the same type of military evidence which would be readily accepted in wartime. This psychological hurdle is a serious problem in reaching warning assessments. In some circumstances, a surprising number of individuals will prove unable to reach straightforward or obvious conclusions from the massive buildup of military power and will offer a variety of other explanations, sometimes quite implausible or illogical, as to why all this combat force is being assembled.

There is one important factor to be considered in the buildup of a combat force prior to the outbreak of hostilities, which differs from the wartime situation. Even if the potential aggressor has decided to carry out military action to secure its objectives, it is always possible that an accommodation will make the military operation unnecessary. There may be a negotiated political settlement, perhaps through mediation, or the other country may simply capitulate in the face of the threatened attack. Such an occurrence, however, does not invalidate a conclusion that the nation in question was determined to obtain its goals by force if needed, or that it had intended to attack unless a solution satisfactory to it was reached.

Obviously, states will not usually undertake costly and dangerous military operations if they can obtain the same objectives without them. It has been argued that, because the U.S. did not attack the Soviet missile bases in Cuba in October 1962, no conclusions could have been drawn as to U.S. intentions—and that the foregoing discussion concerning intentions is therefore invalid. This line of reasoning avoids the issue. The U.S. did not attack the bases because it did not have to; the USSR agreed to remove the missiles because it considered that an attack was likely—as indeed it was.

Another pitfall to be avoided is the tendency to give inadequate emphasis to the capability when its logical implications may be alarming or unpopular. In any crisis or potential crisis situation, the military analyst should be particularly careful that he is in fact making and conveying to his superiors an accurate and adequate assessment of the military situation. He has the same responsibility as the field commander to judge capabilities first without regard to his personal predilections as to intentions. The analyst must not let his preconceptions of a likely course of action for the adversary influence his analysis and reporting of the military evidence. It is regrettable but true that some analysts who have rejected military action by the adversary as unlikely or inconsistent with their preconceptions have also been known to downplay or even fail to report at all some evidence which indicated that a massive buildup of capability was in progress.

Power talks. Realistic descriptions of the buildup of military power often will convey a better sense of the likelihood of action than will a series of estimative judgments which fail to include the military details or reasons on which the assessment is based. To understand the capability, and to be able to view it objectively, is a prerequisite to the understanding of intent.

Chapter 2
INTRODUCTION TO THE ANALYTICAL METHOD

INDICATOR LISTS: COMPILING INDICATIONS

Indicator lists are believed to be a post-World War II development, although it is not unlikely that similar techniques had been used in the past. In about 1948, the intelligence agencies began developing lists of actions or possible actions which might be undertaken by an adversary (specifically the Soviet Union) prior to the initiation of hostilities. From this beginning, the intelligence services of the U.S. (and its Allies) have gradually developed a series of indicator lists.

The earlier lists, reflecting the then-apparent monolithic structure of the communist world, generally were intended to apply to the "Sino-Soviet Bloc" (as it was then called) as a whole. Little effort was made to differentiate actions that might be taken by the USSR from those which might be taken by Communist China, North Korea or the Communist Vietnamese (Viet Minh). In recognition of the differing nature of conflicts and preparations for conflicts in various areas of the world, however, numerous special lists evolved in the 1950's dealing with such topics or areas as Southeast Asia, the Taiwan Strait and Berlin. These early lists had varying degrees of coordination, formality and stature in the community, but most were prepared at the working level as tools for the analysts or by field agencies or commands, primarily for their own use, Since the late fifties, the Intelligence Community has attempted to reduce this proliferation of lists and to use the resources of the community as a whole to prepare single, coordinated and formally issued lists. In recognition both of the Sino-Soviet split and the differing nature of the Soviet and Chinese Communist states and military establishments, separate lists were developed for these areas.

Content and Preparation of Indicator Lists

The philosophy behind indicator lists is that any nation in preparation for war (either general or localized) will or may undertake certain measures (military, political and possibly economic), and that it is useful for analysts and collectors to determine in advance what these are or might be, and to identify them as specifically as possible. Because of the large variety of actions which a major country will or may undertake prior to initiating hostilities or during periods of rising tensions, indicator lists have tended to become quite long and detailed. Thus, instead of referring simply to "mobilization of manpower," the list may have a dozen or more items identifying specific actions which may be taken during the mobilization process. While some of these specifics are intended primarily for collectors, they may also be very useful to the analysts. Because of the length of lists, however, it has sometimes been found useful to issue brief lists of selected or consolidated items as a guide to those actions deemed of most critical immediate importance, if they should occur.

In compiling indicator lists, analysts will draw on three major sources of knowledge: logic or longtime historical precedent; specific knowledge of the military doctrine or practices of the state or states concerned; and the lessons learned from the behavior of that state or those states during a recent war or international crisis. The first of these (logic or longtime precedent) is obviously essential. Regardless of what we may know about the doctrine or recent performance of any country, history tells us that all countries either must or probably will do certain types of things before they initiate hostilities. They must, at a minimum, provide the necessary combat supplies for their forces, redeploy them or at least alert them to varying degrees, and issue the order to attack. Depending on the scale and geographic area of the attack and on the likely resulting scope of the hostilities, they may undertake a large variety of additional military measures, both offensive and defensive. Most states will probably take some measures to prepare their own populace and perhaps world opinion for their action. And, if the conflict is to be of major proportions or is likely to last for a prolonged period, they may also begin major economic reallocations before hostilities are under way.

Both analyst and collector, however, will wish more specific guides than these general precepts. For this, a knowledge of military and political doctrine and practice of the nation in question will be of invaluable assistance. Indeed, most refinements in indicator lists are based primarily on our growing knowledge and understanding of the military organization, doctrine and practices of our potential adversaries, as derived from a variety of sources.

Equally valuable to the compilers of indicator lists, although usually less frequently available, will be the actual performance of a country in a "live" warning situation. No amount of theory replaces the observance of actual performance. Preferably for the analyst, the crisis should have resulted in actual war or commitment of forces, since there will then have been no doubt that it was "for real." A crisis which abates or is adjudicated before an outbreak of hostile action is never quite as useful since there will always be some doubt how many of the observed developments were actually preparations for hostilities. The greater and/or riskier the crisis and the greater the preparedness measures undertaken, the more useful for future indications purposes it is likely to be. In addition, the more recent the crisis, the more likely it is to reflect current doctrine and practice. Because of changes in Chinese Communist military forces and procedures as well as other factors, a study of the Chinese military intervention in Korea, invaluable as it is, cannot be considered an absolute guide to how the Chinese political leadership and armed forces might perform were such a situation to occur again. Some of the most useful intelligence we had since World War II on Soviet mobilization and logistic practice came from the preparations taken for the invasion of Czechoslovakia. A number of refinements in Soviet/Warsaw Pact indicator lists were made as a result of the Czechoslovak crisis. It is thus evident that the carefully researched and well-prepared indicator list will contain a large variety of items, some theoretical, some well documented from recent practice or doctrine, and covering a whole spectrum of possible actions that the potential adversary may undertake. No list, however, purports to be complete or to cover every possible contingency. Each crisis or conflict, potential or actual, brings forth actions or developments that had not been anticipated on an indicator list and which in fact may be unique to the particular situation and might not occur another time.

Still more important, it must be understood that even a major crisis involving a great national mobilization and commitment of forces and many obvious political and propaganda developments may involve only a relatively small fraction of the actions set forth on a comprehensive indicator list. And, of these actions, the best intelligence collection system can reasonably be expected to observe a still smaller fraction. Some of the most important developments, particularly those immediately preceding the initiation of hostilities, are unlikely under the best of circumstances to be detected, or at least to be detected in time. A judgment that a specific indicator is unlikely to be detected, however, should never preclude its inclusion on an indicator list, since there is always a chance that the collection system, perhaps fortuitously, will learn of it. As someone once said, an indicator list is a desideratum, not an absolute guide to what may occur, still less a statement of what we are likely to know.

At one time, it was considered desirable to divide indicator lists, not only into various subject categories (military, political, economic) and sub-categories of these, but also into time phases—usually long-range, intermediate-range and short-range. This procedure rested on the hypothesis, which is not invalid in theory, that some preparations for hostilities are of a much longer term nature than others and require much longer to implement, whereas others could reasonably be expected to occur very shortly before the initiation of the attack. Experience, however, has shown that such pre-judgments of likely time phases of actions are of doubtful practical use, and can be misleading or even dangerous. Some preparations may be so long term (the start of a program to build large numbers of new submarines, for example) that their relevance to the initiation of hostilities at some date in the future is questionable, at best.

Similarly, dependent on circumstances, an action that would usually be considered very short-term in nature may occur weeks or even months before the military attack or action is finally carried out. (Some of the Soviet units that finally invaded Czechoslovakia on 20-21 August 1968 were mobilized and deployed to the border on 7-8 May and were held in readiness for operations for over three months. One regiment reportedly was actually issued the basic load of ammunition on 9 May, but it was then withdrawn.) On the other hand, in a rapidly developing crisis calling for immediate military action, all preparations may be telescoped into a few days, as in the Soviet suppression of the Hungarian revolt in

1956. Still another factor to be considered is that the collection of information on a given action may run days or weeks after the occurrence, so that actions that may appear to be recent have actually been in progress for some time.

Thus, for these and other reasons, most indicator lists today have dropped a distinction between long and short-term preparations for hostilities. At the same time, some preparations judged to be so long term in nature that they are of doubtful validity as indicators have been dropped altogether. The focus today is on the collection and evaluation of all indicators, regardless of timing, which may point to a likelihood or possibility that a nation has begun preparations for the initiation of hostilities.

Uses of Indicator Lists

Any analyst who has participated in the preparation of a detailed indicator list and its coordination with other agencies will have learned a great deal in the process. In fact, the most useful aspect of these lists may be that the analysts who work on them must examine in detail the steps that a prospective adversary is most likely to take before initiating hostilities. For beginners, such experience is invaluable, and even analysts with long experience always learn something new in the process of preparing or revising such lists. The process serves as an extremely useful medium for an exchange of expertise between basic analysts (with their invaluable knowledge of the nuts and bolts) and current indications analysts who may be very knowledgeable on the theory of warning and the general types of things to be looking for but rather ignorant on the specifics. Thus, if nothing further were done with indicator lists, the time spent in preparing them would probably not have been wasted.

The usual reason for preparing such lists, however, is to give them wide dissemination to other analysts, supervisors, collectors and field agencies in order to guide them on what it is we want to know. At least in theory, every field collector is armed with an indicator list (together of course with all his other guidance and directives on what to look for), and each current analyst frequently consults his list to see how many indicators are showing up "positive" or where his collection gaps may be. It is not uncommon for those new to the intelligence process to expect the indicator list to be a kind of bible or at least the master guide on what to be watching for. "Let me see your indicator files" is not an unusual query.

Of course, it is not this simple. To field collectors, the indicator list (even if they have received it which sometimes they have not) is one more piece of collection guidance and one more document to keep in the safe. Practically never will the collector receive a query specifically pegged to an item on the indicator list. He may receive a query on a subject on the indicator list, and quite likely will, but it will not be related to the list and there will be no reason to consult it. What the field collector needs when something begins to happen that has potentially ominous connotations is not to sit down and reread his indicator list, but rather to have specific guidance on exactly what to look for in his area (and where) and to be relieved of a lot of routine requests when he should be concentrating on what is of immediate importance.

In the interests of more specific guidance and of not burdening the field office with a detailed list, some attempts have been made to compile very specific lists of things to took for in specific cities or areas in event of possible preparation for major hostilities. Obviously, such lists can only be prepared by those with the most detailed knowledge of the area. Much more remains to be done in this field, but it is one which might prove to be quite fruitful. By reducing the general to the specific and for a specific area, indicator lists in the future may prove to have a greater usefulness for the field than has heretofore been the case.

And what use is the indicator list to the analyst back at headquarters? What is he doing with it? The chances are that he also has it somewhere in the office but has not looked at it very often. If he has helped to prepare it in the first place, he will probably have very little need to consult it since he will know almost automatically that a given report does or does not fit some category on the indicator list. Hopefully, he will from time to time consult his list, particularly if he begins to note a number of developments which could indicate an impending outbreak of conflict or some other crisis. If he does not expect too much, and remembers that at best he may hope to see only a fraction of all the indicators on the list, he may find that the list is a useful guide to give him perspective on his present crisis.

In normal times, when the situation is reasonably quiet and no disturbing military or political developments are evident, an indicator list is not going to be of much use unless one needs to be reassured periodically that things are pretty normal. An indicator list is really not for all the time; it is a sometime thing. And even when that "some time" occurs, that twice a decade perhaps when we are confronted with a real warning crisis, no one should look on the indicator list as a solution to the warning problem. The mere ticking off of items on an indicator list has never produced warning, and it never will. It is a tool but not a panacea.

Compiling Indications

As all analysts know, it is possible to collect an enormous amount of information in an extremely short time on almost any current intelligence problem, and the greater the current interest in the subject, the greater will be the amount of verbiage. In no time at all, the analyst can collect drawers full of raw intelligence items, current intelligence items and special studies on an ongoing situation like the war in Vietnam. The measure of the importance of a crisis is sometimes the amount of reporting it engenders. The Cuban missile crisis or the Soviet/Warsaw Pact military buildup for the invasion of Czechoslovakia will result in an avalanche of reporting. Unfortunately, not all of these are original reports. Situation reports repeating raw data that was received 48 hours earlier pour in on the analyst who is hard put to read everything, let alone put it into a filing system where information can be easily recovered.

There are no panaceas to this problem, at least none have been found yet, and the following suggestions may not necessarily be the best method in a crisis or even from day to day when things are relatively quiet. Nothing yet has been found to replace a retentive memory, a recognition of what is important and what is not, and a sense of how things fit together. There are perhaps four basic filing or compiling problems that the indications analyst should be prepared to deal with. They are: (1) extracting raw data or information of potential indications significance; (2) compiling the highlights of such data into a readily usable form by topic or area; (3) coping with the sudden but short-term crisis; and (4) maintaining long-term warning or indications files.

Extracting Indications Data

The indications analyst must have the basic raw data, extracted verbatim or competently summarized if the item is very long, with the original source notations and evaluation and the date of the information (not just when it was acquired). The analyst can, if necessary, dispense with all current intelligence summaries, all special situation reports (unless they contain new data), and a variety of other reports, but the analyst cannot do without the basic information. The basic data may be filed in a computer system and recovered under various file headings. Obviously, discrimination is needed to retain what is of some lasting indications interest and to pitch out a lot of current information which may be of no interest next week. When in doubt, however, it is better to retain more rather than less.

For indications purposes, the material should be filed under the date on which the development occurred, not when it was reported or received. You are interested in the interrelationship of events in time, not when the information became available.

The general headings of indicator lists may be good headings for some portions of the file, but specific items from the indicator list usually should not be used as file headings. Above all, however, the analyst should maintain a flexible system, in which new headings are created, titles are revised, or some categories are broken down into subheadings.

The researcher should take care not to be trapped in a rigid system which cannot be readily expanded or modified as new developments occur. The system should be designed to serve the analyst, not to have the analyst serve the system.

The indexing of such files by country and key words has also proved useful in recovering specific items. The analyst should remember, however, that when he keeps his own subject files he is doing much of his research as he goes along. If the analyst relies on any library system he will have to recover each item separately and really do the research from scratch. Where large numbers of items may be involved, this can be very time-consuming.

Compiling Highlights: the Indications Chronology

No indications methodology yet devised is as useful or meaningful as the properly prepared indications chronology. The method is applicable both to relatively normal situations, for recording the highlights, and to budding crisis situations in which large volumes of material are being received. While its advantages are numerous, it must also be observed that it is a very time-consuming task requiring the most conscientious effort, which is probably the chief reason that so few are prepared.

The purpose of the indications chronology is to record briefly in time sequence (by date of occurrence, not date of reporting) all known developments, reported facts, alleged actions or plans, rumors, or anything else which might be an indication of impending aggressive action or other abnormal activity. For the initial chronology, it is not necessary to prove any inter-relationship of the various items, but merely to note them (obviously, there must be some possible connection, even if remote, to include an item). Some notation as to the validity of the information is desirable (particularly unconfirmed or dubious items), and it is often helpful to note the source as well, but the items should be as brief as possible. The chronology should also include significant actions by our side (or allies) that might cause some reaction or help explain some adversarial activity.

In a slow-building crisis of many months (which is the usual, not the unusual crisis) the relationship of old and new material may become immediately evident once the information is approached chronologically. Decision times may be isolated, or the likely reason for some action may become apparent. Where serious military preparations are under way, it will quite likely appear that a number of actions were initiated at about the same time. Events which appeared to have no relationship at the time they were reported may suddenly assume a meaningful pattern. Moreover, the method provides an almost foolproof way that the analyst will not fail to note something, perhaps because he did not understand it when received or did not know where to file it. A chronology is a catch-all for anomalies, and *while not all anomalies lead to crises, all crises are made up of anomalies.*

In addition to insuring that research is done and items not ignored, the draft chronology can rapidly be edited in final form for distribution on a crash basis, and the analyst also can readily produce a written analysis or summary of the evidence from the chronology. Where a great deal of material is coming in, a page for each day can be maintained and new items added as received, and only those pages need be rerun to insure that it is current.

The method is also very handy for just keeping an historical record of major developments in some area or country. Further, once an item has been briefly recorded, a large amount of paper can be thrown away. It is a tremendous saver of file space. Good chronologies of major crises can be kept indefinitely, most of the other data can be destroyed, and the document will remain the most useful record of the crisis which you could have.

Long-term Warning Files

"Unlike current intelligence files, good warning files improve with age."

Unlike current intelligence files, which rapidly become out-of-date, good warning files improve with age. Some of the most valuable files in intelligence are the indications files maintained on major crises, since most analysts' research files will have been destroyed and anyone seeking to review the basic data from the original raw material would have an almost insurmountable task.

One of the most useful things which an indications office can do is to keep files of crisis situations and warning problems. This may include extracts of the original material as described above, and also the chronologies and special studies. Postmortems of what happened and how it was analyzed and reported at the time are extremely useful for future study of indications and warning methodology. If such files are well compiled, virtually all other current information on the problem can usually be destroyed. Don't throw out crisis files and studies just because they are old and there has been no demand for them in years. There was little demand for ten years for studies on the Soviet reaction to the Hungarian revolt of 1956, but interest perked up noticeably in the summer of 1968. Similarly, studies of Soviet reaction in the Suez crisis of 1956 were suddenly in demand at the time of the six-day war in June 1967.

Another type of file which the indications analyst or office should maintain is the basic data on how a nation goes to war: alert and combat readiness procedures, mobilization laws, studies of major war games or exercises, civil defense doctrine and practice, and a host of other similar material which is rarely needed but of absolutely vital importance when there is a threat of employment of military force.

FUNDAMENTALS OF INDICATIONS ANALYSIS

There is seemingly very little difference between indications analysis and the process of developing intelligence judgments in any other field of intelligence; so, why study indications analysis? What's different about it? The difference between warning analysis and other intelligence analysis is largely one of degree or, one might say, of intensity. The analytical factors and techniques most useful or essential for warning also are required in varying degrees in other fields of intelligence analysis. Nonetheless, the analytical problems of warning, if not unique individually, pose a complexity of difficulties in combination which are certainly exceptional and would seem to warrant some special consideration. There are some fundamentals of indications research which analysts (and their supervisors and higher level officials) should understand.

Recognition of the Inadequacy of Our Knowledge

Warning analysis must begin with a realistic understanding of how much—or more accurately, how little—we know about what is going on in the areas of the world controlled by our enemies or potential enemies on a current day-to-day basis. Large numbers of people, in fact probably most people who are not actively engaged in collection or research on these areas, often have quite distorted ideas about what we know about the situation right now or what our current collection capabilities really are.

For the most part, people with a superficial rather than a detailed knowledge will tend to believe that we know more about the current situation than we really do. This tendency to exaggerate our current knowledge or collection capabilities is the product of several factors. Most important perhaps is that our overall, long-term, basic intelligence on other countries is often quite good, or even excellent. We may really know a good deal about the Chinese transportation system, the locations and strengths of Syrian units, military production in Poland and innumerable other subjects all pertinent in some degree to the capabilities and intentions of these states. What the inexperienced observer may not realize is how long it has taken to obtain such information, or that our knowledge is the product of literally years of painstaking collection and meticulous analysis. He may not understand that some of our best information may be months or even years old before we obtain it, and that it is rare that information of such quality is available on a current basis.

It cannot be denied also that the managers of certain collection systems may tend to create the impression that they really know far more—or have reported far more—on a current situation than is actually the case. Post-mortem and retrospective analyses are notorious vehicles for setting forth all sorts of detailed military facts and interpretations as if all this had really been available and in the hands of the intelligence users at the time the event occurred. Such self-serving reporting may be useful for budgetary purposes (indeed, this may be the most frequent reason for this type of distorted reporting) but it does a real disservice to the rest of the Intelligence Community. Small wonder that outside investigators (and congressional committees) may have an altogether erroneous impression of our current collection capabilities—and thus may tend to blame the analytical process for errors which were only in part its fault.

Some finished reporting of intelligence agencies also contributes to the impression that our knowledge is more current than is actually the case. Order-of-battle summaries will "accept" the existence or move of a unit months or sometimes even years after it has occurred—but often without mentioning the actual date of the event. Similar time lags in the acquisition and reporting of other important basic data may be well understood by the analysts immediately concerned but not by most readers.

The Intelligence Community is expected to make daily judgments about the current situation, such as the state of military preparedness or combat readiness, in a variety of countries which habitually conceal or attempt to conceal nearly all strategic information. Nonetheless, the community—looking at the overall situation insofar as it can perceive it and seeing nothing obviously abnormal—may conclude that the situation is generally normal and that all forces are in their usual locations and in a relatively low state of combat readiness. In fact, such judgments if made on a daily or weekly basis, may be based on the most superficial knowledge of what is actually happening at the time and can be quite erroneous. However, the chances are high that such judgments are right, but this will not necessarily be because we know what is happening but rather because about 95 percent of the time things really are pretty normal. Thus, even if no current information were being received, the odds are that the statement would be correct. The impression nonetheless is left, probably in the minds of most readers, that these judgments are the product of considerable evidence. And if we know when things are "normal," then clearly we should also know when something is "abnormal."

Now, there are some types of developments—both military and political—which we have a fair chance of detecting on a current basis in many countries and which, if they occur, can often be regarded as abnormal. In the case of military activities, these will most often be major deployments of large military units, particularly in open terrain, along major transportation routes, or in forward areas where detection capabilities are usually the best. Certain very obvious political anomalies—such as cancellations of planned trips by the leadership, or extraordinary diplomatic or propaganda developments—also can often be described as abnormal even though their purpose may not be clear. But these obvious developments may be only the smallest fraction of what is really going on, and the activity could well include the initial preparations for future hostile actions which could be totally concealed.

What we observe from day-to-day of what goes on in foreign states—even in those areas in which our collection and basic intelligence is the best—is actually something less than the tip of the iceberg. Disasters—natural and man-made—insurrections, major internal struggles even including the ouster of key officials, mobilization of thousands of men and a host of other military preparations have been successfully concealed from us and almost certainly will be again. The capabilities of our adversaries for concealment are probably fully appreciated or recognized only by a relatively small percentage of those associated with, or dependent upon, the intelligence process. It may take a really surprise hostile action by our adversaries right under our noses for us to realize that fact.

The spectacular aspects of the Cuban missile crisis and the delay in detection of the strategic missiles in Cuba have tended to overshadow the important question of what was going on in the Soviet Union in the spring and summer of 1962 as the USSR was making its preparations for the deployment of the missiles and the accompanying military forces to Cuba. We tend to overlook the fact that our appreciation of what was happening was almost entirely dependent on what we observed on the high seas and in Cuba.

Thousands of combat troops were moved from the USSR to Cuba, together with the equipment for entire SAM battalions and MRBM regiments, as well as tanks, short-range missiles and quantities of air, naval and electronic equipment—all without a discernible ripple in the USSR itself, without a rumor of the movement ever reaching the West. Only the fact that this small expeditionary force was then moved by ship permitted us to recognize that anything unusual was under way. Even by Soviet standards this was perhaps an extraordinary accomplishment in security.

A second example of a very well-concealed move was the closure of the Berlin sector borders in the early morning hours of 13 August 1961. The warning analyst who often complains that the available indications were overlooked or not appreciated is hard put to find the evidence that was ignored in this case. In fact, the available indications were carefully analyzed and did not *in themselves* support a likelihood that the Soviets and East Germans would move to close the sector borders. Such evidence as was available tended rather to indicate that they would seek to cut down the enormous flow of refugees to the West by closing the zonal borders (access to Berlin from East Germany itself), a less drastic but also less effective move which would not have violated the four-power agreements on the status of Berlin. The preparations for the closure of the sector borders were actually carried out almost under the eyes of Western patrols and yet achieved almost total surprise. This success was the more remarkable in that our collection capabilities in East Berlin and through it into East Germany were then considered superior to those in any other area of the communist world. At all levels, the community suffered from a misplaced confidence that this collection would give us insight into what the communists were most likely to do, that there would be a leak of some kind as to their plans.

The lessons that the analyst should derive from such experience are:

a. The observed anomalies—those which are apparent—will likely be only a small fraction of the total, and it must be presumed that far more is under way than is discernible to us;

b. Even in areas or circumstances where collection is very good and we may have much information, our seeming knowledge may be deceptive and the adversary may be capable of far greater concealment than we would normally expect.

The Presumption of Surprise

Closely related to the recognition of the inadequacy of our knowledge, and fundamental to the indications method, is the presumption that the adversary usually will attempt to surprise us. If he cannot or does not attempt to conceal completely what he is getting ready to do, he will of least attempt to deceive us on some aspects of his plans and preparations.

It follows that the warning analyst must be inherently skeptical, if not downright suspicious, of what the adversary may be up to from day to day whether or not there is any great cause at the moment to be particularly worried about his intentions. The indications analyst will examine each piece of unusual information or report for the possibility that it may be a prelude to hostile action or some other surprise move, even though the situation at the moment gives no special cause for alarm. He will not discard information of.potential warning significance until he can be sure, or at least reasonably sure, that it is erroneous or that there is some really satisfactory "other explanation" for the anomaly. He will not accept the most reassuring (or least worrisome) explanation for some unusual development which could prove to be ominous. He will endeavor consciously to go through this analytical process and to maintain his alertness for unexplained anomalies, and he will hold on to those fragments of information that are potentially of indications significance.

"It is the function of the warning or indications analyst to be alert for the possibility—however remote it may seem now—that some other nation has begun preparations for hostile action."

This approach is thus somewhat different—in some cases markedly different—from that of the current or basic analyst, or even from that of the estimator, though all are using the same basic information. It is the function of the warning or indications analyst to be alert for the *possibility*—however remote it may seem now—that some other nation has begun preparations for hostile action. At least in theory, the indications analyst will be running ahead of the rest of the analytical community in his perception of this possibility. It is his function, if the system operates as it should, to be continually raising questions concerning the adversary's possible motives, to be reminding others of pieces of information which they may have overlooked, to be urging more collection on items of possible warning significance. He is the devil's advocate, the thorn in the side of the rest of the community. This method is sometimes also described as assuming "the worst case."

"He is the devil's advocate, of the Intelligence Community."

There has been much misunderstanding about this, and many have derided indications analysts for their presumed proclivity for crying "wolf! wolf!" Warning intelligence is held in ill repute by some—often those with the least contact with it—because they assume that indications analysts are continually putting forth the most alarmist interpretations, in part to justify their existence or because that is what they feel they must do in order to earn their pay. Thus the indications analyst proposes, but fortunately wiser heads prevail and the current intelligence or estimative process disposes and puts those scaremongers in their place.

It is necessary emphatically to dispel the idea that the perceptive and experienced warning analyst is continually rushing to his superiors with the most alarmist interpretations or is an irrational and undependable character. No responsible indications analyst takes the "worst possible" view of every low-grade rumor or is continually searching for the worst possible explanation of every anomaly. Rarely if ever will he regard a single report or indication as a cause for alerting the community. To maintain an open and skeptical mind and to be diligent and imaginative in the collection and analysis of evidence against the possibility of the unexpected does not require that one go off halfcocked.

Indeed, experience has shown that qualified warning analysts, well-versed in their facts, often have been able to play the opposite role; they have sometimes been able to dampen down potential flaps engendered by a few alarmist rumors or unconfirmed reports, particularly when the international situation is tense or a general crisis atmosphere prevails. One product of the diligent collection of facts is that the analyst is able to make a reasoned and hopefully more objective analysis than he would otherwise be able to do.

The Scope of Relevant Information

"Warning intelligence must deal not only with that which is obvious but with that which is obscure."

As a product of the diligent collection of facts, and possible facts, the indications analyst hopefully should be able to assemble and analyze all the available information which may bear on the problem and not just that received most recently or that which is most apparent or readily acceptable. Warning intelligence must deal not only with that which is obvious but with that which is obscure. It must consider all the information which may be relevant to the problem at hand. If one accepts the premise of surprise, it will follow that what the adversary is preparing to do will not necessarily be that which is most obvious or seemingly plausible.

We earlier discussed the importance for warning of the exhaustive research effort and the requirement that the analyst have available the basic raw data. The preparation of chronologies is one very useful method whereby the analyst can assemble in readily usable form a variety of reports and fragments of information which may relate to the problem even though their relevance cannot yet be positively established.

It is a characteristic of impending crises or of periods of great national decisions and extraordinary preparations that there are likely to be a large number of unusual developments and often a still larger number of unconfirmed, unexplained and otherwise puzzling reports or rumors. Some of these will be true but unimportant. Some will be false but—had they been true—potentially important. Some will be true, or partly true, and very important. But a lot of these reports simply cannot be determined with any certainty to be either important or unimportant. It cannot be demonstrated with any certitude whether they are or are not relevant. And, interestingly enough, this may never be established. Time will neither prove nor disprove the relevance of some information. This is one reason that postmortems, even with all the benefit of 20-20 hindsight, often do not reach agreements either.

The problem of what facts, what known occurrences, what reported developments, which rumors, and how much of what is happening in general are actually pertinent to what the adversary may be getting ready to do is one of the most difficult problems for warning intelligence. It is probably safe to say that no two people are likely to reach complete agreement on what is relevant in any really complicated situation. One of the most frequent criticisms levied against the indications method is that it tends to see all unusual or unexplained developments not only as potentially ominous but also as related to one another. This same criticism is often made against chronologies on the grounds that they tend to pull together a lot of developments or reports simply because they occurred at the same time when there is actually no such demonstrable causal relationship between them. Obviously, such criticisms can have much validity if in fact the indications analyst has been tossing in everything but the kitchen sink in an effort to demonstrate ominous connections between a variety of reports and developments of uncertain validity and/or significance.

Nonetheless, in justice to the indications method, it must also be said that in retrospect—when the crisis is over—more rather than less information is nearly always judged to have been relevant than was appreciated by most people at the time. The imaginative rather than restricted or literal approach has almost invariably proved to be the correct one. The ability to perceive connections, or at least possible connections, between events and reports which on the surface may not seem to be directly related is a very important ingredient in the warning process, and one which has probably been given too little attention. The formal process of intelligence and the emphasis on coordination and "agreed positions" have tended increasingly to suppress the independent and often more imaginative analysis. "Think pieces" and speculative analyses need to be encouraged rather than discouraged. Information which may be relevant to the problem, whether or not it can be "proved" to be, must be considered in coming to warning assessments. It was the inability to see the relevance and interconnections of events in the Soviet Union, Germany and Cuba which contributed in large part to our slowness to perceive that the USSR was preparing for a great strategic adventure in the summer of 1962.

When we are attempting to assess what may and may not be relevant in a given situation, it may be well to be guided by an important and usually valid precept. As a general rule, the greater the military venture on which any nation is preparing to embark, and the greater the risks, the more important the outcome, the more crucial the decisions—the wider the ramifications are likely to be. And the wider the ramifications, the more likely it is that we will see anomalies in widely varying fields of activity as the nation prepares for the great impending showdown. In these circumstances, many seemingly unrelated things really do have relevance to the situation—if not directly, then indirectly. They are part of an atmosphere; they contribute to the sense of unease that things just are not right or normal, and that something big is brewing. To discard a series of such fragments as irrelevant or unrelated is to lose that atmosphere. The intelligence system will usually come out ahead if it is prepared in these circumstances to consider as relevant a broader field of information than it might in other circumstances. It will be better prepared to accept the great dramatic impending event if it has already perceived a series of anomalies as possibly relevant to such a development. In the words of Louis Pasteur, "Chance favors the prepared mind."

Objectivity and Realism

No factor is more important for warning than objectivity in the analysis of the data and a realistic appreciation of the situation as it actually is. The ability to be objective, to set aside one's own preconceptions of what another country ought to do or how it should behave, to look of all the evidence as realistically as possible—these are crucial to indications analysis and the ultimate issuance of the warning judgment at every stage of the process. The greater experience any individual has in the warning field the more likely he is to believe that objectivity, and the accompanying ability to look at the situation as the other fellow sees it, is the single most crucial factor in warning. There have been too many warning failures which seemed attributable above all to the failure of people—both individually and collectively—to examine their evidence realistically and to draw conclusions from it rather than from their subjective feelings about the situation.

One of the foremost authorities on warning in the U.S. Government, when told by this writer that she was planning this book, said, "So what have you got to write about? It is the same thing every time. People just will not believe their indications."

The rejection of evidence incompatible with one's own hypotheses or preconceptions, the refusal to accept or to believe that which is unpleasant or disturbing or which might upset one's superiors—these are far more common failings than most people suspect. One of the most frequent, and maddening, obstacles which the warning analyst is likely to encounter is the individual who says, "Yes, I know you have all these indications, but I just do not believe he'll do that." Korea, 1950; Suez, 1956; Hungary, 1956, Czechoslovakia, 1968, and the Egyptian attack on Israel, 1973: In none of these cases did we lack indications—in some of them, there was a wealth of positive indications—it was that too many people could not or would not believe them.

Now, the reaction of most people to the mere suggestion that they may not be thinking objectively is one of high indignation, it is an insult both to their intelligence and their character to imply such a thing. Of course, they are thinking objectively; it's you or the other fellow who is not, or it is you who is leaping to conclusions on the basis of wholly inadequate evidence while they are maintaining an open mind. In these circumstances, the atmosphere often becomes highly charged emotionally. Positions tend to harden, and with each side taking a more adamant position, reconciliation of views becomes less likely, and objectivity more difficult to obtain.

One of the first things which we all must recognize if we are to understand the warning business is that nobody achieves total objectivity. We are all influenced in some degree by our preconceptions, our beliefs, our education, early training, and a variety of other factors in our experience. Some people—for reasons yet to be fully understood—are capable of more objectivity than other people. Perhaps more accurately, they are capable of more objectivity on some subjects which other people find it difficult to be objective about. But no one is perfect.

We must also recognize that the ability to think objectively is not necessarily correlated with high intelligence, and that objectivity in one field may not necessarily carry over into other fields. The history of both religion and of politics provides ample illustrations of men of great intellectual achievements who were nonetheless totally biased and dogmatic in their outlook. Cases can be cited also of brilliant scientists—presumably capable of very objective analysis in their fields of specialization—who have seemed almost unbelievably naive or unrealistic when they have attempted to engage in other pursuits. Whole communities and even nations (Salem, Massachusetts, and Nazi Germany) have been victims of mass hysteria or guilty of such irrational conduct that it is difficult for the outsider to comprehend it at all. None of us is immune. We are all emotional as well as rational.

It is important, both for the analyst and the Intelligence Community as a whole, to recognize and face this problem. It should not be a forbidden subject. The rules of the game generally have precluded challenging a colleague publicly, and certainly not one's superiors, as to why they will not accept certain evidence or why they think as they do. Yet this may be the most crucial factor in their assessment. It would help greatly in such cases if people could be induced to explain their thought processes as best they can, or what is really behind the way they feel. The mere process of discussing the subject, dispassionately one would hope, may help them to see that they are not really assessing the evidence on its merits, but evaluating it in the light of their preconceptions. Still better, other listeners less involved in the problem may perceive where the difficulty lies. For years, experienced indications analysts have maintained, and not facetiously, that warning was a problem for psychologists. What is it that does not allow some people to examine evidence with greater objectivity, even to the point where they will consistently reject indications which seem self-evident to another analyst? Why will one analyst view certain information as tremendously important to the problem and another tend to downplay it as of not much importance or discard it altogether? How can there be such a wide divergence of views on the same information—not little differences, but 180-degree differences?

The thought that psychological, rather than strictly intellectual, factors are involved in warning has support from the academic community. Social scientists have inquired into the formation and nature of individual and group beliefs and their relationship to national decisionmaking. Some conclusions from these studies are that: (1) individuals do not perceive and evaluate all new information objectively; they may instead fit it into a previously held theory or conceptual pattern, or they may reject the information entirely as "not relevant"; (2) if the individual has already ruled out the possibility of an event occurring, or considers it highly unlikely, he will tend also to ignore or reject the incoming data which may contradict that conclusion; (3) a very great deal of unambiguous evidence is required to overcome such prejudgments or to get the analyst to reverse his position even to the point of admitting that the event is possible, let alone probable; (4) if the individual is unable to assimilate this contradictory information into his existing frame of reference or cannot be brought to modify his opinion, the extreme result may be a closed-minded concept of the situation with a high emotional content.

All of the foregoing reactions have been observed in warning situations. It is unquestionably true that this is precisely what has happened in more than one crisis.

The Need to Reach Immediate Conclusions

> "The warning analyst usually does not have the luxury of time, of further collection and analysis, of deferring his judgment 'until all the evidence is in.'"

The problems of indications analysis, which at best are complex, are immeasurably compounded by the requirement to reach conclusions or judgments long before all the evidence is available or can be adequately checked, evaluated or analyzed. The warning analyst usually does not have the luxury of time, of further collection and analysis, of deferring his judgment "until all the evidence is in." In many ways, he must act in defiance of all that he has ever been taught about careful research—to be thorough, to wait until he has looked at everything available before making up his mind, to check and recheck, to take his time, to come to the "definitive" rather than the hasty judgment. The more extensive his academic training, the more he may be dedicated to these principles or habits, and the more difficult it may be for him to revise his methods when confronted with the real life of current or indications intelligence. Some analysts are never able to make this adjustment. They may make good analysts on some long-term aspects of basic intelligence, but they should not be assigned to the indications field.

The tenuousness of it all, the uncertainties, the doubts, the contradictions are characteristics of every true warning problem. Only in retrospect can the relevance, meaning and reliability of some information ever be established, and some of it (often a surprising amount) is never established. In retrospect, however, much of the uncertainty is either forgotten, or it seems to disappear. Even those who actively worked the problem tend, after the event, to think that they saw things more clearly than they really did at the time. And outsiders—including those assigned to do critiques of what went wrong or to investigate the intelligence "failure"—can never truly see how complex and difficult the problem was at the time.

SPECIFICS OF THE ANALYTICAL METHOD

Inference, Induction and Deduction

The analysis of indications and the reaching of the warning judgment almost always will be a process of inference. Also, it will in large part be the result of inductive rather than deductive reasoning. Or, to simplify what is a very complex problem, the warning judgment will be derived from a series of "facts" or more accurately what people think are the facts, and from the inferences or judgments which may be drawn from these conceptions of the facts, leading to a final conclusion or series of conclusions which will be expressed as probabilities rather than absolutes. The process is highly subjective; neither the inferences nor the final conclusion necessarily follow directly from the facts, and, as a result, individuals will vary widely in their willingness to reach either specific inferences or general conclusions.

This is not a treatise on the nature of logic, and so we may use the simple dictionary (Webster's) definitions:

Inference: the act of passing from one or more propositions, statements or judgments considered as true, to another the truth of which is believed to follow from that of the former;

Induction: reasoning from a part to a whole, from particulars to generals, or from the individual to the universal;

Deduction: reasoning from the general to the particular, or from the universal to the individual, from given premises to their necessary conclusion.

An analyst may have no choice about what evidence is available in the warning situation. In such a case, he must proceed from fragments of information and from particulars to general conclusions, and he will not have developed logical premises which will lead logically or necessarily to certain conclusions. (On the other hand, if his anticipation of a situation gives sufficient lead time, he may be able to influence intelligence information collection, either directly or indirectly.[2]) He must normally come to his judgments, both as to the facts in the case and their meaning, on the basis of very incomplete information, on a mere sampling of the "facts," and often without knowing whether he even has a sampling of some of the potentially most important data.

The problem of how much evidence is necessary in order to make certain inferences or to some type of generalized conclusions is peculiarly applicable to certain types of military information—above all, to order-of-battle and mobilization. There is a fundamental difference in analytical approach between the conventional order-of-battle method and the indications method.

The normal order-of-battle approach to assessing the strength and locations of foreign forces is to examine each unit individually. Ideally, the order-of-battle analyst seeks the total sample before he wishes to make a judgment on total strength. He usually requires positive evidence for each individual unit before he is willing to make a judgment (to "accept") that the unit has been re-equipped with more modern tanks or higher performance aircraft, or that it has been mobilized with additional men and equipment to bring it to wartime strength. The conventional military analyst normally will be extremely reluctant to accept that any new military units exist or are in process of formation until he has positively located them and identified them—until they meet some type of order-of-battle criteria. This is likely to be the case even if there is a great deal of other information to indicate that a major mobilization of manpower is in fact in process.

The same general precepts apply to movements of units. It is not enough that there are numerous reports of movements of ground units and aircraft; what the order-of-battle analyst wants is evidence that this or that specific unit has moved. His method is thus essentially restrictive rather than expansive. He will not normally conclude that more units have moved than he can identify, or that several units have been mobilized because he has evidence that one or two have.

The indications analyst, on the other hand, must consider that what he sees or can prove may be only a fragment of the whole and that he may have to come to

---

[2] In such a case, he would be in a position to adopt a deductive approach to the analysis of disconfirming information, as was done hypothetically but convincingly by an Israeli intelligence analyst who looked back at the information available to military analysts prior to the surprise attack on the Israelis in the 1973 Middle Eastern October War. See Isaac Ben-Israel, "Philosophy and Methodology of Intelligence: The Logic of Estimate Process." *Intelligence and National Security* 4, no. 4 (October 1989): 660-718.

more general conclusions about what the adversary is doing from his sampling of the evidence. If available information—unspecific though it may be—suggests that large-scale call-ups of men to the armed forces are in progress and if some units which he can observe are known to be mobilizing, the indications analyst will consider it a good chance, if not certain, that other units also are being mobilized. If one unit in the crisis area has issued the basic load of ammunition, it will be likely that others have. If some units are known to be deploying toward the front or crisis area but the status of others is unknown, the indications analyst will be inclined to give greater weight to the possibility that additional units are deploying than will the order-of-battle analyst. At least he will consider that what is provable is probably the minimum that is occurring, rather than the maximum. The warning analyst does not take this approach because he wants to draw broad judgments from inadequate data or because he is inherently rash and likes to jump to conclusions. He takes this attitude because this is the nature of warning problems. In times of crisis, the more leisurely and conventional analysis may be a luxury which we cannot afford. Much as we might wish to have all the data before we draw our conclusions, we may have to make general judgments based on only a sampling of the potentially available data, or whatever we can get. How great a sampling is needed before a general conclusion can be drawn will vary with the circumstances and is likely in any case to be a hotly debated subject between warning analysts and more conventional military analysts. The point here is that the principle of inductive (or more expansive or generalized) analysis must be recognized as valid in these circumstances, even though judgments will necessarily be tentative and subject to some margin of error. Historically intelligence has usually underestimated the scale of mobilization and troop deployment in a crisis situation.

The problems of reaching general judgments from limited data are of course applicable to other types of information which are received in a potentially critical situation. Even assessments of the meaning and significance of political information or propaganda trends must be based on a sampling of what is actually occurring and are essentially inferential or inductive in nature. Because so much political planning and preparation may be concealed, however, and because other political evidence may be so ambiguous or uncertain, political analysis in a crisis situation may be even more complex and subjective than the ascertainment of the military facts.

Acceptance of New Data

It is a phenomenon of intelligence, as of many other fields of investigation and analysis, that the appearance of new types of information or data of a kind not normally received poses difficult problems—and that the reaction is likely to be extremely conservative. This conservatism, or slowness to accept or even to deal with new information, is a product of several factors. One is simply a basic tenet of good research—that judgment should be withheld in such cases until sufficient unambiguous data are available that we can be sure of the meaning and significance of the information. A related factor often is that there is no accepted methodology for dealing with new types of information; since it is new, the analyst is not sure how to tackle it analytically, and he wants more time to think about it and to confer with other analysts. Still another and often very important factor may be that the intelligence organization is not prepared to handle this type of information or analysis; there is no one assigned to this type of problem, so that it tends to be set aside or its existence may not even be recognized. And finally, there is an inherent great reluctance on the part of many individuals and probably most bureaucratic organizations to stick their necks out on problems which are new, controversial, and above all which could be bad news for higher officials and the policymaker.

The effect of these factors and possibly others, individually and collectively, can be to retard the analysis and acceptance of data in the intelligence system by weeks, months and sometimes even years. Few people outside the analytical level have probably ever recognized this, but examples can be cited of delays in the analysis and reporting of data which seem almost incomprehensible in retrospect. Even normally perceptive and imaginative individuals seem to have lapses in which they are unable to perceive that something new is occurring or that things have changed. They may be reluctant to accept evidence which in other circumstances, particularly when there is adequate precedent, they would accept without question.

Lest the writer be accused of exaggerating all this, a few examples may be in order. A very intelligent and sophisticated supervisor of political intelligence on the Soviet Union resisted for weeks (and finally took a footnote in opposition to) a judgment that the USSR was preparing in the mid-1950's to export arms to the Middle East. His reason—although the evidence was almost overwhelming and no one would question it today—was that the USSR had never exported armaments outside the communist world, and therefore never would.

Numerous examples could be cited of delays in the acceptance of information on troop movements, other order-of-battle changes and mobilization, which were attributable to the fact that the evidence was new rather than insufficient by criteria later adopted. Two instances from the Vietnam war may suffice here.

It required ten months for order-of-battle analysts to accept the presence in South Vietnam of the first two North Vietnamese regiments which arrived there in the winter of 1964-1965 (one other which arrived slightly later in February was, however, accepted in July). With the acceptance at the same time of several other regiments which had arrived in 1965, and with it the acceptance of the fact that North Vietnam was deploying integral regiments to South Vietnam, the time lag between arrival and acceptance thereafter rarely exceeded two months and was often less.

North Vietnam began an expansion of its armed forces in 1964 and conducted a major expansion and mobilization in 1965. Much of the evidence for this mobilization was derived from public statements and other indirect evidence of large-scale callups to the armed forces, rather than from conventional order-of-battle information. (Confirmation by order-of-battle ran months and in some cases years behind what could be deduced from what Hanoi was saying about its mobilization effort.) Just why there was so much reluctance to accept Hanoi's transparent statements that thousands (sometimes tens of thousands) of men were required to fight at "the front" in South Vietnam was then and is now very difficult to understand. Over-reliance on order-of-battle methodology and mistaken notions that anything said by the adversary should be dismissed as "propaganda" no doubt contributed. In time, however, the value of Hanoi's press and radio comments came to be recognized.

A few years later, public statements that callups to the armed forces were being increased were routinely accepted as evidence that this was in fact under way, whereas much larger volumes of similar evidence were not considered acceptable in 1965-66.

These examples are cited for purposes of illustration only. Many other instances, some probably more serious, could undoubtedly be found from the annals of warfare. The fact is that the reluctance to cope with or accept new types of data is a very serious problem for warning intelligence, and one to which supervisors in particular should be constantly alert. A review of draft indications items, when compared with what was finally accepted for publication, will consistently show that indications analysis tends to run ahead (sometimes weeks ahead) of what is usually acceptable to the community as a whole, particularly on new intelligence. One is happy to note, however, that this gap appears to be narrowing—which may reflect somewhat greater willingness to use indications methodology and new types of data than was once the case.

Together with the need for objectivity, the ability to perceive that change has occurred and that new information must be considered even though it may not yet be fully "provable" is a fundamental requirement for successful warning analysis. In warning, delay can be fatal. Both the analyst and the system as a whole must be receptive to change and the acceptance of that which is new.

"Experience suggests that experts in their fields are not necessarily the most likely to recognize and accept changes or new types of data."

Interestingly enough, experience suggests that experts in their fields are not necessarily the most likely to recognize and accept changes or new types of data. The greatest resistance to the idea that China would intervene in Korea in 1950 came from "old China hands," and by and large it was Soviet experts who were the most unwilling to believe that the Soviet Union would put strategic missiles in Cuba. There seems to be something to the concept that experts tend to become enamored of their traditional views and, despite their expertise, are less willing to change their positions than those who are less involved with the matter.

Understanding How the Adversary Thinks

This heading may be a bit misleading. No one can aspire to total understanding of how someone else, and particularly the leadership of another and hostile country, actually thinks. A sophisticated student of the Soviet Union (the remark is attributed to Chip Bohlen) once observed that his favorite last words were: "Liquor doesn't affect me," and "I understand the Russians." To which the warning analyst should add a fervent, "I understand the Chinese."

The path to understanding the objectives, rationale, and decisionmaking processes of foreign powers clearly is fraught with peril. Nonetheless, it is important to try. The analyst, the Intelligence Community, the policymaker or military planner may have to make a conscientious and imaginative effort to see the problem or situation from the other side's point of view. Fantastic errors in judgment, and the most calamitous misassessments of what the adversary was up to have been attributable to such a lack of perception or understanding. An examination of such errors in perception—both by individuals and groups—which have been made over a period of years in warning situations indicates that this is a problem to which we must be particularly alert. The ability to perceive, or to attempt to perceive, what others are thinking may be the mark of an expert in more than one field. This ability does not seem to come easily to some people, even when the opponent is making no particular effort to conceal how he feels about the matter, and indeed may be making it quite obvious. Why did so many analysts—after months of evidence that the Soviet Union was determined to maintain its political hold on Czechoslovakia and in the face of a massive military buildup—nonetheless bring themselves to believe that the Soviet Union would not invade? One can only conclude that they had not really tried to understand how the USSR felt about it, how important the control of Eastern Europe was to Soviet leaders, and that these analysts had somehow deceived themselves into believing that a détente with the U.S. was more important to the USSR than its hegemony in Eastern Europe and the preservation of the Warsaw Pact.

The root causes of such lack of perception—whether it be an inability or unwillingness to look at it from the other fellow's standpoint—are complex. Individual, group and national attitudes or images are involved as well as relatively more simple questions such as how much education the analyst has on the subject, how many facts he has examined, and how much imagination he has. The problem of objectivity and realism obviously is closely related; misconceptions, based on subjective judgments of how the other nation ought to behave rather than objective assessments based on how it is behaving, have much to do with this problem.

While one hesitates to suggest that there may be certain national characteristics of Americans which tend to inhibit our understanding of what our adversaries may be planning, one is struck by two prevailing attitudes.

Perhaps because of our historic isolation, prosperity and democracy, Americans traditionally have been optimistic, and often unduly so, about world affairs. A reluctance to believe that World War II would come or that we could become involved lay behind much of the isolationist sentiment of the thirties. We couldn't believe that Japan would be so treacherous as to attack Pearl Harbor, that the Chinese would intervene in Korea, or that our close friends the British would move against Suez in 1956. And so forth. Healthy and admirable as such attitudes may be in private life, we need to guard against such false optimism in professional intelligence analysis.

Many Americans also—and this has sometimes been particularly true of military men—are so convinced of the superiority of American military forces and technology that they cannot bring themselves to believe that ill-prepared nations would dare to oppose U.S. military power. Perhaps more than any other factor, this lay behind the unwillingness to believe that China would throw its poorly equipped and ill-educated troops against the armed forces of the U.S. in Korea. Much of the same attitude prevailed in the early days of the Vietnam War.

Consideration of Various Hypotheses

The consideration of alternative or multiple hypotheses to explain sets of data is a fundamental of the scientific method which, curiously enough, often is given scant attention in intelligence problems. Various alternative explanations or possibilities may be offered for particular facts or bits of information (that is, this photography of new construction activity could be a missile site in its early stages but it may be an industrial facility). Often, however, no particular effort will be made to itemize all the available pieces of information on any complex current situation with a view to considering their relevance to various alternative possible courses of action of the adversary. Even special national intelligence estimates (SNIEs), prepared sometimes to address alternative possibilities, usually do not attempt to deal with all the facts or possible facts before coming to judgments. They are much more apt to be generalized discussions of alternatives, rather than detailed analyses of the relevant information. There have been certain exceptions to this—on particularly critical military subjects, for example—but as a general rule estimates do not involve a critical examination of a mass of detailed information and a consideration of various hypotheses to explain it. Still less are other forums of the Intelligence Community likely to provide an opportunity for detailed consideration of various alternative hypotheses unless a special effort is made to do so and the forum is opened to all who may have something to contribute.[3]

---

[3] For one of the rare exceptions, see Robert D. Folker, Jr., *Intelligence Analysis in Theater Joint Intelligence Centers: An Experiment in Applying Structured Methods* (Washington, DC: Joint Military Intelligence College, 2000). Folker's experiment involved the retrospective examination of competing hypotheses for two well-documented international scenarios. In these scenarios, strategic warning decisions had to be made by intelligence analysts. Folker's work indicates that familiarity with structured comparative methods, such as formal "analysis of competing hypotheses," provides an advantage to analysts, ideally resulting in greater warning accuracy.

Ideally, the warning system should operate to provide a forum for this type of analytical effort, but often it does not. The analysts who have the most detailed knowledge should but often do not get together on warning problems with analysts of other agencies. More often, each agency considers the evidence and comes to its "position" and the various "positions" are what are discussed at the interagency forum rather than the detailed evidence itself. The result is that various alternative hypotheses may not be given adequate consideration, or even sometimes considered at all, and no systematic effort is made to insure that some group really goes through all the evidence and considers the various alternative explanations in exhaustive detail.

One reason for this, which we have noted before, is that in crises, or budding crisis situations, there is likely to be an overwhelming quantity of information, the mere scanning and preliminary processing of which is consuming most of the analysts' time. There are simply insufficient resources to cope with all the information in any manner, let alone go through a time-consuming process of evaluating each item of information against several alternative hypotheses.

This is a serious matter. Most of all, in such situations, people need time to think and to really take the time and effort to look at the available information and to consider what it does mean, or could mean. As we have observed in preceding chapters, facts are lost in crisis situations, and sometimes very important facts whose adequate evaluation and consideration would have made a great difference indeed to the final judgment.

The most useful thing which an administrator or committee chairman can probably do in such circumstances is to devise some method to insure that all the relevant information, or possibly relevant information, is being brought together and that it is really being looked at and considered against various hypotheses or possible courses of action. Before the validity of various hypotheses can be considered, we must insure the examination of the facts.

Assuming that this can be accomplished, an objective consideration of the meaning and importance of individual pieces of information in relation to various alternative hypotheses can be a real eye-opener. Almost any method which will require the analyst or analysts collectively to examine the data and evaluate each piece will help. One does not need for this purpose some mathematical theorem or other statistical method to insure "reliability" or "objectivity." The purpose is to look at the information and to say yes or no or maybe to each piece (to each indication) as to whether it is or is not a likely preparation for (a) hostilities, (b) peace, (c) various stages between full-scale war and total peace, of which of course there may be many, or (d) not significant for any of these hypotheses.

The idea that the analyst should be required to look at each piece of information and to come to a judgment on it and its validity or relevance to various hypotheses is the essence of various systems or theories which have been devised for the purpose of helping to improve objectivity in analysis of information. The best known of these systems, which enjoys considerable popularity today in the information-handling field, is "Bayes' Theorem" (See Index).

The outstanding successes of warning analysts, and of watch committees, have usually been those which involved the meticulous and objective evaluation of each piece of information and its relevance to war or peace. Any system which requires people individually and collectively to apply some such quasi-scientific method to their data and their analysis is almost certain to be of positive benefit to warning. A distinguished former chairman of the U.S. Watch Committee repeatedly observed that what the report included and how it was organized was infinitely less important than that the committee painstakingly examine each potential indication and evaluate it.

The advantage of such methods is not just to insure that facts are not ignored, valuable as that is. An even more important result should be that certain hypotheses are not ignored or swept under the rug—particularly those which are frightening, unpopular, or counter to the prevailing mood or "climate of opinion." It is essential for warning that the intelligence system be able objectively to consider the hypothesis which is contrary to the majority opinion or which runs counter to hitherto accepted precepts or estimates. In addition to an extraordinary analytical effort, this may require an exceptional degree of objectivity and willingness to consider the unpopular thesis, and the one which might require us to take some positive and difficult or dangerous action.

For warning, we rarely need to be concerned about the "idea whose time has come." It is the fate of the idea whose time has not yet come—the hypothesis which is in its infancy and has yet to gain adherents—that should most concern us. There is indifference to new ideas; long-held opinions are extremely slow to change except in the face of some extraordinary development or unambiguous evidence. This is true even when the issues are not important. When the matter is exceptionally important and the new judgment is unpopular or contrary to going national policy, indifference to new ideas or hypotheses may change to outright hostility. The warning system must insure that this does not happen and that new hypotheses and ideas are given "equal time" on the basis of their merits, no matter how unpopular or contrary to prevailing opinion they may be.

Chapter 3

MILITARY INDICATIONS AND WARNING

THE NATURE OF MILITARY INDICATORS

For various reasons, some obvious and some less well-recognized, the collection and analysis of military data or indications has been the predominant element in warning. By far the greater number of items on indicator lists deal with military, or military-related, activities. By far the greater portion of the collection effort, and particularly the most expensive collection, is devoted to obtaining data on the military strengths, capabilities and activities of foreign forces. This collection effort has greatly increased, largely as a result of breakthroughs in technology, and the future promises a still greater expansion in the volume of military data. Whether this necessarily results in a great improvement in our so-called "warning capabilities" is uncertain, although improvement in the timeliness of our evidence appears unquestionable. What does appear certain is that military information will continue to consume much of the intelligence effort in the future, and hence that military indications may assume an even more important role, or at least will take more of analysts' time, than in the past.

Primary Reasons for Importance of Military Indicators

First, and most obvious, military preparations are a necessity for war. There would be no warning problem, in the sense we use it in warning intelligence, if it were not that states have armed forces and arsenals of modern weapons which they could commit against us or our allies. The index of our concern about the intentions of other nations is largely how much military damage they can do to us, rather than just how politically hostile they may be, and our collection effort is usually allocated accordingly.

Secondly, many military preparations, although far from all, are physically discernible or at least potentially discernible to us. They involve movements of troops and weapons, or augmentations of them, which we can observe provided our collection is adequate. As a general rule (at least this has been true historically), the greater and more ominous the scale of military preparations, the more discernible they have been. The advent of weapons of mass destruction and long-range delivery systems has potentially altered this. It is now theoretically possible for a nation so equipped to make almost no physically discernible preparations for a devastating nuclear strike. Few analysts now believe, however, that there would not also be other potentially discernible military, and political, indications before any nation undertook so terrible and perilous a course of action. The concept of a totally surprise nuclear attack (that is, the attack out of the blue without any prior deterioration in relations or military preparations of various types) no longer enjoys much credence. The problem of providing warning that the situation had deteriorated to the point that nuclear attack might be imminent is, of course, another problem. The effect of the advent of the nuclear age, in any case, has hardly been to reduce the importance of military indications! The result has been quite the contrary, the community has devoted far more effort to attempting to determine what ancillary military indications might be discernible and to devising methods to collect such information.

One lesson we have learned is that discernible military preparations—the type of preparations that have traditionally preceded the outbreak of hostilities—have by no means lost their validity as indicators. The effect of such military episodes as the Chinese military intervention in Korea and the Soviet military intervention in both Hungary and Czechoslovakia has been to reinforce confidence in the value of military indications as less ambiguous and probably more dependable gauges of impending action than political indicators. The amount of preparation undertaken by the Soviet Union and its allies for the invasion of Czechoslovakia probably served to reduce fears—once quite prevalent—that the USSR from a standing start and without a discernible change in its military posture might launch a devastating attack against the West. That portion of intelligence sometimes defined as "hard military evidence" has gained stature for warning.

Another factor which lends importance or credence to military indications is that so many of them are so expensive to undertake—and that this is becoming increasingly so. It is one thing to undertake a relatively inexpensive propaganda campaign of bombast and threat or to alert forces for possible movement, or even deploy several regiments or so. It is quite another to call up a half million reservists for extended active duty, or to move a number of major ground force units hundreds or thousands of miles, or to initiate a crash program of production of new combat aircraft or naval landing craft.

Such serious, expensive, and often disruptive military preparations—and particularly those which take a real bite out of the taxpayer's income or which involve a commitment of national resources from civilian to military effort at the expense of the consumer—these are measures of how a nation or at least its leadership really feels about a problem and how important it is to it. These are the hard indications of national priorities. They are rarely undertaken lightly, or just for political effect or as a "show of force." There are cheaper ways to bluff or to make idle threats one has no intention of carrying out.

This is not to say, of course, that such major military preparations or reallocations of national resources are necessarily unequivocal indications of preparations for aggression. They may be defensive, or a recognition that the international situation is deteriorating to a point that the state against its will may become involved in conflict. But such preparations are real and meaningful and important—a kind of barometer of what a nation will do and what it will fight for. And they are evidence that important decisions have been taken.

Such major changes in military allocations or posture or priorities are not only substantial or "concrete" indications; they may also be particularly valuable as long-term indications. They often give us lead time—time to readjust our own priorities and preparations, not only in intelligence collection and analysis, but more importantly our own military preparations and allocations of resources. Provided we have recognized and understood them correctly, they may prevent our being strategically surprised even though our short-term or tactical warning may fail us.

Understanding the Basics: How a Nation Goes To War

Know your adversary. This basic tenet is nowhere more applicable in intelligence than to the problem of strategic military warning. The analyst who would hope to understand what his adversary is up to in time of crisis should begin his education with the study of all that he can possibly find on the subject of how that adversary will prepare his forces for war.

This principle underlies the preparation of indicator lists. The well-prepared and well-researched indicator list should incorporate not only theoretical or general ideas of how the adversary nation will get ready for war; it should also include, insofar as is practicable, some specifics of what we know of the potential enemy's doctrine, practice and plans. As our knowledge of these things increases, we are likely to prepare better and hopefully more usable indicator lists.

It would be virtually impossible, however, to include in any indicator list everything which might occur if a major country were preparing its forces for war. A list that attempted to incorporate all that we know, or think we know, about war plans, missions of specific units, wartime organization and terminology, civil defense preparations and any number of other subjects would become too cumbersome to cope with. Except possibly for very specific problems or areas, indicator lists are likely to remain fairly generalized. The warning analyst needs far more than this.

Other things being equal, the individual best qualified to recognize that a nation has begun serious preparations for possible hostilities should be the analyst who best understands its military doctrine and is best read in its military theory and practice. One unfortunate consequence of the separation of basic and current intelligence (when they are separated) is that the analyst who must make quick judgments on the significance of current information may not be well-grounded or up-to-date in such basic material.

> *"The distinguishing characteristic of preparations for hostilities is that they are real and that they will therefore include activities rarely if ever observed in peacetime."*

The distinguishing characteristic of preparations for hostilities (versus preparations for exercises or other relatively normal peacetime activities) is that they are real—and that they will therefore include activities rarely if ever observed in peacetime. Various exercises or mobilization drills or the like no doubt have rehearsed part of the plan, often in miniature form as a command post exercise, but almost never will the adversary have rehearsed in full force all the preparations that he will undertake when he is actually preparing to commit his forces. (Those who doubt this should reexamine the preparations for the invasion of Czechoslovakia.) An understanding of his doctrine and military theory, of what he did the last time that he was involved in a real combat situation and of what changes there have been in his military practice since then will be invaluable, indeed indispensable, to an understanding of what he is up to now.

The military forces of all nations are slaves in large degree to their doctrine and theory. What the staff officer has been taught in school that he should do in a given situation is likely what he will do. If doctrine calls for the employment of airborne troops in a given tactical situation, the chances are they will be employed. If the unit mobilization plan calls for the requisitioning of trucks from a local economic enterprise, the chances are very high that they will be requisitioned before that unit is committed to combat. If contingency wartime legislation provides for the establishment of a supreme military council (or some such super body), or for the re-designation of military districts as field armies, the warning analyst and the community should instantly recognize the significance of such developments should they occur. If the national military service law (normally unclassified) provides that reservists should be recalled for no more than three months in peacetime, evidence that they are being held longer could indicate that emergency secret wartime decrees had been passed. And so forth. Innumerable and much less obvious examples could no doubt be cited by experts on such topics.

Unfortunately, the experts on such topics are often scattered and engaged in long-term basic research, even when a crisis is impending. Means must be established so that this information is not overlooked or forgotten, or filed in the library, when it is most needed.

How many analysts assigned to the current or indications effort at various headquarters or various echelons in the national Intelligence Community have read or studied much of the basic material that might be so crucial to the understanding of actual preparations for hostilities? How many have it catalogued or readily available or know where they could immediately obtain the answers they might need?

Some offices and analysts no doubt are much better prepared than others, but experience suggests that no intelligence office is really fully prepared now for the contingency of real preparation for hostilities by one of our major potential enemies. Every major crisis, at least, has shown this to be true. And those at the supervisory or policy levels, for obvious reasons, are quite likely to have minimal knowledge of a great deal of basic information which could be crucial in a real crisis.

Warning specialists and current military indications analysts could make no greater contribution over the long term than to do their best to review, study and compile the rarely reported and often obscure basic data which might some day be so essential for warning. The scope of potentially relevant military information is vast: doctrine, theory, logistics deficiencies and wartime requirements, applicable legislation, mobilization theory and practice, military terminology, major military exercises and war games, combat readiness and alert procedures, and other similar basic topics. The study of the performance of our potential enemies in relatively recent live crises, as we have noted before, is also invaluable even though the situation the next time will doubtless not be identical. It is not even too much to suggest that there are still many useful lessons in warning to be derived from a study of World War II.

The Soviet buildup for the attack on Japanese forces in Manchuria in August 1945 is a useful example of the difference in strategic and tactical warning. And the campaign itself, as well as earlier operations of Soviet forces in the same area, provides potentially useful lessons in how Russia today might go about conducting operations against Chinese forces.

ORDER-OF-BATTLE ANALYSIS IN CRISIS SITUATIONS

It is readily apparent that a determination of the order-of-battle (OB) of foreign forces is of decisive importance for warning intelligence. Indeed, insofar as warning rests on a determination of the facts—as opposed to the more complex problem of determining what the facts mean and issuing some interpretive judgment—the order-of-battle facts will often be the single most important element in warning. Whatever other facts may be relevant or significant for warning, nothing is likely to be so critical as the locations, strengths and equipment of the adversary's military forces, for these determine what the adversary can do. Understanding or a correct assessment of the enemy's capability is a prerequisite to the assessment of intentions, and the failure to recognize the capability is fraught with peril. Thus, obviously, at every step in the process, order-of-battle analysis will play a crucial role in the issuance of warning. And order-of-battle analysts will carry a heavy responsibility.

Order-of-Battle Methodology

Since most countries are usually at peace and the strengths and locations of their military forces are relatively static, or at least the changes are fairly gradual, order-of-battle analysis normally tends to be a rather slow and hence conservative process. Over a period of time, certain methodologies or criteria are established (again rather conservative ones) which determine, by and large, whether a given unit can be "accepted" in the order-of-battle. While the methodologies will vary somewhat from country to country and among various types of forces (that is, the same criteria for "acceptance" may not apply to a Chinese ground force unit as to a North Korean air unit, still less to a guerrilla unit), the criteria nearly always are relatively rigid. In particular, they call for a relatively high degree of substantiation or "proof" that the unit does in fact exist, is of a certain strength or echelon, and is located in some specific area. Also, some unit number (hopefully the correct one, but at any rate some identifying number or designation) is highly desired by OB analysts. A unit which must be described as "unidentified" (u/i) lacks status, as it were, and is a little suspect. There is always a possibility that it is already carried elsewhere in the OB as an identified unit and has moved without detection. The analyst always seeks to "tidy up" his order-of-battle so as not to have such loose ends. Ideally, all units are firmly identified and located on a current basis, together with their correct designations, commanders and equipment, and their manning levels are consistent with the accepted table of organization and equipment (TO&E) for that type of unit. Everything fits. No problems. All units have been "accepted" and we have confidence in the OB.

Now, this ideal OB situation, of course, is rarely met—and almost never so for hostile states which are attempting to conceal such military facts from us. For a number of reasons—the difficulties and slowness of collection, the conservative criteria for acceptance of units, the personal views of analysts, the requirements for interagency or sometimes international consultation, and even the slowness of the reporting, editorial and printing process—the accepted order-of-battle is almost invariably out-of-date. For some units, it may be years out-of-date. Order-of-battle analysts are normally loath to admit it and few outside their immediate circle probably realize it, but it has by no means been unusual to have delays of two and three years in the acceptance of new units, determination that units have been inactivated, or recognition that they have been upgraded or downgraded in strength or relocated, redesignated, resubordinated, converted to another type, or split into two or more units. Incorrect numerical designations of units have been carried in OB summaries year after year; only by chance will it sometimes be found that units have been incorrectly identified for five or even ten or more years. Quite often, the last thing we can learn about a unit is its numerical designation.

In short, the "accepted" order-of-battle and the real current order-of-battle for adversaries probably never are identical. The most we can hope for is that it is reasonably close to the facts and that we have made no serious misjudgments of the enemy's strengths and capabilities. In time, we will usually obtain the data which we need to correct the OB—and we can change the location, designation or whatnot on the next printing. It is better to be slow or late with a change than to make a judgment too soon that may be erroneous and which we will have to retract later. Such, in general, is the philosophy of OB analysis. This is not intended as criticism; it is a statement of fact.

And most of the time, it does not really matter that it is like this, which is probably the chief reason that this normal lag in OB acceptance is so little recognized.

No one suffers from errors in the order-of-battle or from delays in information that a unit has been formed, upgraded or moved. Even egregious errors in estimating the strength of foreign forces (or particular components of foreign forces, like the great overestimate of Soviet missile strength in the late 1950s) have not caused us any real harm. Some might even say that the effects for budgetary purposes have been beneficial. Few care and no lives have been lost.

Except when there is a warning problem—when we or our allies are in danger of being attacked. Then these order-of-battle "details" can matter and matter decisively. When units are being upgraded or moved or mobilized or otherwise prepared for combat, then the accuracy and currency of order-of-battle do matter and lives can be lost, and many have been, because of incorrect details.

Often, however, sudden changes in the enemy's military situation, including a redeployment of units for possible commitment to combat, have not brought forth imaginative and responsive changes in methodology by order-of-battle analysts. It is in fact the usual case that the criteria for "acceptance" of changes in unit strengths and locations are not modified—even when it is clear that major troop movements are in fact in progress.

Sudden changes in unit locations, particularly large and secret redeployments, admittedly pose tremendous problems for order-of-battle analysts. It is rare indeed that the initial evidence will be so good, or accurate or complete that it will be possible to determine with any confidence how many troops are involved, what types or how many units are deploying, still less their unit designations or where they come from. Time is required to sort out the data, to attempt to obtain coverage of the home stations of the more likely units to see if they have in fact departed, and it will probably be weeks or months (even with good collection) before some of the needed information can be obtained. It may even be years— or never.

Confronted with initial reports, which may include some highly reliable observations and other good evidence as well as hearsay and unconfirmed reports that large numbers of troops of unknown designation are moving from unspecified locations toward undetermined destinations, the reaction of the normal OB analyst not surprisingly is to wait. What units can be moved on his situation map? He has no identifications, no firm evidence precisely what area the troops have come from; he may not be sure whether one or ten divisions could be involved although he usually suspects the lower figure and that many of his sources are greatly exaggerating the facts. The whole situation is anathema to him; it would be in violation of all his criteria to move any unit until he knows which units to move.

It may be all right for current or indications analysts to talk vaguely about large but unidentified troop movements, but the OB analyst must be specific and precise. He must "accept" or decide not to accept the movement of specific units (and this might well include new units of whose existence he has yet to learn). Confronted with this dilemma, he moves nothing—not yet.

The Indications Approach to Order-of-Battle

On the other hand is the indications analyst, sometimes but not always supported by other current analysts, who cares less for the order-of-battle details than that the community and the policymaker recognize, and recognize now, that the adversary is deploying major forces and that there is grave danger that this buildup is preparatory to their commitment. He implores his colleagues and superiors to see what is happening—and he is driven half frantic when they turn to the order-of-battle "experts" whose reply is that they "cannot accept" that yet. And the indications or current analyst may even be told that he cannot report a possible increasing threat. How can the threat be increasing when the order-of-battle (OB) map does not show any buildup of forces in that area? Perhaps it does not even show any units there.

This is not a hypothetical fiction or an indications analyst's nightmare. This is what can happen unless an impartial arbiter in position of authority intervenes to hear both sides. It is unquestionably true that the rigid criteria of order-of-battle acceptance have held back warning for weeks, and that this can be the most serious single impediment to the issuance of military warning. A few examples will illustrate the point more convincingly.

Not long after U.S. and UN forces intervened in the Korean conflict in June 1950, reports began to be received of northward troop movements on the Chinese mainland. Many of these reports indicated only that large numbers of troops were leaving the southernmost provinces of China (there had been a substantial buildup in this area to complete the conquest of the mainland the preceding year).

By late July, it was clear that substantial elements of the Fourth Field Army had left South China. Meanwhile, there were numerous although somewhat conflicting reports concerning troop movements farther north—while there were many reports which indicated that troops were moving to Manchuria, it could not be confirmed how many of the troops were proceeding that far and how many might have deployed to intermediate locations, including Fukien Province, for a possible assault on Taiwan. Even as reports of heavy northward troop movement continued to mount during August (some reports claimed that troop trains were moving northward day and night), there was little evidence on the whereabouts of specific units or sufficient data to make a reliable estimate of the number of troops involved.

Indications and order-of-battle analysts locked horns over the issue, with warning analysts pleading that the community recognize the likelihood of a major buildup in Manchuria, while OB claimed that there was "insufficient evidence" to move any units to Manchuria. Not until the end of August were watch reports (reviewed by OB) permitted to go forth stating that any elements of the

Fourth Field Army had moved to Manchuria (attempts to say that "major elements" could be there were vetoed). Not until about 1 October did order-of-battle "accept" that elements of some six armies of the Fourth Field Army were in Manchuria and make its first increase in estimated strength in that area. The criteria for OB "acceptance" actually held back warning of the buildup in Manchuria for at least six weeks, and this discrepancy as to what could be reported or "accepted" as evidence continued to a lesser degree up to and after the major Chinese offensive in late November. Who can say whether or not an earlier acceptance of the buildup would have increased the likelihood that U.S. and UN forces would have been better prepared for the Chinese onslaught?

A simpler and less damaging example of the difference between the order-of-battle and indications approach to troop movements may be derived from the Hungarian revolt in 1956. The Soviet response to this unexpected explosion was to pour troops into Hungary over virtually every road and rail connection from adjacent areas of the USSR. There was no reliable information on the total forces involved in the buildup; it was only clear that there were a lot. Concurrent with this heavy troop movement from the Carpathian Military District, an extraordinary travel ban was imposed in Romania, prohibiting all official Western travel to rail centers north of Bucharest—while several sources reported that Soviet troop trains were moving northwestward through Romania during the some period. By the criteria of indications analysts—for warning purposes—this was sufficient evidence to justify a statement that Soviet troops from the Odessa Military District (from unknown units and in unknown strength) were probably deploying to Hungary.

To order-of-battle analysts, such a conclusion could not be justified. They stated flatly that they could not accept information of this kind. About six months later, a unit number associated with a Soviet division from the Odessa Military District was identified in Hungary, and the division was immediately accepted in the order-of-battle.

By the time that Soviet forces were deploying for the invasion of Czechoslovakia in the summer of 1968, our collection and analysis had seemingly improved, or perhaps because we had more time we were able to do better. At any rate, the usual conflict between indications and order-of-battle analysts was subdued, and there were fewer (one cannot say no) complaints from warning analysts that too few units were being accepted by order-of-battle or accepted too late. A controversy did arise, however, over the Soviet troop movements into Poland which began in the last few days of July, which illustrates that this question of troop movements when unit identifications are not available remains a potentially serious problem for warning. The initial sources of information on these Soviet troop movements into Poland were primarily tourists and other travelers in Poland. Within 48 to 72 hours after the initial movements into Poland began, there were a half dozen voluntary reports from travelers of sightings of heavy troop movements at several road crossing points from the USSR. Within a few days, Western observers had located two holding or assembly areas for these forces—one to the north of Warsaw and one to the south—to which they were denied access. Indications analysts, and to a lesser degree other current analysts, were prepared to "accept" or at least to report that substantial Soviet forces were entering Poland that were apparently backup forces (not part of the concurrent buildup directly along the Czechoslovak border). Even indications analysts, however (usually considered alarmist or prone to exaggerate by their more conservative colleagues), would hardly have been willing to accept in early August what later proved to be true, that some 11 or 12 Soviet divisions all told were then in Poland, as compared with the normal two. Order of battle analysts, using their criteria, were not willing to accept any units which they could not identify, or whose movement from home stations had not been confirmed, which resulted in some delay in acceptance of additional Soviet divisions in Poland.

Analysis of Mobilization

Closely related to order-of-battle and usually handled by the same analysts is mobilization. Traditionally in expectation of war, although sometimes not until it has broken out, countries mobilize their forces. Historically, the declaration of general mobilization often was the decisive indication of the imminence or inevitability of war.

Nearly all nations have mobilization plans to cover a range of contingencies. Mobilization can range from a partial or selective callup of reservists to fill out existing units, to a full mobilization of the armed forces and formation of additional units, to a general or total mobilization of the entire populace and economic resources of the entire country.

There is little chance any state would try to conceal a full mobilization; it would be too obvious. Experience teaches us, however, that in closed societies substantial augmentation of the armed forces often has proved extremely difficult to quantify or detect. Surprising as it may seem, intelligence often has been more likely to obtain data and report promptly the movement of a single submarine or the redeployment of a squadron of aircraft than the call-up to the armed forces of a half a million troops. Information which could never be concealed in this country is routinely held secret in a dictatorship and protected by highly effective security measures.

Estimates of the total strength of the armed forces of foreign states have proved to be extremely elusive and have sometimes been wide of the mark. While U.S. intelligence was greatly overestimating the strength of the Soviet missile forces in the 1950s, it was greatly underestimating the strength of Soviet ground forces, quite likely by a third or more.

In 1968, despite a great improvement in collection, U.S. intelligence did not detect the call-up of Soviet reservists to fill out the units deployed to the

Czechoslovak border in May, and it recognized the mobilization of the invasion forces in July largely because of Soviet announcements.

Of still greater importance was the failure to recognize the substantial mobilization of North Vietnamese forces in 1964-1965. The evidence of this was derived in large part from Hanoi's public calls for enlistments. While order-of-battle analysts, lacking specific evidence of the formation of new units or upgrading of existing ones, could accept only a very small increase in North Vietnamese forces, indications analysts argued that a doubling of the armed forces was not an unreasonable estimate—an assessment which, a year later, was accepted as correct.

It is thus evident that assessments of mobilization—a key indicator of hostile intent—are subject to the same problems and potential errors as order-of-battle. When mobilization is in progress, we are almost certain to be running behind the facts. Where there is a good reason to believe that mobilization is under way, warning cannot wait for "proof' which may be long in coming.

Needed: a Voice for Warning in the Order-of-Battle Buildup

The differences in approach, in criteria, in analytical techniques between indications and order-of-battle analysts are serious, and they are potentially as damaging for warning in the future as they have been in the past. Indeed, a dependence on the strict criteria of order-of-battle in a genuine crisis in which the adversary was employing his most sophisticated security and deception techniques could be catastrophic. At the same time, few would presume to suggest that the normal analytic techniques of order-of-battle (which have generally worked well, if slowly, in peacetime) should be tossed overboard for more imaginative, less precise and more "indications-oriented" techniques.

What is the answer to this serious dilemma? The answer is that both sides should be given their say, but that order-of-battle analysts should not be permitted in the crisis situation to have the last word on what can be "accepted" or what can even be reported to higher authority. There are things more important in an impending showdown with the adversary than the purity of order-of-battle techniques. It is more important that superior authorities know that some enemy troop buildup is under way, even if we cannot be too precise about it, than that they be led to believe that there is no such buildup.

The arbitration of such disputes belongs at the supervisory level. The system must not work, as it has sometimes worked in the past, so that the order-of-battle analyst is permitted to review and to veto what indications and current analysts, in their best judgment, believe to be of warning significance. For the most part, order-of-battle analysts are accustomed to a degree of autonomy and independence on what they will decide or "accept" which is probably unparalleled at the analytical level of intelligence. Often the basis or reasons on which such judgments are made, or not made, goes unquestioned by higher authority. Conventional order-of-battle methods must not be permitted to hold back warning. To insure that the indications of a military buildup are being adequately reported, and not just that which has been "accepted," is a constant and most important responsibility of the supervisor. He must not attempt to resolve the argument by turning it back to the order-of-battle analysts for decision on the grounds that they are the "experts." To do so may be fatal to the warning judgment. Over a period of years, this issue has probably been the single greatest bone of contention between the indications system and the rest of the community. To deny the warning analyst an equal hearing on the all-important issue of the military buildup is to make a mockery of the whole indications system.

It would be misleading not to note that progress has been made on this problem. Perhaps most important, major improvements in technical collection have greatly increased the accuracy and currency of our information concerning the locations, strengths, equipment and movements of military units. This is particularly true of large formations with heavy equipment operating in relatively open terrain. Detection is less certain for smaller, poorly equipped units (particularly guerrilla forces) and in heavily forested or mountainous areas. In addition, poor weather can impede collection.

Over a period of years many people have come to recognize that normal order-of-battle methods may be inadequate and too slow in crisis situations. Postmortems have often confirmed the contentions of indications analysts that their methods, in these circumstances, are more accurate and responsive to the problem than waiting for all the order-of-battle "proof" to come in. The proliferation of operations and alert centers and general dispersion of the military analytical effort in the community, although probably excessively duplicative in some respects, also has done much to insure that order-of-battle analysts do not have a monopoly on reporting military movements, and their techniques have come under increasing scrutiny by other analysts. Nonetheless, this is a problem to which the community at all levels needs to be constantly alert. Particularly when an abnormal situation is developing, and it becomes evident that unusual troop movement is or could be in progress, the intelligence system may need to take specific steps to insure that indications of order-of-battle changes, as well as confirmed deployments of known units, are being adequately analyzed and reported.

LOGISTICS IS THE QUEEN OF BATTLES

The extent and variety of logistic preparations for modern war are reflected in the number of logistic and transportation items carried on indicator lists, which usually equal or exceed the number for any other topic. If we could be sure of knowing the extent, level and variety of logistic preparations at any time we would not only have a very accurate grasp of the adversary's capabilities, we would probably also have very precise insight into his intent.

Countries are Not Logistically Ready for War

It is easy to gain the impression that states with large and well-equipped military forces are also in a high state of readiness logistically for hostilities, and would need to undertake little additional preparation for war. As with many other things, some experience with live crises and improved collection have given us a better appreciation of reality. It was true, of course, that the USSR did produce large quantities of weapons and equipment and it had substantial stocks of many items in reserve depots—some in forward areas and others further to the rear—which would be drawn upon in the event of hostilities.

However, the USSR clearly felt its logistic preparations to be inadequate for the possibility of hostilities. Not only did the Czechoslovak crisis reveal a requirement to mobilize Soviet combat units, still more striking was the requirement to mobilize rear services support units. In order to support the forward movement of combat units, it was necessary to requisition transport vehicles and their drivers from their normal civilian activities, and this at the height of the harvest season when they were most needed. These reserve transport units were then employed in shuttling supplies from the USSR to forward bases both prior to and after the invasion of Czechoslovakia and were only demobilized in the autumn when the situation had stabilized sufficiently to permit a withdrawal from Czechoslovakia of a substantial portion of the original invasion force. There are some indications that, even with this effort, supply shortages were encountered although there was no active resistance.

These points are made here to emphasize that these activities bore no similarity to an exercise (although in a pro forma deception effort the Soviets called much of their logistic activity an exercise) and were clearly distinguishable from the type of activity normally conducted in Eastern Europe. To those analysts who were convinced of the likelihood of a Soviet invasion, the logistic preparation above all was perhaps the most decisive evidence. Even more persuasive than the deployment of Soviet divisions to positions around Czechoslovakia (which conceivably, albeit with some difficulty, could have been explained away as mere "pressure" on Czechoslovakia) was the reality of the logistic buildup. There was no conceivable need for it except for an actual invasion.

This is but one of innumerable examples which could be found to demonstrate the validity of logistic preparations as a barometer of preparations for hostilities. Numerous instances could be cited from the Vietnam war, ranging from such relatively long-term preparations as the construction of new roads in the Lao Panhandle to handle the truck movements to the South, to such short-term tactical preparations as the commandeering of the local populace to porter supplies in preparation for an attack on a fortified village. In large part the history of the war was a chronicle of ingenious and unrelenting North Vietnamese efforts to sustain their logistic movements and of our attempts to disrupt them. With few exceptions, major new logistic projects or exceptionally heavy movements of supplies proved to be valid and reliable indications of enemy preparations for forthcoming operations. In short, the type of logistic preparations undertaken by any state in expectation of early hostilities is different in both quantity and quality from what goes on in a time of peace. And we can, if we have enough evidence and understand our adversary's methods of operation, usually see the difference.

Key Warning Factors in Logistic Preparations for Combat Operations

From the multitude of potential logistic indications of impending hostilities, some of which may be quite specific for particular nations, we may generalize on several of the more important aspects of logistic preparations, some or many of which will nearly always be undertaken prior to military action. Clearly, the extent and variety of such preparations will be dependent on the type and scope of expected hostilities, their likely duration, and the degree of counteraction which is anticipated.

Logistic preparations are an integral part of any mobilization plan. When the impending military operation requires any degree of mobilization, as it usually will, the mobilization also will involve some type of logistic preparations, since the two are inseparably connected. Reserves called up must have weapons and ammunition, expanded units must obtain or remove equipment from depots, additional transport (rail cars, trucks, aircraft and sometimes ships) is needed to move both troops and their supplies and equipment, more fuel is needed both to move the units and to support them in the impending action, and so forth. Even the mobilization of a single reserve or under-strength unit in a modern army will require a whole series of logistic support measures if the unit is to move anywhere or have any combat capability when it gets there. The more troops involved, the more extensive the logistic and transport support which will be needed, and the more disruptive or apparent the fulfilling of this requirement is apt to be. Logistic planning for the mobilization and deployment of modern forces is enormously complex and, indeed, the greater part of the mobilization plan actually comprises the details by which the supply, support and transport of forces is to be accomplished rather than the mere call-up of the reservists themselves to their units. The more carefully the mobilization plan is prepared and the more rapidly it is to be implemented, the greater will be the meticulous attention to every detail of logistic support, since any shortage or bottleneck can disrupt the whole system.

Impact on civilian life and economy. The mobilization of additional logistic support on any scale is likely to have an early and sometimes serious impact on the life of the ordinary civilian. Certain factors of course will mitigate these effects: well-placed and large reserves of military supplies and equipment may permit a unit to mobilize locally with no seeming impact on the community; some types of foods can be preserved for long periods; fuel depots reserved exclusively for a military emergency will reduce the need to requisition it from the civilian economy; and very affluent nations (such as the U.S.) may have such a general abundance that a relatively small mobilization will have little or no immediate impact on civilians.

Nonetheless, all countries have some bottlenecks and shortages, and in a mobilization of any scope the effect of these will be felt, and often immediately, on the life of civilians. Warning analysts should be cognizant of what these potentially critical shortages are and collectors should be prepared in advance to concentrate on some of these, since a coincidence of several of them may be either long-term or short-term evidence of mobilization or of unusual military requirements. Some of the types of shortages indicative of military requisitioning which have shown up most frequently have been: food (particularly meats and other choice items which are nearly always diverted to the military in time of need); fuel (despite reserve depots for the military, crises involving military deployments are usually accompanied by reports of fuel shortages for civilian use); and transportation and medical supplies (both of such critical importance that they are further discussed below).

Impact on transportation. One of the most immediate and most disruptive effects of logistic mobilization measures is likely to be on the transportation system, and it is also one of the most likely to be detectable. No country has a transportation system adequate to take care of any substantial increase in military requirements without either requisitioning from or otherwise having some effect on normal civilian transport. The mobilization plans of all states call for the commandeering in one way or another of civilian transport facilities. These measures may range all the way from simply giving priority to military shipments (by rail, truck, water or air) over civilian shipments up to extensive requisitioning of trucks from the civilian economy and/or the takeover by the military of the entire transportation system.

The most extensive mobilization plans in the world for the takeover of civilian transport by the military were probably those of the USSR and its Eastern European allies (which had closely integrated plans). Any significant or sudden increase in military requirements will usually have an immediate impact on the transportation system. Reports of shortages of rail cars for normal use and the requisitioning of trucks from the civilian economy have sometimes been a key indicator that abnormal military movements were impending, as they were for the buildup of forces around Czechoslovakia in the last week of July 1968.

For a major mobilization in expectation of large-scale hostilities, some nations plan a virtual total takeover of the transportation systems—ground, air and water. However effective or ineffective the implementation of these plans, we could hardly fail to detect some aspects of it, particularly in a drastic and sudden military takeover accompanied by heavy military use of rail and road transport. In other key areas as well, major disruptions of transportation as a result of military movements have been key indications of preparations for hostilities. The heavy

Chinese troop movements to Manchuria in the summer and fall of 1950 caused extensive disruption of normal freight movements—and there were a number of reports of this. Less extensive troop and supply movements in China also have occasioned sporadic reports that civil transport has been curtailed.

Heavy movements of rear service elements and supplies. However many supplies may have been stocked in forward depots or in reserve to the rear, no commander probably ever thought he had enough. The additional buildup of supplies for the forces to be committed in initial operations (whether they be ground assault forces, air, naval, air defense or even missile forces) is a virtual certainty for any country which has time to make such preparations. Unless forces are taken by total surprise, some logistic buildup prior to operations is to be expected, and usually it will be very heavy. In fact, the logistic buildup often will be as heavy and demanding of resources as the troop buildup, if not more so, and, moreover, will require a longer time. The problem of the "logistic tail" is well known, and many a commander has been ready to go before his supply buildup has been completed, or has been forced to halt his offensive for lack of such key items as fuel. A delay in attack after the combat forces are seemingly ready and in place therefore may not mean any hesitancy or indecision on the part of the adversary so long as the supply buildup is continuing. It should not be regarded as a negative indication, as it so often has been. Rather, a most close watch should be maintained on the logistic buildup in the hope of determining when in fact the adversary will be ready to jump off. (This may not be easy to determine, but it will probably be somewhat better than total guesswork.)

In World War II, the Japanese watched the buildup of Soviet forces in the Far East for about six months. They had estimated that the facilities of the Trans-Siberian Railroad would have to be concentrated on military shipments for at least 100 days before a Soviet attack on the Japanese forces in Manchuria. By late July 1945, their intelligence was reporting that continued heavy movements now consisted almost entirely of supply and rear service troops, which they correctly interpreted to mean that the buildup of combat forces was complete. They concluded that the Soviets could initiate the attack at any time after 1 August and received no further warning of the attack which occurred on 8 August.

In the Soviet buildup for the attack on Czechoslovakia in the summer of 1968, most of the combat forces which participated in the invasion appeared to have completed their deployments by 1 August (this excluded the backup forces which entered northern Poland whose movement was still in progress well into August). The intelligence judgment was that Soviet forces were in a high state of readiness (if not their peak readiness) for invasion on about 1 August. In fact, however, the logistic buildup in Europe was still continuing and the Soviets themselves did not announce the completion of their professed rear services "exercise" until 10 August. The invasion began on 20 August. It is likely that Soviet forces really were not ready, or at least not as ready as their commanders would have wished, at the time that the community judged them to be. Had there been a real threat of serious opposition, the logistic buildup probably would have been of even greater importance and presumably might have required a longer time. In any case, the relaxation of concern over a possible invasion of Czechoslovakia when nothing occurred in the first few days of August was not warranted by the military evidence. The threat not only remained but was increasing.

The problem of assessing logistic readiness, and hence actual readiness for attack, was a difficult intelligence problem in Vietnam and Laos, where the problems of estimating supply movements at all were compounded by the effects of air strikes, road interdictions, poor weather and jungle terrain. In these circumstances, however, as in more conventional warfare, the continuing effort to build up supplies and the evident great importance attached to keeping the roads open were indications of impending operations even when their scope or timing might be elusive.

Drawdown on existing depots. Another aspect of the abnormal requirement of military units for supplies is likely to be the drawdown on supplies in depots, both in forward and rear areas. In the forward area, it will be for allocation to the troops for combat. In rear areas, a sudden emptying of reserve depots, particularly if several are involved, is a likely indication that equipment is being issued to reserve or under-strength units.

Medical preparations. One of the most obvious requirements of forces going into combat as compared with their needs in peacetime is in medical support. Indeed, of all fields of logistic support, this may be the one in which there is the greatest difference between war and peace. Not only do combat units require vastly greater quantities of drugs and medicines, but also different types of drugs. The requirements for doctors and medical technicians will multiply, as will the need for field hospitals, evacuation facilities, and the like. Even in nations which do not traditionally place a high value on saving the lives of wounded enlisted men (among which have been several important Communist nations), the need for increased drugs and medical support facilities of all types will skyrocket in the event of hostilities. As in other logistic preparations, these changes will affect not only the military forces themselves, but also are likely to have a serious impact on the civilian populace. Shortage of drugs and hospital supplies, sudden callups of physicians to the armed forces, and greatly stepped-up blood collection programs are some of the obvious effects.

In addition, belligerents may have to make very heavy purchases of drugs abroad (as did North Vietnam, assisted by China, in the early stages of U.S. involvement in the Vietnam war). Occasionally, heavy acquisition of drugs for particular ailments (such as, anti-malarial) may provide a tip-off that military forces are being readied for movement into particular areas.

Some analysts feel that medical preparations are an aspect of war planning which have been given too little attention, and that this is a field in which our data base and collection planning could well be improved. It is a field in which some preparedness measures would appear to be unique to hostilities and thus of very high specific value for warning.

Logistic preparations for survivability. Another important logistic preparation likely to distinguish war from peace is the stockpiling of equipment and other measures to insure the survivability of the logistic system itself. Such measures, particularly if undertaken in any great number or in marked contrast to normal practice, carry high validity as indications that a nation is preparing for some action for which it expects retaliation. (Unless, on the other hand, an adversary is clearly getting ready to initiate the action.) Rail and road facilities are, of course, highly vulnerable to interdiction, and aggressors normally will take some measures to protect them and to provide for their repair before they embark on hostilities. In addition to obvious measures such as increased air defense protection at bridges and rail yards, extraordinary logistic preparedness measures will be suggested by the stockpiling along the way of railroad ties and rails, emergency bridging equipment, bulldozers, road-building machinery and other material for the rapid repair of damaged transportation routes. Rarely, if ever, do nations undertake emergency steps of this nature when they are expecting a prolonged period of peace. Another measure to insure the survivability of critical transportation routes is the construction of numerous road bypasses, extra bridges, and the like at bottlenecks—a procedure at which the North Vietnamese were adept.

Logistic preparations for specific operations. In addition to the value of logistic preparations as indications in general, certain types of activity may provide very specific indications of the nature of impending attacks. An extraordinary standdown of transport aircraft or their assembly at bases near airborne forces is a good indication that airborne operations are impending. A large buildup of amphibious equipment and landing craft probably signifies impending waterborne attacks, and the detection of large quantities of mobile bridging equipment probably indicates major river-crossing operations. These highly specific logistic operations are of great value for warning, provided they are detected, since they give us not only generalized warning but often specific warning of how and where attacks may be launched. Thus, once again, we can demonstrate the value for warning of the identification of the enemy's logistic preparations.

One final note of guidance can be offered. The analyst should not forget or overlook the logistic items in the mass of other indications. In a major buildup, a great deal will be going on—large-scale ground force movements, lots of fighter aircraft redeployments, dozens of political items and rumors, accurate and planted reports of enemy intentions. All these are heady stuff and make fine current items, and the order-of-battle buildup looks great on the map. But, sometimes in all this, those little logistic fragments get lost which might have confirmed that the military buildup is genuine—that is, involves bona fide preparations for combat and is not an exercise or an idle threat for our benefit. In all the excitement, it is important not to lose these gems of intelligence so rare and invaluable to the assessment of the enemy's real intentions.

OTHER FACTORS IN COMBAT PREPARATIONS

The preceding sections have addressed some of the major types of activity that precede or accompany the commitment of forces to combat. Preparations for hostilities, however, will likely be marked by a number of other anomalies or highly unusual activities which will further help to distinguish the situation from that which is normal. In this section, we will consider in general terms some of the things that we should watch for, or which have been noted in past crises, as they characterize true preparations for hostilities.

Preoccupation of the High Command

War is the business of generals and admirals and, when preparations are in progress for war, they will be very deeply involved indeed in the planning, even to the consideration of the most minute details of the impending operation. Their staffs will be putting in long hours of planning and paper work, and more officers will likely be needed to cope with it. For reasons of security and secrecy, as few officers as possible may be informed of the full plans, but it is inevitable that the preparations will affect the activities of many, if not all, components of the military establishment in one way or another. This will be true, although in varying degrees, whether a deliberate surprise attack is being planned for some months ahead (as in Japan's preparations before Pearl Harbor) or whether the military leadership is preparing to respond to a relatively sudden and unexpected crisis (such as the U.S. when the strategic missiles were discovered in Cuba).

It is a myth "That our enemies have all their contingency plans ready and that great hostilities could start at the drop of the hat without any further planning or consideration."

One of the great myths perpetrated by some analysts (sometimes in the name of warning) is that our enemies have all their contingency plans ready and that great hostilities could start at the drop of the hat without any further planning or consideration of the details by their general staffs. This is ridiculous. No state can be ready for every contingency, and even if it does have a specific plan for the particular crisis at hand, the high command or general staff assuredly will want to review it and to be sure that all the subordinate commands are fully prepared to play their roles and there are no bottlenecks. More likely, they will have to modify the plan or prepare a whole new one, since the situation almost inevitably will be a little different, or someone questions part of it, and so forth. In any case, the result is a virtual certainty: the military establishment at its highest levels will be extraordinarily involved and preoccupied with planning and staff work, intensive activity will be under way, the command and control system will be tested to its fullest, and the ramifications of all this are likely to be reflected in high volumes of communications and a general atmosphere of crisis in the military establishment. We have learned from experience that even major exercises are likely to require the attention and presence of top military leaders. Where the preparations are real, the requirement for their participation will be infinitely greater. A knowledge of their whereabouts and some information on their activities may be invaluable. From a variety of sources, both military and political, we hopefully will gain some sense, however inadequate, that the military establishment is immersed in great and extraordinary activity, or is devoting an inordinate amount of attention to a particular area or subject.

Alerts and Combat Readiness

The declaration of the real (not practice) alert and the raising of forces to very high (or the highest) levels of combat readiness is a major indication of preparedness for combat or possible combat. Like mobilization or major redeployments of units, the true combat alert will be reserved only for the extraordinary situation in which hostilities are either planned or there is reason to fear that deteriorating international conditions entail a risk of hostilities in the near future.

Forces of major countries usually have prescribed degrees or conditions of readiness ranging upward from their normal day-to-day condition to the highest degree of readiness which is full readiness for imminent hostilities. In the U.S. forces, these stages are known as DEFCONs (Defense Conditions) which range from 5 (lowest) to 1 (highest).

The raising of DEFCON status is a serious matter and involves specific prescribed steps which materially increase the readiness of men and materiel for combat. Imposition of the highest DEFCON status would indicate a national emergency.

These steps entail a series of specific measures by the various components of the armed forces which, when fully accomplished (that is, when full readiness is implemented), will have brought both combat and supporting units to readiness for immediate commitment to combat. These readiness conditions are to be distinguished from routine alerts or exercises, which are frequently carried out to test the ability of units to respond quickly. As in the U.S. forces, the raising of readiness conditions is a serious step, undertaken rarely. Indeed, there is reason to believe that the imposition of full readiness conditions throughout the armed forces, with all the steps that would presumably be entailed, is a step (like our DEFCON 1) which would be undertaken only in expectation of hostilities. Although aspects of the combat alert plan are undoubtedly tested frequently, the widespread implementation of full readiness is reserved for the genuine combat situation, or expectation of such a situation.

The declaration of full combat readiness is thus a matter of highest concern to warning intelligence. There is nothing too trivial for us to know about so important a subject: the precise terminology, the mechanics by which such a condition would be ordered, or the exact measures which follow from such an order. Because of the rarity with which even increased (as opposed to full) readiness conditions are imposed, most analysts will have had little experience with such circumstances, and there is likely to be considerable uncertainty about what we can or cannot detect or about what precisely will occur. The warning student, however, should make a study of all available evidence on this subject, for in the hour of crisis the ability to recognize that full combat readiness was being implemented could be of decisive importance.

Exercises versus Combat Deployments

Both compilers and users of indicator lists are frequently puzzled by the fact that an abnormally high level of exercise activity and a virtual standdown of normal exercise activity both appear as indicators. This is not a real contradiction provided that the circumstances in which each of these may be valid indicators are understood. An exceptionally high level of training, and particularly very realistic or specialized training for a specific type of operation or against a specific target, of course may be a valid indication of preparations for combat operations. Obviously, troops need training, and very intensive training, if they are to accomplish their missions effectively, and the scope and type of training in the armed forces of any country is a very useful guide indeed to the type of operations it expects to conduct. If our collection is adequate, we may also be able to tell from specific training exercises exactly what combat operations are being planned. The North Vietnamese Army traditionally held detailed rehearsals with sand tables before launching attacks on specific targets in South Vietnam and Laos. For larger, more conventional operations, extensive command post and staff exercises, supplemented by drills of the troops in their specific roles, are the normal procedure. No commander would choose to launch combat operations until he had satisfied himself that both his officers and troops were reasonably well trained in what they were to do, and the more specific the training for the particular type of warfare or target, the better.

Thus, as a general—and sometimes quite specific—guide to the plans of the potential adversary, the type of training is an indication not to be ignored. Such training activity, however, is often a relatively long-term indication, which may precede the actual initiation of hostilities by weeks, months or even years. It may, in fact, not indicate an expectation of hostilities so much as a desire to be prepared for them if they should occur.

Over the shorter term, perhaps a period of some weeks—although it may be much less—extraordinary changes in the pattern of training activity, and particularly cessation or near standdown of normal training, have usually proved to be a much more specific or valid indication of hostilities. The genuine alert of forces in a crisis or for possible hostilities is nearly always marked by abrupt curtailment of routine training, usually accompanied by a recall of forces in the field to their home stations in order to place them in readiness. In a real combat alert, missile troops will not be sent to remote ranges for training nor antiaircraft units to firing areas; they will be needed either at their home stations or wartime deployment areas. Similarly, much if not all routine ground, air and naval activity will be terminated, although defensive measures such as air and naval patrols will probably be stepped up. Such variations in training patterns are likely to be evident and they are a distinguishing characteristic of genuine crises—a true sign that combat readiness of potential enemy forces is indeed being raised. The Intelligence Community, based on growing experience, will often be able to recognize such situations, but we need constantly to be alert to what is not happening (but ought to be happening) as well as to what is. This is particularly true when there are no overt tensions which might alert us—when the adversary is preparing in secret.

Statements that "Things look pretty quiet," or "There doesn't seem to be much going on," can be dangerously misleading. Intended as reassurance to the listener, they may in fact mean that normal activity has been curtailed because of an alert.

Once it is under way, an exercise is something of a negative indication in the short term. When troops and logistic resources have been committed to an exercise, they are not as ready to respond to a combat situation as they were before they deployed for the exercise. The problem for intelligence is to be sure that the buildup phase for an "exercise" is really for an exercise and not a cover for a deployment of forces for an attack. In many exercises, this will be little if any problem since the exercises probably will not be conducted in the area in which the troops would have to be deployed for an actual attack, but farther back from the line of confrontation or even some distance to the rear.

There are few deception measures so simple to carry out or seemingly so transparently evident as a series of false statements on the nature or purpose of military activity. Despite this, such falsehoods have sometimes proved effective, and we have no assurance that the Intelligence Community as a whole will necessarily recognize them for what they are. During the summer of 1968, the USSR announced a whole series of "exercises" that Soviet and Warsaw Pact forces were said to be undertaking either in or adjacent to Czechoslovakia. In fact, these forces conducted no real exercises all summer long, and the alerting and deployments of forces for the Czechoslovak crisis totally disrupted the summer training program. These "exercises" were announced solely to provide a pretext for the introduction of Soviet forces into Czechoslovakia in June and, still more importantly, as a cover for the major mobilization and deployment of Soviet forces after mid-July. The USSR even announced an elaborate scenario for its so-called "rear services exercise" under cover of which combat units and their logistic support were deployed. Yet, despite the circumstances and the obvious fact that all this activity was clearly related to Soviet efforts to bring the Czechoslovak situation under control, much current intelligence reporting accepted Soviet statements on these "exercises" as if they were valid descriptions of what was occurring. Even after the invasion, a number of post-mortem studies persisted in referring to the "exercises" without qualification, and even repeated (as if valid) the scenarios which had been carried in the Soviet press.

In the case of Czechoslovakia, there was ample evidence at hand to make a judgment that the Soviets were not engaged in genuine "exercises" and that Soviet tactics all summer long were designed to bring Czechoslovakia into line by one means or another. Thus the situation called for exceptional care and sophistication in reporting to insure that the real Soviet purpose and objective were not obscured by rote-like repetition of Soviet statements

Offensive versus Defensive Preparations

In an impending crisis, when war may be about to break out or when there is a fear of escalation of hostilities already in progress, the Intelligence Community often is required to come to some judgment as to whether preparations are to be considered offensive or defensive in nature—in short, does fear of attack by us or some other adversary account for the observed military activity, or is it in preparation for offensive action?

This analytical problem is encountered both with respect to buildups of forces that could be used for offensive action (particularly ground force combat units) and to activity clearly of a defensive nature (such as increased antiaircraft defenses and fighter patrol activity). There are instances in which the seemingly offensive buildup of ground combat force, and even a considerable one, may be entirely for defensive purposes because of a valid fear of attack. And there are instances in which the seemingly defensive action, the buildup of forces which could never be used in an attack, is in fact part of the offensive preparations undertaken solely in expectation of retaliation for the impending offense. How can we tell the difference? When should accelerated military activity, of either type, be considered a manifestation of offensive preparations, and when not?

There can be no categorical answer to this question and each case must be separately considered. The following, however, are some general guidelines to be considered:

- Any large-scale buildup of combat strength, particularly major deployments of ground force units, which is in excess of a reasonable defensive requirement for the area, should be considered a probable preparation for offensive action. Experience, in fact, teaches us that it will often be the best single indicator of aggressive intentions.
- Other extensive military preparations (such as a major mobilization effort and a large-scale buildup of logistic support) will reinforce the likelihood that the troop deployment is probably for offensive purposes.
- Preparations which are seemingly "defensive" (particularly air and civil defense measures) can be accurately evaluated only in the light of the buildup of capabilities for offensive action. Where the offensive capability is being rapidly or steadily augmented, the probability is that the concurrent acceleration of defensive measures is in fact in preparation for an expected retaliation for the planned offensive.

- In the absence of a buildup of offensive capabilities, the defensive preparations are probably indeed just that.
- The speed and urgency of both offensive and defensive preparations must also be considered. When an offensive action is imminent, the aggressor is likely to be most urgently concerned with the security of his homeland and its populace, and the defensive measures against possible retaliation may be truly extraordinary and greatly accelerated (such as those in mainland China shortly prior to the Chinese intervention in Korea, after a summer in which Beijing had shown no great concern with civil defense).

Coping with Extraordinary Military Developments

The military situation which prevails in the course of preparations for hostilities is extraordinary. It is not a question of degree alone—not just more high command activity, more communications, more alerts, and so on. It will also involve unprecedented activity that would never occur except in preparation for or expectation of hostilities.

Compilers of indicator lists have devoted much effort to attempting to isolate and to define accurately those preparations unique to hostilities, or at any rate highly unusual in time of peace. Heading any such list, of course, would be obtaining by any means the order of attack. Second only to this is the plan to attack (without the order to implement it). It may be noted that in the history of warfare such intelligence coups have been accomplished more than once, but not always recognized as such.

In addition there are indicators of such specificity and value that they can only be interpreted as preparations for offensive action. These actions would never be required for defense or precautionary purposes and are rarely undertaken in peacetime. In some cases, such information may be even more valuable or convincing than the plan or order to attack—since the latter will often be suspect, and with cause, as a plant or deception effort.

Among the types of military indicators of such high specific value are:

- The redesignation of administrative military commands as operational commands, or the change from peacetime to wartime organization.
- Widespread activation of wartime headquarters or alternate command posts.
- Release to control of commanders types of weapons normally held under very strict controls, particularly chemical or nuclear weapons.
- Minelaying in maritime approaches.
- Assignment of interpreters or prisoner of war interrogation teams to front-line units.

- Evidence of positive military deception—as opposed to increased security measures.
- Imposition of extraordinary military security measures—such as evacuation of military dependents or removal of border populations.
- Greatly increased reconnaissance by any means, but particularly against likely targets of initial surprise attack.
- Sudden adoption of extraordinary camouflage or other concealment measures.

When the intelligence system is so fortunate as to obtain indications of such high specificity, it will be most important that they be recognized as such and accorded the weight they deserve, rather than lost in a mass of other incoming data. Some seemingly small developments (in the total scope of activity) may be of the greatest importance. If one is attempting to compute probabilities, they will rate very high on the scale.

Magnitude and Redundancy of Preparations

No matter how many unusual or highly specific indications may be noted, assessments in the end will often depend heavily on the sheer magnitude of the military buildup of the potential aggressor. And rightly so. The massive buildup of military power, out of all proportion to anything required in normal times or for defensive purposes, has proven time and again to be the most valid indication of military intent. Many have learned to their regret that they had made a great error to write off an overwhelming buildup of military force as "just a buildup of capabilities" from which no conclusion could be drawn.

A manifestation of this phenomenon was the Soviet invasion of Czechoslovakia. Essentially, the misjudgment was to regard the massive buildup of Soviet and Warsaw Pact forces as equally compatible with an intention to invade and a mere show of force or attempt to threaten the Czechoslovaks. This was the largest buildup of Soviet combat power since World War II, exceeding considerably the force which had been brought to bear to suppress the Hungarian revolt in 1956. Experienced military analysts on the Soviet Union had literally never seen anything like it and could hardly believe the evidence at hand. This was a force which met Soviet doctrinal concepts for offensive operations even when resistance might be expected. Sheer logic, not to mention the lessons of history, should teach us that a force of this magnitude was never required just to put more pressure on Dubcek.

It is a feature both of the buildup of combat forces and of logistic preparations for war that the aggressor will seek a great superiority of power and ability to sustain combat in comparison with that of his adversary—that is, if the military planner has his way. All commanders want an abundance of everything before they attack. They are practically never satisfied that they have enough. Occasionally, military forces will have to operate on a shoestring, but rarely at the choice of their commanders.

Thus, a redundancy of supplies and a great superiority in equipment, as well as massive troop deployments, may be the mark of a true buildup for attack. The aggressor sometimes may appear to be inordinately long in his buildup and to be undertaking seemingly excessive preparations. The intelligence analyst in these circumstances should take care to avoid the pitfall into which more than one has fallen, which is to conclude that all this buildup does not mean anything because the adversary already has more than enough on hand to attack. This argument has been seriously advanced and even propounded as a *negative* indication ("he would not do all this unless he was bluffing"). This kind of inverse reasoning is the death of warning.

Massive buildups of military power and logistic support are never negative indications. They may occasionally not be followed by military action, but the odds are high that action will follow. As a general rule, the greater the ratio of buildup in relation to that of the opponent, the greater the likelihood of attack. It is fatal to ignore evidence of this kind.

Chapter 4

POLITICAL FACTORS FOR WARNING

It is easy to demonstrate the importance and relevance of military developments for warning. Anyone can recognize that the numerous military preparedness steps identified on indicator lists bear a direct relationship to a capability, and hence at least a possible intention, to commit military forces. Many military developments, including some of the most important, are physically measurable or quantifiable, assuming, of course, that the collection capability exists. There are so many tanks deployed in this area, which represents such-and-such a percentage increase over the past two weeks, for example. Such information, factually speaking, is unambiguous; its interpretation is not dependent on subjective judgment.

AMBIGUITY OF POLITICAL INDICATORS

> *"The potential for concealment of intention in the political field is much higher than for military preparations."*

In contrast, the relevance of political developments or political indicators to warning is often not so readily apparent, is not factually demonstrable, and interpretation of specific developments is likely to be highly subjective. The potential for concealment of intention in the political field, not to mention for deception, is much higher than for military preparations. At least in theory, it is possible for a closed society to conceal completely its decisions, to fail to take measures to prepare its own populace psychologically for war, and to handle its diplomacy and manipulate its propaganda so that there is virtually no discernible outward change in the political atmosphere which might alert the adversary. In practice, of course, this virtually never occurs. But, even when there are numerous political anomalies and significant changes in diplomacy and propaganda, the interpretation of their significance may be difficult and elusive. Short of old-fashioned ultimatums and declarations of war, or the collection pipeline into the adversary's decisionmaking councils, nearly all political indications are subject to some degree of ambiguity and uncertainty. It follows, of course, that interpretations of political indications are likely to be much more variable and controversial than those of military developments.

One manifestation of this is that there are usually fewer political and civil developments on indicator lists and that they tend to be much vaguer and imprecise in wording. An illustration or two will suffice to make this point. Indicator lists usually carry such political items as: "Protracted high-level leadership meetings," and "marked intensification of internal police controls." Such developments are, of course, potentially significant indications that decisions on war are under consideration or have been taken, but they may also be attributable entirely to domestic developments, such as civil unrest. Even political indicators tied directly to foreign affairs, such as "A general hardening of foreign policy" or "Significant increases in propaganda broadcast to or about a critical area," are not in themselves necessarily manifestations of any decision or intention to resort to conflict. Such developments are significant even as possible indications only in relation to what is sometimes called "the overall situation." Although not all political indicators are so unspecific, it has not been possible to define potential political indicators with precision: there is no political "Table of Organization and Equipment" (TO&E). Nor is it possible to forecast in advance whether an adversary will choose to publicize his objectives and intentions, seek to conceal them almost totally, or, as is most probable, take some intermediate course. Thus the number of political indications is almost impossible to anticipate for any hypothetical future situation. We can forecast with some degree of confidence that some specific military preparations will be undertaken, but we cannot forecast or at least cannot agree what manifestations of the political decision may be evident, or how such manifestations should be interpreted.

This ambiguity and non-specificity of political indicators also often means that our sense of "political warning" is likely to be much more subjective, and hence more difficult to define or explain to others, than is the military evidence. Sometimes, there is little more than an uneasy sense or intuitive "feeling" that the adversary is up to something, which of course is not provable or even necessarily communicable to others who are not thinking on the same wave length. The analyst or military commander who attempts to put this sense of unease into words may feel almost helpless to explain his "feelings," if not downright apprehensive that he is making a fool of himself. Yet, often these "feelings" have been generally accurate, if not specific, barometers of impending developments. Thus, General Lucius Clay, a few weeks before the start of the Berlin blockade, dispatched a cable to Army Intelligence in Washington, which said in part: "Within the last few weeks, I have felt a subtle change in Soviet attitude which I cannot define but which now gives me a feeling that it [war] may come with dramatic suddenness. I cannot support this change in my own thinking with any data or outward evidence in relationships other than to describe it as a feeling of a new tenseness in every Soviet individual with whom we have official relations."[4] Or, as General Clay later recalled his feelings at the time: "Somehow I felt instinctively that a definite change in the attitude of the Russians in Berlin had occurred and that something was about to happen. I pointed out that I had no confirming intelligence of a positive nature."[5]

---

[4] *The Forrestal Diaries*, ed. Walter Millis (New York: The Viking Press, 1951), 387.

[5] Lucius D. Clay, *Decision in Germany* (New York: Doubleday and Company, Inc, 1950), 354.

Much the same sense of unease that something was about to happen has haunted perceptive intelligence analysts on other occasions—such as the spring of 1950 prior to the North Korean attack on South Korea, and in the early months of 1962, even before the marked upsurge of Soviet shipments to Cuba was begun. Even when political warning is less vague and subjective—that is, when the political atmosphere is clearly deteriorating and tensions are rising over a specific situation which may lead to war—the political indicators still may be imprecise and not measurable or quantifiable evidence of a specific course of action. There are, of course, exceptions to this, in which the enemy may make no attempt to conceal his plans, or in which direct warnings are issued to the intended victim, both privately and publicly. Often, however, political indications can give us only generalized warning, such as a recognition that the dangers of war are increasing substantially, or that the adversary is clearly committed to some course of action which entails a grave risk of hostilities.

Critical Role of Political Factors for Warning

In large part because of these uncertainties, there exists a fundamental mistrust and misunderstanding of the importance of political factors for warning. Particularly among military officers, although by no means confined to them, there has been a tendency to downplay the significance of "political warning." Because political indications are less precise, less measurable and less predictable than military indications, it is an easy step to conclude that they matter less, and that we can give them only secondary or incidental attention in our assessment of the enemy's intentions. Warning papers and estimates, in some cases, have seemed to place undue emphasis on the detection of military preparations, with only passing reference to the political problem.

The importance of the political assessment has rarely been so well defined as in the following perceptive comments written years ago by one of the real warning experts in the U.S. Intelligence Community, "We query whether the critical role of the political factors in warning may not warrant somewhat more emphasis or highlighting."

We appreciate that, in the warning process, the political factor—or "posture"—constitutes one of the most esoteric and elusive fields, The very term "political posture" remains essentially ambiguous. Nevertheless, elusive, ambiguous or no, its critical role in warning must be duly weighed. We discern the implication that the political factor somehow constitutes a separable category, distinct from that of physical preparations; that when joined with the latter at some point well along in the game, it may, mathematically, add to or subtract from the sum of our physical holdings. Actually, the political context is determinative of whether at any and every given point in the process of the enemy's preparations, you indeed hold any sum at all in the "preparations" category.

The political context to us is not merely another increment to the warning conveyed by a particular pattern or patterns of observed physical "preparations." It is rather the essential, *a priori*, context which establishes that a particular physical activity may have any possible relevance to a real, live warning issue; it gives or denies to the physical "preparations" their presumed evidential value as indications. In any discussion of a hypothetical future warning problem, there is, of necessity, present an exquisitely subtle subjective assumption. Any discourse on what indications or evidence one expects to receive, how one will handle these, etc., assumes the very point at issue—that one is dealing with activities recognized as "preparations." Now, logically, there cannot be "preparations" for something that in fact the enemy has no conscious design of doing; there cannot be a valid "indication" of that which does not exist in reality (much less a whole compendium of such "indications" sampled from a cross-section of the attack-bound enemy national entity). Unless and until, and then only to the degree that, the intelligence community's intellectual assumptions and convictions as to the enemy's political posture can rationally accommodate at least the *possibility* that the enemy just *might really* be preparing to attack, there is not likely to be acceptance—even contingent and tentative—of any enemy activity whatever—specific or in pattern—as reflecting or indicating "preparations" to attack. So long as the prevailing political assessment of the enemy's foreign policy objectives, motivational factors, etc., confidently holds that the course of action for which alleged "preparations" are being made is inconceivable, or impossible (or even unlikely), there has not even been a beginning of the cumulative process [of indications intelligence]. Thus the political factor invariably stands athwart the warning exercise from the very outset, and represents a constant, vital ingredient in the warning process from beginning to end.

Our remarks above derive primarily from our cumulative experience in the warning process. The same conclusion, however, follows from the intrinsic logic of the problem itself. The very end to which warning generally addresses itself—enemy intent to attack—is fundamentally a political issue, involving a political decision of the highest order, made by the political leadership of the enemy state (we are excluding here, of course, the "Failsafe" issue of some military nut just arbitrarily pushing a button). The working rationale underlying the exercise discussed throughout this estimate is simply the presumed existence of:

(a) an enemy decision to attack;

(b) a plan of measures/preparations to be taken to insure success of the attack;

(c) implementation of the plan.

The intelligence processes involve basically our attempt to detect, identify, and place in order fragmentary manifestations of the process actually under way in (c), with a view toward reconstructing and authenticating the essential outlines of (b), from which we hope to derive and prove (a) which equals classic warning. We cannot hope to reason effectively from (c) to (a), without a correct, albeit hypothetical, appreciation from the outset of (a). Here again, then, we find that in theory as well as in practice the crucial, final link is entirely political. Whether viewed from Moscow or Washington, the political context is the capstone: for the enemy—the beginning of that fateful course; for U.S. intelligence—the end.[6]

Political Perception Fundamental To Warning

> *"The perception of the adversary's fundamental goals and priorities is the sine qua non of warning."*

The perception of the adversary's fundamental goals and priorities is the *sine qua non* of warning. It constitutes the most significant difference between those who "have warning" and those who do not. No amount of military evidence will serve to convince those who do not have this political perception of the adversary's objectives and national priorities, or those who cannot perceive that military action may be the rational outcome of the adversary's course of action to date. The validity of this point can be demonstrated in instance after instance; it is the problem of "those who cannot see," and more "facts" will have little effect on their ability to see. Just as some could not see that Hitler was bent on conquest in Europe, others later could not see that China would or even might intervene in Korea, or that the USSR would or even might invade Czechoslovakia. All were fundamentally problems in political perception, rather than the evaluation of military evidence. An indications study on the Czechoslovak crisis (written after the event) described the analytic problem as it existed in mid-July (just prior to the start of Soviet mobilization and major troop deployments) as follows:

> It is important to note that, while current intelligence reporting at this time clearly and explicitly recognized the gravity of the crisis and the nature of Soviet tactics, there was also a fundamental difference of opinion among analysts. The point at issue was the means which the Soviet Union could and would use to accomplish its objectives and whether it would, if faced by continuing Czechoslovak intransigence, ultimately resort to overt intervention in Czechoslovak affairs.
>
> On the one hand, there was a group of analysts who questioned whether there was anything that the Soviet Union really could do,

---

[6]Frank Denny, Director of the National Indications Center, early 1960s, unpublished manuscript.

including employment of military force, to reverse the trends in Czechoslovakia. This group was also inclined to the view that the USSR, if unable to secure Czech compliance by political means, would not jeopardize its international image, its relations with western Communist Parties and its progress toward coexistence with the United States by direct military action. It believed that the USSR had changed or matured politically since the days of the Hungarian intervention and was unlikely to take such action again. For these reasons, direct Soviet action against Czechoslovakia was viewed as somewhat "irrational" and therefore unlikely. This group was thus predisposed, in varying degrees, to regard subsequent major Soviet military moves as more pressure on Czechoslovakia rather than as bona fide preparations for military action.

On the other hand was a group of analysts who inclined to the belief quite early in the summer that the USSR was deadly serious in its determination to maintain control of Czechoslovakia and would ultimately use any means, including military force, to insure this. They believed that the USSR, not just for political but also for strategic reasons, could not tolerate the loss of Czechoslovakia and that Soviet security interests were the paramount consideration. The USSR therefore would decide, if in fact it had not already decided, that military action against Czechoslovakia was the lesser of the evils which confronted it. These analysts thus did not regard such a course of action as irrational, and they were predisposed earlier rather than later to regard the Soviet military moves as preparations for direct intervention. Such judgments or estimates by individuals are crucial to the warning process, and each person makes his own regardless of whether there is an agreed national estimate. Each analyst is influenced, perhaps unconsciously, by his preconceived views or his opinion of what is rational or logical behavior on the part of the adversary. His judgment on this will help to determine, sometimes more than he may realize, not only how he interprets a given piece of information but what he selects to report at all.[7]

The foregoing discussion should help to explain why some critics object to the terms "military warning" and "political warning" as if they were separate processes. There are indications which are essentially military, and those which are primarily political, but there is only one kind of warning. It is the perception of the significance of all these developments in toto. Warning, like beauty, lies in the eye of the beholder.

It is highly erroneous to presume, as many do, that political analysts (or even political agencies, such as the Department of State) make political analyses, and that military analysts (and military agencies, such as the Department of Defense)

---

[7]Cynthia Grabo, 1968, unpublished manuscript.

make military analyses. The intelligence offices of the Department of State do a great deal of essentially military analysis and must constantly take military factors into account in making political assessments. Still more pertinent, perhaps, is the fact that military analysts are constantly making essentially political judgments about the likely military courses of actions of our potential enemies. They may not recognize that this is so; it may be entirely unconscious, but assessments of political factors underlie virtually all military estimates and other analyses of enemy courses of action.

It may be extremely important for warning that gratuitous political judgments of intent do not creep into military assessments of the enemy's capabilities, or at least that the political judgment be clearly separated from the statement of the military capability. This point was well illustrated in judgments made prior to the outbreak of the Korean War in June 1950. By March, Army Intelligence was correctly reporting that the steady buildup of North Korean forces gave them the capability to attack South Korea at any time—but then undercut this significant military judgment (a warning in itself) with the judgment that it was not believed that North Korea would do it, at least for the time being. The same positive military but negative political judgments were being made by General MacArthur's intelligence in the Far East. Thus, the gratuitous political judgment (the basis and argumentation for which was never really set forth) tended in effect to dilute or even negate a highly important military estimate.

"Warning has failed more often for political perception than it has for lack of military evidence."

Warning has failed more often for lack of political perception than it has for lack of military evidence. When I have pointed this out to military officers, their reaction often is that you really cannot trust these political people, and if more heed had been paid to the military people, all would have gone well. In some cases this may be true (it is at least partly true for Czechoslovakia in 1968), but in other cases it has been the military themselves who have permitted their own political misperceptions to override the military evidence. And there are cases in which political officers have been well ahead of the military analysts in perception of the likely course of military action. In warning, where we have so often been wrong, there is blame to go around. The point is that the political judgment, no matter who makes it, will likely be even more important than the military analysis for the assessment of the adversary's intentions.

A PROBLEM OF PERCEPTION

Presumably, few persons would take exception to the general thesis set forth in the preceding section that the perception of another country's intentions is essentially a political judgment of developments in given circumstances, and that this understanding of national priorities and objectives is fundamental to any warning judgment. In this section, this problem will be examined in more detail, with some specific illustrations of how it may affect our appreciation of the adversary's course of action.

Perceptions of the Likelihood of Conflict

In normal circumstances, the likelihood or improbability of conflict between two or more states is fairly well understood, not only in government circles but by the educated public, and these judgments are usually quite accurate. They are derived from our recognition that the basic conditions for war between two or more states either do not exist at all, or are present in varying degrees of probability ranging from a very small chance that war would occur to the situation in which virtually all political signs of ultimate hostilities are positive.

Between these two extremes, there are all sorts of gradations of our assessments of the probabilities of conflict between nations, or of our perceptions of whether a given nation is or is not inclined to resort to hostilities, or of how aggressive or cautious it may be in pursuit of its aims. Our understanding of these questions are basic not only to our intelligence assessments (particularly our national intelligence estimates) but also to our national political and military policies.

Such attitudes are crucial to our views as to the nature, and amount, of the political warning we may perceive and articulate. If the opinion prevails that the national leadership of any country is essentially aggressive and bent on expansion or conquest, then it follows that there need be no basic political changes in the attitudes or behavior of that country before it attacks. In this case, the *casus belli* already exists; it is not brought about by some observable change in circumstance.

Priorities and Traditional Behavior

How any country may react in a particular situation will usually be predicated, at least in part, on its traditional national objectives and past performance. It is thus essential to understand what the national objectives or priorities of the potential adversary have been in the past. This, of course, assumes a rationality and consistency of national behavior which have not always been the case, but the premise nonetheless is usually valid. It is from such concepts of likely national behavior in certain circumstances that we derive our judgments of what a nation will fight for and what it will not.

It is virtually impossible for any country (or leader) to conceal for long what its basic philosophies and national objectives are. Deception and concealment cannot extend this far. All leaders need some popular support for their programs, particularly programs that may ultimately lead to war. History shows that most leaders, even those bent on a course of aggression, rarely have made much effort to conceal their intentions, and some leaders (for example, Hitler in *Mein Kampf*) have provided us with virtual blueprints of what they planned to accomplish, If we do not, in such cases, correctly perceive the enemy's general course of action, it is often because we did not wish to believe what we were being told—just as many refused to accept the clear warnings from Hitler's own writings.

Unfortunately, however, political warning is not this simple. While it is essential to understand fundamental objectives and priorities, those are not likely to provide us with specific warning of what another state will do in some particular situation. It usually cannot tell us how great a risk it is prepared to run to achieve its objectives, how far it may seek them by political means before it will resort to military action or whether it will, in fact, ever finally take the military course. In short, even when our understanding of the adversary's philosophy and objectives is pretty good, we must still have some more specific understanding of his objectives and decisions in the specific situation in order to predict a likely course of action.

Strategic Importance of the Particular Issue

Except in instances of long-planned deliberate aggression, the possibility of conflict usually arises over some particular issue or development, and the potential aggressor may have had very little control of it. Or, if the situation is largely of his own making, development of the situation and the reactions of others may be different from what he had expected. There are potentially, and often actually, a vast number of complicating factors which may influence his political decisions. It will not be enough just to have a general estimate of how he should react in such circumstances, or how he has reacted in the past. It is important to understand how he views the situation now and to interpret how he will behave in this particular instance. We are confronted now with a condition and not a theory. We thus move from the long-term estimative approach to the specific and more short-term indications approach.

How much weight are we going to give, in these circumstances, to our traditional concepts of this country's objectives and likely courses of action, and how much to the specific indications of what he is going to do this time? In a fair number of cases, there is not apt to be a great deal of conflict here—the traditional or seemingly logical course of action will in fact prove to be the right one. In this case, the current political indications will be generally consistent with how we expect this particular country to perform. This will be particularly true if both past behavior and current indications call for an essentially negative assessment—that is, that the state in question will not resort to military action in these circumstances.

The difficulties in warning are likely to arise when some of these factors are not consonant with one another, and particularly when standing estimates or judgments would dictate that the adversary will not take military action in this situation, but the current indications, both military and political, suggest that he will. Which is right, and what validity should be given our current indications as against the established estimate? Any answer without numerous caveats is likely to be an oversimplification and subject to rebuttal with examples that will tend to negate the general conclusion. History nonetheless suggests that the greater weight in these cases should be given to the current indications. In other words, it is usually more important to understand the strategic importance of the particular issue to the nation than it is to place undue weight on traditional behavior and priorities. This is, after all, the fundamental cause of warning failures—that the behavior of the aggressor appeared inconsistent with what we would normally have expected him to do, or with our estimate of what he would do. Thus, we were "surprised." He did not do what we thought he would do, or should do.

In some instances, a country's course of action truly does appear irrational. It is a misjudgment of the situation, in either the long or short term, or both, and in the end it is counterproductive. Two conspicuous examples which come to mind are Pearl Harbor—which was a short-term triumph but long-term misjudgment on the part of Japan—and the Cuban missile crisis, which was a gross miscalculation in the short term. In both, the indications of what the adversary was doing were more important to an assessment of his intentions than any intelligence estimates, which in fact proved to be wrong. It was later observed that, in the Cuba situation, we had totally misjudged Khrushchev's sense of priorities (just as he had misjudged ours) and that there must have been an overriding requirement in his mind to achieve some degree of strategic parity with the U.S. which would have led him to take such a risk.

"The perception of what the adversary is thinking and how important the current issue is to him is fundamental to our ability to understand what he will do."

In lesser degree, this may be said of many crises. The perception of what the adversary is thinking and how important the current issue is to him is fundamental to our ability to understand what he will do. It was a lack of such perception that lay behind much of our misjudgment of North Vietnamese intentions and persistence in the Vietnam war. As has subsequently become obvious, both U.S. intelligence and perhaps to a greater degree policy level officials (there were individual exceptions, of course) vastly underestimated the determination and ability of the North Vietnamese leadership to sustain the war effort. No doubt this attitude contributed materially to the reluctance to believe in 1965-66 that Hanoi was mobilizing its armed forces for the conduct of a prolonged war in the South.

We should note here also that it may require no particular collection effort or sophisticated analytic talent to perceive how nations feel about particular issues. Even our security-conscious adversaries whom we characteristically suspect of all kinds of chicanery are not necessarily engaged in devious efforts to conceal how they feel on great problems and issues vital to their national security or objectives. It will often be quite obvious how they feel about something and how important it is to them, if we will only take the time to examine what they are saying and try to see it from their viewpoint. In some cases—such as China's intervention in the Korean war and North Vietnam's general program for the conduct of the war in South Vietnam—they have virtually told us what they intended to do. In others—such as the Soviet invasion of Czechoslovakia—they have made no secret whatever of the criticality of the issue and of its overriding importance to them, and have strongly indicated that force would be used if needed.

Influences in Political Perception

Objective perception of the adversary's attitudes and the ability to look at things from his point of view are crucial to warning, and above all to political analysis, since this will necessarily be more subjective than the compiling and analysis of military data.

The "climate of opinion" also strongly influences political perception. It is not only very difficult for an individual to maintain an independent viewpoint against a widespread contrary view about another state, it may prove almost impossible to gain acceptance for such a view, even when there may be considerable evidence to support it. Time is needed to change national attitudes.

A somewhat related factor may be the influence of our own national policies and military plans on our judgments of what the adversary may do. Once a national decision has been made on a certain course of action—such as whether a particular country is or is not vital to our defense and hence whether we will or will not defend it—there will almost inevitably be some impact on our assessments. It is not so obvious as simply saying what the policy level would like to hear (or not saying what it would like not to hear); there tends also to be a more subtle influence on our thinking and analyses. Various historical examples could be cited, Vietnam for one. Our concepts of North Vietnam as an aggressive nation bent on conquering the South almost certainly were influenced, or at least reinforced, by the U.S. decisions in 1965 to commit forces to defend the South; it then become acceptable to talk of North Vietnam as an aggressor and hence to think in such terms.

Judgments concerning North Korean intentions in the period prior to the attack of June 1950 also were materially influenced by U.S. policies in that area. For at least three years before that attack, it had been officially recognized that there was grave danger that North Korea would seek to take over the South if U.S. forces were withdrawn. Nonetheless, it was decided to withdraw U.S. forces, partly on the grounds that South Korea was not essential to the U.S. military position in the Far East, and to hand the Korean problem to the United Nations. Once having decided to write off South Korea as a U.S. military responsibility, the U.S. made no military plans for the defense of South Korea against an attack from the North, and seemingly it became U.S. policy not to defend South Korea. The effect of this on intelligence assessments, and thus indirectly on warning, was two-fold: as a low priority area for U.S. policy, Korea became a low priority collection target; and intelligence analysts, believing that the U.S. would take no military action if North Korea attacked, tended to downplay both the importance and by implication the likelihood of the attack in their assessments. Even those who expected the attack and predicted that it was coming (not necessarily in June, of course), saw the possibility as a relatively unimportant development in comparison with other potential Communist military threats in Europe and the Far East, and hence gave it little attention in their assessments. They saw no urgency in warning the policymaker about Korea, since nothing was going to be done about it anyway. It was only one of many areas where the so-called Communist Bloc (meaning the Soviet Union and its obedient satellites) might strike, and apparently one of the least important.

A related factor influencing assessments on Korea in that period was the concept that only the Soviet Union was a real military threat against which U.S. military forces should be prepared to act. The concept of limited "wars of liberation" or indirect aggression through third parties was vaguely perceived, if at all. North Korea, like Communist Europe, was seen only as a pawn of Moscow; war, if it came, would be on Soviet instigation and part of a much larger conflict. Intelligence assessments, as well as military planning, reflected this view of the Communist threat and scarcely hinted at the possibility of a Communist attack, which would be confined to the Korean peninsula. General Ridgway has well described the then prevailing concept as follows:

> By 1949, we were completely committed to the theory that the next war involving the United States would be a global war, in which Korea would be of relatively minor importance and, in any event, indefensible. All our planning, all our official statements, all our military decisions derived essentially from this belief.[8]

Finally, we may note the effects on judgments of the likelihood of attack of the unwillingness to believe it or to accept it—the tendency to push the problem aside as too unpleasant to think about, in the hope that it may just go away. This tendency, which all of us have in some degree, may be accentuated by a sense of hopelessness and inability to do anything about it, or by a desire not to rock the boat or stir the waters lest the potential aggressor be even more provoked. This last consideration possibly was a major factor in Stalin's apparent failure to have anticipated the German attack on the Soviet Union in June 1941, and his seeming dismissal of the numerous warnings of the coming attack. There is no doubt that the USSR had ample long-term strategic warning of the German offensive, and some observers have felt that Stalin was blind to this, suffering from a megalomania almost as great as Hitler's. But an alternate thesis holds that he did foresee the attack but, believing that nothing further could be done to prevent it, he sought to delay it as long as possible by trying to appease Hitler and thus publicly refusing

---

[8]Matthew B. Ridgway, *The Korean War* (Garden City, NY: Doubleday and Company, Inc., 1967), 11.

to concede that there was danger of attack. Whether true or not—we shall proba-bly never know what Stalin really thought—the effect of his policies was to decrease the preparedness of the Soviet public and particularly the armed forces for the attack when it finally came.

CONSIDERATIONS IN POLITICAL WARNING

Diplomacy and Foreign Policy

Since war is an expression of political relations by other means and states resort to war only when they have failed to secure their objectives by political means, foreign policy and diplomacy are highly important indications of national objectives. It is difficult to conceive of hostilities breaking out between nations today without some prior crisis or at least deterioration in their diplo-matic relations. Indeed, historically, the most obvious early warning of approaching hostilities has usually been in the field of foreign political rela-tions. The outbreak of both world wars in Europe was preceded by marked deterioration in the international political climate, which made the threat of war apparent to all, if not "inevitable." Even Japan's surprise attack on Pearl Harbor was preceded by a crisis in U.S.-Japanese political relations, which had greatly raised U.S. fears of war, although specific Japanese intentions were not foreseen. Those who are confident that the coming of future wars also will be foreshadowed by international political crises and developments in the conduct of foreign policy unquestionably have the lessons of history on their side.

Nonetheless, there is a substantial body of opinion which questions the likeli-hood that wars of the future will necessarily be preceded by such obvious changes in the political atmosphere. Moreover, it is our uncertainty that political indications of this nature will provide us warning that largely accounts for the existence of indications intelligence at all. If we could be confident of having this type of political warning, not to mention direct ultimatums and declarations of war, then obviously there would be little need for much indications analysis. We could confine ourselves to assessments of the enemy's capabilities. The circum-stances surrounding the outbreak of some conflicts since World War II certainly justify this concern. The North Korean attack on South Korea, the most conspicu-ous example, was not preceded by any political crisis or diplomatic warning in the near term, although the political atmosphere had long been highly strained, and of course the two sections of the country had no diplomatic relations. The diplomatic warnings of Chinese intervention in Korea, although they were issued, fell short of what might have been expected if the Chinese objective was truly to deter the advance of U.S./UN forces toward the Yalu. The Middle East conflicts of 1956 and 1967 were both preceded by international political crises, but spe-cific political indications that Israel had decided to attack were largely lacking.

There are perhaps three major reasons why we have less confidence that we will receive specific political warning through developments in foreign policy and diplomacy than has been true in the past:

- Modern weapons, even non-nuclear weapons, have given a greater advantage to the attacker, thus increasing the value of political surprise. The Israeli attack of 1967 is a prime example. Probably in part because of this, it is no longer considered desirable to break political relations or to declare war prior to attacking, and few countries today would probably do so.

- It is the doctrine of our major potential enemies to attack without diplomatic warning, and they almost certainly would do so, however much generalized political warning there might be beforehand of their intentions. In the short term, this is one of the easiest and most common means of deception.

- The pressures brought by other states, through the United Nations or otherwise, to forestall conflicts are such that countries today increasingly feel compelled to act without diplomatic warnings so that the international peacemaking machinery will not be brought to bear before they achieve their objectives.

Altogether, it is probable that specific warning of impending attack through diplomatic channels is largely a thing of the past. This does not necessarily mean, however, that more generalized indications of intention will not continue to be evident through the conduct of foreign policy and diplomacy. Indeed, as the dangers and costs of war increase, there is considerable reason to believe that there will be ample evidence that international political relations are seriously deteriorating before wars break out. In other words, we should still expect generalized strategic warning, if not short-term warning of imminent attack, from such developments. This may, however, require increased sophistication of analysis to recognize that war is imminent.

Public Diplomacy, Propaganda and Disinformation

The term "propaganda" here is used in its broadest sense, to cover all information put forth by any means under national control or direction, which is designed to win over or influence the intended audience. Propaganda can be either true or false, or somewhere in between, and it can be intended for domestic or foreign consumption or both. It can be disseminated through private channels (that is, to the party faithful or non-government organizations in briefings, directives, or "resolutions") or through the mass media to the domestic population or the world at large. The term "public diplomacy" can be equated with "propaganda" when there is a factual basis for the information. If the information is based on falsehoods, it may best be labeled "disinformation."

The potential value, and difficulties, of propaganda analysis for assessment of intentions (that is, for warning) are well recognized. Propaganda analysis became recognized as an art, if not a science, during World War II, when specific efforts were made to analyze Nazi pronouncements for indications of possible forthcoming German military moves, as well as for other purposes.

There are two prevalent misunderstandings about propaganda and its relationship to, and value for, warning. First is the widespread tendency to mistrust or reject almost anything our adversaries say as "mere propaganda" and hence to regard it as meaningless if not completely false. This tendency to disparage the usefulness of propaganda is most unfortunate, for the record shows that propaganda trends, and specific pronouncements, are often very valuable indications of intentions.

A second tendency, almost the opposite of the above, is to expect too much warning from propaganda, that is, to expect it to be highly specific or to provide virtually unequivocal evidence that military action is impending, perhaps even specific warning of the time and place. People who expect this kind of warning from propaganda are almost certain to be disappointed, and they may therefore conclude that the propaganda provided "no warning" when in fact the propaganda provided considerable indirect or less specific evidence of what an opponent might do.

The following general comments on the usefulness of propaganda are derived from experience in many crises. We are here discussing the propaganda put out by closed societies through controlled media, where both its quantity and content are carefully regulated and designed to achieve specific goals.

Propaganda reflects concern. Propaganda is a very useful barometer of how concerned the country's leadership is about particular issues. Marked upsurges in propaganda on a particular subject or area do generally reflect genuine preoccupation with it, particularly if sustained over any period of time. Similarly, a very low level of propaganda attention to an issue usually indicates very little concern with it. A drop in meaningful comment however, can signify that the issue is so important that all comment is being withheld pending guidance from the top. Finally, deliberate inattention to an area or an issue can be used for deception, generally in the relatively short term.

Most propaganda is "true." Here we are using "truth" in a relative, not absolute, sense. We mean that states cannot continually distort their objectives and policies, and particularly not to their own people. To put out totally false statements or misleading guidance is self-defeating and will not evoke the desired response. It is important, when hostilities may be impending, to instill the proper degree of hatred or fear of the adversary. The leadership cannot afford to give a wholly false picture of the situation to the populace.

To illustrate the point further, there was a major argument in 1965-66 over the meaning and significance of a heavy barrage of North Vietnamese statements aimed at their own populace, which called for large-scale enlistment in the armed forces, longer working hours, greater sacrifices, recruitment of more women so that men by the thousands could be sent "to the front." There was a group in the U.S. Intelligence Community that rejected all this as "mere propaganda" for our benefit and would not credit it as evidence that North Vietnam was preparing to send large numbers of troops to South Vietnam. The contrary argument, which of course proved to be the correct one, maintained that just the reverse was true, that this intensive internal indoctrination was the true barometer of Hanoi's intentions, and that the official propaganda line (that there were no North Vietnamese troops in South Vietnam) was the false one put out for our benefit. The refusal to believe this internal propaganda campaign possibly was the single greatest obstacle to the recognition that Hanoi was mobilizing for a major military effort in South Vietnam.

Official, authorized statements are unusually significant. In the former communist states of Europe the press operated under a set of prescribed rules which proved very consistent over a period of years. Routine, day-to-day events were handled under established guidelines; more important developments called for articles by particular commentators (sometimes pseudonyms for top officials); major issues evoked authorized or official statements from the highest level. These latter statements were important not only for themselves, but because they set forth the "party line" for the rest of the propaganda machinery and thus were carefully adhered to by the faithful. These statements always warranted the most careful study and analysis, and when they bore on war or peace were of particular significance for warning. This does not necessarily mean that they were easy to interpret. It became clear in retrospect that some of the fine points in one of these communist classics—the 11 September 1962 TASS statement which unknown to us really ushered in the Cuba crisis—were not given sufficient attention in the community.

Propaganda warning is usually indirect, rather than specific. As a general rule, statements such as the foregoing are about as specific propaganda warning as we are likely to receive of military action. It will be observed that it would be difficult to be much more precise without describing specific military preparations or directly threatening to intervene with military force. I cannot recall an instance after World War II in which a communist country publicly stated that it would intervene, invade or attack with its regular forces, even when such action was imminent. The closest any communist country came to such a direct statement was China's open calls for "volunteers" for Korea in the fall of 1950. In most cases, communist nations liked to maintain the pretense that their forces were either "invited in" or weren't there at all. China has never acknowledged that anything other than "volunteer" units were sent to Korea; North Vietnam never acknowledged the presence of its forces in South Vietnam until the 1972 offensive, when this was tacitly although not explicitly admitted; Soviet troops, of course were "invited" to enter both Hungary in 1956 and Czechoslovakia in 1968.

Political Warning Through Third Parties

No discussion of the type of developments that can give us political warning would be complete without some attention to the usefulness of intermediaries or third parties. This applies both when they are deliberately used as a channel to convey a message and when they serve as leaks, inadvertently or otherwise.

When deliberately used, it is often for the purpose of arranging discussions or negotiations, but it may also be to convey a direct warning. The Indian Ambassador in Beijing was selected as the first channel to convey warning to the U.S. that Chinese forces would intervene in Korea if U.S./UN forces crossed the 38th Parallel. Most people were inclined to dismiss this as bluff at the time. Still more useful may be the unintended, or at least only semi-intended, leak through third parties. It is axiomatic that the more people, and particularly the more countries, brought in on a plan, the more difficult it is to keep it secret.

Because of the very tight security on the introduction of Soviet missiles into Cuba, the USSR is believed to have informed very few foreign communist leaders, probably only the heads of the Warsaw Pact countries under rigid security admonitions. This adventure was solely a Soviet show. On the other hand, the preparations for the invasion of Czechoslovakia required a high degree of cooperation and planning among five states, and numerous people were cognizant of the general nature of the plans if not the details.

Internal Factors: Assessing the Views of the Leadership

Few subjects have proved more elusive to us than a true understanding of the character, attitudes and proclivities of the leaders of foreign countries. This can be true even for those with whom we have friendly relations and numerous cultural contacts. When the nations are essentially hostile, or at least not friendly, and their leaders have been educated in entirely different traditions or ideologies, the potential for misunderstanding them rises dramatically. Of the communist leaders since World War II, Khrushchev almost certainly was the most outgoing, garrulous and willing to meet with foreigners. If we thereby felt we understood him, we were disabused by the Cuban missile episode. Brezhnev, on the other hand, had apparently never met with an American other than Gus Hall prior to preparations for his Summit meeting with President Nixon in May 1972.

Where the leadership is essentially collective, we often have very little if any perception of the lineup on particular issues. Despite several reports on the subject, we really do not know how the Soviet leadership voted with respect to an invasion of Czechoslovakia. Nor do we know which of the leaders of North

Vietnam at any time favored various tactics, such as prolonged guerrilla warfare versus large-scale conventional offensive operations. It is possible to get widely varying opinions from professed experts on where General Giap really stood on this question at various times. As a general rule, therefore, the attempt to second-guess our potential enemies based on any professed insight into their characters or attitudes is likely to be a risky business.

When sudden changes in leadership occur and relative unknowns move into positions of power, the difficulties are compounded. The death of Stalin brought about a period of great uncertainty, and there was a brief period of intelligence alert against the contingency that the new Soviet leaders might undertake some hostile act. Of course, the reverse proved to be true. Stalin's successors were somewhat less hostile and aggressive and probably were instrumental in bringing about the armistice in Korea shortly later. Nonetheless, there are instances in which a change in leadership has been of warning significance, and has been indicative of a change toward a more aggressive policy or even of a clear intent to initiate hostilities. The change of government in Japan in October 1941 is universally recognized as one of the key developments which foreshadowed a more aggressive Japanese policy. The formation of a new government under the militarist General Tojo set in motion the chain of events which culminated in the attack on Pearl Harbor.

Coups and Other Political Surprises

Intelligence personnel, particularly the chiefs of intelligence agencies, become used to being blamed for things for which they were not responsible and which they could not conceivably have predicted. (This is partly compensated by the mistakes made by intelligence which are not recognized or brought to light.) Nothing is more exasperating to members of the intelligence profession than to be charged with failing to predict coups and assassinations, which they rightly consider as "acts of God" somewhat less predictable than tornadoes, avalanches and plane hijackings. It is ridiculous and grossly unfair to expect the intelligence system to anticipate such acts, which are plotted in secrecy and sometimes by only one individual. Forecasts of this type are not within the province of strategic warning—however serious the consequences of such acts may be—and they really are not within the province of intelligence at all. The most that can reasonably be expected is that the intelligence system recognize that, in certain countries or situations, such acts if they should occur might precipitate riots, revolts or other crises inimical to our interests. But even this is expecting a good deal, as the police record in this country of attempting to anticipate urban riots should demonstrate.

Chapter 5

WARNING FROM THE TOTALITY
OF EVIDENCE

In real life, developments do not occur separately but in conjunction or simultaneously. Moreover, they relate to each other in some more or less logical fashion if in fact a country is preparing for hostilities.

THE RELATIVE WEIGHT OF POLITICAL
AND MILITARY FACTORS

At the risk of an oversimplification of this problem, we may note certain generally valid precepts. First, political indications alone—in the absence of any significant military preparations or without the capability to act—are not credible and we will virtually always be correct in dismissing them as so much bombast or propaganda. For years, The People's Republic of China had a propensity for reserving some of its most violent propaganda for situations half way around the globe in which it had absolutely no capability to act—for example, Lebanon in 1958. In the years following its decisive defeat by Israel in 1967, Egypt's repeated calls for the recovery of its former territory carried little weight in the absence of a capability to defeat the Israelis in the Sinai. Similarly, the anti-American propaganda put out by North Korea over a period of years has been so intense and vitriolic that it has been meaningless as an indication of an intention to take military action within any foreseeable time period. We must always remember, however, that the national attitudes reflected in such propaganda are significant, and that such bitter hostility will make the military preparations (if or when they occur) potentially more meaningful and dangerous than might otherwise be the case, as was demonstrated in the Egyptian attack on Israeli forces in the Sinai in 1973.

At the other extreme, military indications alone—in the absence of any signs of political crisis or a deterioration in the international situation—also will tend to lose credibility. In such circumstances, we will be inclined to regard even quite extensive and unusual military activity as an exercise or test of some kind, rather than a bona fide preparation for early military action. For example, a partial mobilization, which in time of political crisis would cause grave concern, would probably be dismissed as only an exercise in a period of political calm. In the absence of any crisis, even a highly unusual and potentially very ominous development may not cause much alarm; it will rather be regarded as a mistake of some kind, or an error in reporting, as in fact it often is. Whereas in a crisis such a development would likely be assessed as even more ominous than the fact alone might warrant, it will probably require quite a number of unusual military developments to disturb our complacency if we see no positive political indications.

Although this is in part a psychological phenomenon, it is also historically valid. Very few wars have started without some deterioration in the political situation or some development which would increase the possibilities that a nation might decide to launch military operations.

There is, however, some limit to the number of major military preparations which may be undertaken in a period of political calm without arousing concern. In real life, we rarely see the situation in which political and military indications are totally out of phase or contradictory. Each will be contributing, in varying measure perhaps, to our assessment of the enemy's likely course of action. It has been observed that, in normal times, we will usually give somewhat greater weight to political indications than to military developments; this reflects our general sense of the attitudes and intentions of our adversaries, usually borne out by many years of experience. It is also essentially our national estimate—that they are not going to go to war without some reason, and that we will have some indication that the situation has changed before they would take such a decision. On the other hand, once the situation has changed and the political atmosphere is deteriorating, we will probably give greater weight in the crisis situation to the military indications as our best guideline to the enemy's intentions. This in turn reflects two historically valid principles: political indications can be ambiguous or even misleading, particularly if the adversary is seeking to confuse or deceive us; and the extraordinary buildup of military capability is likely to be the best single indication of the enemy's course of action, a point made several times previously in this work.

ISOLATING THE CRITICAL FACTS AND INDICATIONS

"Whereas the inexperienced tend to believe that warning 'failures' arise from totally inadequate information, experienced analysts have learned that the reverse may be the case; there is almost too much information, too many reports, too many military preparations, too much 'warning.'"

Individuals lacking experience with real warning situations nearly always have considerable misconception about the nature and quantities of information that are likely to be received, and the problem of interpreting it. Whereas the inexperienced tend to believe that warning "failures" arise from totally inadequate information ("we didn't have warning"), experienced analysts have learned that the reverse may be the case; there is almost too much information, too many reports, too many military preparations, too much "warning."

In any large volume of political and military reports or indications, some obviously will be of far greater importance than others for the judgment of the enemy's intentions. In the preceding sections, a number of such critical facts and indications have been discussed, particularly highly unusual military developments that can be expected to occur only in preparation for combat.

These particularly meaningful preparations should be singled out and accorded the attention they deserve. The question should not be simply, is this a likely preparation for war? There will probably be a great many developments in this category. The crucial question may be, how rare is it? How often has it occurred at all in peacetime, including crises which did not lead to conflict? How likely would it be to occur except in preparation for war? If the answers show that even a few critical or nearly unique indications are showing up, the odds of course are materially increased that the country in question is preparing for and will probably initiate hostilities. The more advanced and sophisticated the military forces and the economy of a country, the more such distinctive preparations will be required for war. Preparations for nuclear war would involve an unprecedented range of activities, some of which would probably never be seen except in preparation for that contingency. It follows, therefore, that:

All Indicators are Not Ambiguous

A great disservice has been done the community and the warning system by some rather casual statements that "all indicators are ambiguous." Such comments are not dissimilar in lack of perception to the claim that "We can judge the enemy's capabilities but we cannot judge his intentions."

It is probably true that there is only one totally reliable, unequivocal indication of an intention to attack and that is instantaneous access to the enemy's decision to do so and/or the order to implement it. Even where total preparations for war have been accomplished, where all military indications are "positive," and even when the political decision has already been made in principle to attack, there is always the possibility that the leaders will change their minds or that some last minute event will cause them to postpone or to call off the operation entirely. In this sense, it may be said that all indications but the one are subject to some measure of doubt or uncertainty and can never be viewed as absolutely conclusive evidence of intent.

But there are a number of military indications which are not in themselves ambiguous. That is, they are the steps that are undertaken only in preparation for hostilities, that virtually never occur in peacetime, that are not just "more of the same" but different from what goes on from day to day. They do not occur for exercises, they do not occur (or only to a very limited extent) in practice mobilizations or other drills. They are the developments which truly distinguish war from peace. They are the manifestations of the implementation of the war plan, and they include such developments as: full national mobilization; the institution of full combat readiness in all military forces; the formation of wartime commands; the release of nuclear weapons to the authority of the commander; and a number of other similar although less dramatic measures.

There are further a number of lesser military developments which, although not necessarily indicative of imminent hostilities, are positive indications that the combat readiness and capabilities of forces are being raised, or that they are being deployed into positions for attack. To call these measures "ambiguous" is highly misleading, for the military measures themselves are not. They are not exercises but bona fide measures to raise the combat capabilities and readiness of forces for a particular action.

Negative Indications and Problems of Concealment

In assessing the adversary's intentions, it is necessary not only to take note of what he has done, but also of what he has not done. If we can determine for sure that he has not taken certain essential preparations for conflict, or even has taken some that might reduce his readiness for combat (such as releasing seasoned troops), this will materially influence our conclusions. In some cases, knowing what has not occurred can be the most important factor of all. Unfortunately, it is often very difficult to find out that something has not happened. This is particularly true of the whole range of preparations, both military and civil, that are not readily discernible or which involve relatively little overt activity. There are other preparations, particularly those involving major deployments or changes in the normal patterns of military activity, on which we often can make a judgment with some degree of confidence that certain things either have or have not occurred.

In compiling a list of what is often called "positive" and "negative" indications, therefore, great care should be taken to distinguish true negative indications (things that we expect to happen prior to hostilities but which have not) from just plain lack of information. In some cases, a large portion of the seeming negative indications will turn out to be in the "no information" category. On some of these, we may be able with sufficient collection to make a determination one way or the other. On many others, however, our chances of finding out anything are poor, and sometimes very poor. We must be careful not to mislead our consumers into believing that we know more than we do, and it may be necessary to point this out quite explicitly.

The indications or current analyst should avoid phrases such as "we have no evidence that" when the chances of getting the evidence are poor, and he should not otherwise imply in any way that the information he is presenting represents the sum total of what the adversary is up to. It may be helpful just to compile a list of the things that logically could or might have happened which we cannot tell about one way or the other. The consumer of intelligence in his turn must have a realistic understanding of indications intelligence and our collection capabilities lest he equate a lack of reporting with lack of occurrence. Reporting from field collectors also should be geared to insure in a crisis situation that those at headquarters know what the collector has covered or even can cover, when he files his "negative" report or fails to send a report at all. A true "negative indication" from a field collector is not the absence of a cable, from which we assume that all is well, or even the report which reads: "Troop movements, negative; mobilization, negative." We may need to know what parts of the country he and his colleagues have covered, and whether any troop induction stations or reserve depots have been reconnoitered to be sure what "negative" means. Subject to these provisions, the careful compiling and reporting of true negative indications can be a most important portion of the totality of evidence and hence of the final judgment of the adversary's intentions.

Urgency

A distinguishing feature of most crises which result in hostilities and of the preparedness measures that accompany them is urgency. There is an atmosphere which surrounds the bona fide prewar situation which differentiates it from exercises, shows of force, or even political pressure tactics. Although it is somewhat difficult to define this atmosphere, or to explain exactly what makes it seem "real," an important ingredient nearly always is urgency. This sense that there is a race against time, that things are being done on an accelerated schedule, that the pressure is on, is likely to be conveyed to us in a variety of ways. It usually will affect both military and political activities and be evident in a number of anomalies or indications that plans have been changed, trips cut short, exercises canceled, propaganda changed abruptly, and so forth.

Only in rare instances—and those usually where our collection is poorest—do we fail to obtain some evidence of this urgency. Where the pace is leisurely and there appears to be no deadline for completion of the activity, we will usually be correct in judging that it represents a long-term or gradual buildup of capabilities rather than preparation for early hostilities. The general absence of urgency or hurried preparation was one of the major differences, for example, between the Soviet military buildup along the Chinese border over a period of years, and the precipitate movement of forces prior to the invasion of Czechoslovakia.

One note of caution is in order, however. There are instances of long pre-planned and deliberate attack—the North Korean attack on South Korea in June 1950 is a prime example—in which evidence of urgency or even any particular sign of crisis at all may be lacking. Where a country has more or less unlimited time to prepare and is practicing a deliberate political deception campaign designed to lull the adversary, it may under favorable circumstances be successful in concealing or suppressing any signs of urgency. In the case of the North Korean attack, our very limited collection capabilities undoubtedly also contributed heavily to the surprise; we were not even alerted to the possibility of the attack when it occurred.

SOME GUIDELINES FOR ASSESSING THE MEANING
OF THE EVIDENCE

Crises are marked by confusion, by too much raw information and too little time to deal with it, by too many demands on the analyst and so forth. It would be nice to have lots of time for the interested and knowledgeable analysts to assemble and review their evidence, make their arguments, reexamine the facts, and revise their judgments and conclusions, much in the same laborious fashion in which national estimates are prepared. In warning, unfortunately, time often does not permit this and it frequently does not even permit some of the less time-consuming means of getting analysts together to discuss the material and exchange views on what it all means.

In these circumstances, analysts and consumers alike may profit from some relatively simple guidelines designed to assist in evaluating the evidence and the intention of the adversary. We begin by assuming that the adversary is behaving rationally and that he is following some logical and relatively consistent pattern of action in achieving his objectives. Although this may not always be the case (states as well as individuals have sometimes acted irrationally and inconsistently), it is well to start with the logical analysis of the country's behavior before assuming that its leaders are acting irrationally. As a result, we also assume that war is not an end in itself for them and that they will not resort to hostilities so long as there is some reasonable chance of achieving their objectives by means short of war. We therefore start with the five following questions designed to clarify our own thinking about what the adversary is up to:

1. Is the national leadership committed to the achievement of the objective in question, whatever it may be? Is it a matter of national priority, something the leadership appears determined to accomplish?

2. Is the objective potentially attainable, or the situation potentially soluble, by military means, at least to some degree?

3. Does the military capability already exist, or is it being built up to a point that military action is now feasible and victory likely to be attainable? Or, more explicitly, does the scale of the military buildup meet doctrinal criteria for offensive action?

4. Have all reasonable options, other than military, apparently been exhausted or appear unlikely to have any success in achieving the objective? Or, more simply, have the political options run out?

5. Is the risk factor low, or at least tolerable?

If the answer to all the questions is a firm "yes," logic would dictate that the chances of military action are high. If the answer to any one of them is "no," then it would appear less likely, or even unlikely, that the nation will resort to military action now, although of course circumstances might change so that it would decide to do so in the future. If two or three answers are "no," the chances of military action would logically appear to drop drastically to the point of highly improbable if four or all answers are negative.

The application of these guidelines to some real crises yields some interesting results:

- For the Soviet invasion of Czechoslovakia, the answer to all five questions is "yes"—although some persons might maintain that Soviet political options were not entirely exhausted by 20 August 1968, a series of political measures had failed to bring the situation under control, and there was little reason to believe that more such pressures would succeed.

- For the Arab-Israeli conflict of June 1967, the answers from Israel's standpoint also are "yes" to all five, although slightly less clearly or categorically perhaps than for the USSR in 1968; that is, the risk factor was seemingly a little higher and the exhaustion of political solutions perhaps a little less certain.

- The case of Egypt, in the years preceding the October 1973 war, presents an interesting problem. With respect to Egypt's desire to recover the territory lost to Israel in the 1967 war, the answer to questions one and two was at all times emphatically "yes" and to question four also "yes" (from a realistic standpoint). Yet, the likelihood of a major Egyptian attack on Israel appeared to drop drastically because it was generally assumed (particularly by the Israelis) that Egypt lacked the capability for successful military action and that the risks were high. In large part, this Israeli assessment was right, for Egypt did lack the capability to defeat Israel. It averted disaster in the conflict only because the Israeli counterattack was brought to a halt, largely as a result of the diplomatic intervention of the superpowers. What both Israel and the U.S. failed to perceive was that Sadat had estimated (correctly) that the Egyptian attack even if unsuccessful militarily would achieve the sought-for political outcome. Further, the Israeli judgment that Egyptian forces could not even cross the Canal was, of course, erroneous. There was thus a partial and very important misjudgment of the Egyptian military capability as well.

- In the Sino-Soviet border controversy (which reached its most critical point in 1969), we can come to a firm "yes" only on question one—the Soviet leadership did appear committed to "doing something" about the China problem, particularly after the Damanskiy Island incident in March. To all other questions on this thorny problem, however, the answer is either "no" or at least uncertain. It was highly doubtful that a Soviet military attack would have "solved" or even lessened the China problem. The Soviet Union could not build up sufficient military force actually to conquer the Chinese people in war, except possibly by the use of nuclear weapons. The employment of these, in turn, would make the risk factor very high—both militarily and politically. And finally, difficult as the Chinese might be to negotiate with, the political options had not run out.

Because of the different nature of the Soviet actions in Cuba in 1962 (obviously, the Soviet Union never intended to go to war over Cuba), the foregoing questions cannot all be literally applied to the Cuban missile crisis. Insofar as they are applicable, however, the answers do not yield a positive "yes" which would have made the Soviet action logically predictable or consistent with previous Soviet behavior. In particular, the risk factor, from our standpoint and in fact, was extremely high, and the Soviet action is explainable only as a gross miscalculation of what the U.S. reaction was likely to be.

Thus these questions, although useful as a logical starting point for the examination of the meaning of our evidence, are not a foolproof guide to an assessment of intention. For there will also be the cases in which the adversary's action will not necessarily be logical—where he may resort to military action, even though the answer to one or even more of the five questions is "no." For a variety of reasons—miscalculation of the opponent's strength or reaction, overestimation of one's own strength, frustration, internal domestic pressures, patriotic hysteria, revenge, a fit of pique, or just plain desperation—a nation's leadership may decide on imprudent or even disastrous courses of military action which are clearly not in its national interest.

Probably most conflicts are final acts of desperation when other means of solution have failed. In many cases, the instigator of the military action nonetheless has followed a rational and consistent course of action, and, after due deliberation and all other options have failed to yield results, has decided on military action as the only method which will achieve the desired result. Military solutions are not inherently irrational acts, particularly if they are likely to succeed. The Soviet invasion of Czechoslovakia, for example, was a carefully deliberated, meticulously planned, coldly rational, and entirely logical course of action; although there were political (but not military) risks, they were far less from the Soviet standpoint than permitting Czechoslovakia to pass from control of the communists.

Before we conclude that some other nation is acting "irrationally" in going to war, we should carefully examine our own attitudes and make sure we are not rejecting such action as illogical because we either do not fully appreciate how strongly the other country feels about it, or because we are just opposed to war on principle as an instrument of national policy. I believe that the systematic application of the method described above will more often than not yield positive and correct results. At a minimum, it is a method of helping ourselves to think objectively about the evidence as a whole and to avoid, insofar as possible, substituting our own views for those of the other guy.

But there will remain those cases, like Cuba in 1962, that are not logical and do not meet objective criteria for rational action. It is this imponderable, of course, which so vastly complicates warning. We must allow for those cases where the risk factor is high or where military action is not likely to solve the problem and may even be potentially suicidal. When there is good reason to suspect that the leadership of the state in question may be acting irrationally, the two most important questions are slightly modified versions of one and three:

1. Is the national leadership so committed to the achievement of the objective, or so obsessed with the problem, that it may even act illogically in an effort to achieve its goals?

2. Is the military capability being built up to the maximum possible for this action, even though the chance of success is doubtful?

RECONSTRUCTING THE ADVERSARY'S DECISIONMAKING PROCESS

If the final objective of warning analysis is the understanding of what the adversary is going to do, then the knowledge or recognition that he has decided to do something is the ultimate achievement. The highest goal of every espionage service is the penetration of the enemy's decisionmaking machinery—the hidden microphone in the conference room, or the agent with access to minutes of the conference. To have this type of access is to be sure, or nearly sure, of the enemy's intentions, and will make superfluous a vast amount of information, however valuable in itself, from lesser or secondary sources.

Since we are most unlikely to have such access to the highest councils of our adversaries—or if it could be obtained, it would be a highly vulnerable and perishable asset—we must try to do the next best thing. We seek sources and information that will best permit us to deduce what may have been decided or to infer what the adversary's objectives and plans may be. In practice, in a crisis or warning situation, this will mean that we must examine virtually all the available evidence in an attempt to perceive what the pieces both individually and collectively may tell us about the adversary's decisions.

Obviously, this is both a highly sophisticated and very difficult analytic problem. It is also one of the most controversial aspects of the warning problem, on which there is apt to be the widest divergence of opinion in a live situation. Moreover, very few guidelines appear to have been devised to assist the analyst or the policymaker to follow some logical process in reconstructing the adversary's decisionmaking process. In the pressures of a crisis situation, and lacking any body of experience or agreed "rules" that might be of assistance, there has been some tendency in the Intelligence Community to ignore this problem. What should be of highest priority in the analytic process—the attempt to decide what the adversary has decided—is often shunted aside in favor of mere factual reporting of what is going on, which is obviously much easier and less controversial. Too often, the reconstruction of another country's decisions and planning is attempted only after the crisis has been resolved, and thus becomes one more piece of retrospective or historical analysis, rather than something which might have helped us to foresee what was going to happen. Some brilliant postmortems have been produced, which have revealed that there is considerable talent for analyzing the decisionmaking process by inferential means. Such studies almost invariably also dig up pieces of information which were not considered at the time. But they nearly always are produced too late to help analysis in the current crisis and hence to be of any assistance to our own decisionmakers.

Clearly, it would be very useful to have some type of methodology which would help us to deal on a current basis with this elusive, but highly critical and sometimes decisive, factor in warning. It would be presumptuous to suggest that the remainder of this section is going to provide the answers, or some kind of simple and foolproof methodology. Its purpose rather is to assist the analyst to ask the right questions and to point out some of the more obvious aspects of this problem which have often been overlooked.

Some Elementary Guidelines for Decision Analysis

Actions flow from decisions, not decisions from actions. On the surface, this appears to be a truism, and almost an insult to the intelligence of the reader. Yet experience shows that this elementary principle is often not understood in crisis situations. In case after case, there has been a tendency to project into the future decisions which must in fact already have been taken. The impression is left that the adversary is highly confused, hasn't decided anything yet, and is just doing things with no plan behind them. Thus, even major deployments of military forces may be downplayed or written off in such commonly used phrases as: "The deployment of these units significantly increases the enemy's capability to attack, if he should decide to do so."

The last phrase is not just gratuitous, it can be downright misleading. It suggests that the forces are being moved without any plans in mind, that the adversary does not know yet what he is going to do with them, that major actions have been taken without any reason for them and that the adversary is going to make decisions later. Whether the writer of such phrases consciously realizes it, he is probably using this device to avoid thinking about the problem or coming to any decisions himself. This phrase will help him to "be right" no matter what happens later. Whether it will help our own decisionmaker to "be right" is another matter, since the effect of this soothing language will probably be to reassure him that he has lots of time still and there is nothing to be alarmed about yet. He may even infer that when the adversary makes his decision, the intelligence system will know it and tell him.

All non-routine or unusual actions emanating from the national level result from some kind of decisions. They don't just happen. This is true of both military and political actions. When something unusual occurs, particularly something that increases the adversary's capability to take military action or is otherwise potentially ominous, the analyst should ask such questions as: What does this suggest of the adversary's plans? What prompted him to do this? What kind of decision has been taken which would account for this action? He should avoid suggesting that the adversary does not know why he did it or that we are waiting for him to make his decision. It will often be helpful at this point to try and look backward and see what may have gone before which could account for the current development or which may indicate that there is a connection between a number of developments.

Isolating or estimating decision times. Major national decisions, and sometimes even minor ones, are likely to result in actions in various fields, all of which flow from the same source or cause and are thus related to one another. They are designed to achieve the same ends or to be complementary. Where the decision is concerned with hostilities or preparations for possible hostilities, it will nearly always be followed by a series of both military and political actions which differ markedly from the norm. In some cases, it will require only a minor amount of backtracking or retrospective analysis to perceive that the actions were probably initiated at a recent publicized meeting of the national leadership, military leaders, or whatever. This will be particularly true if there is some sudden, unexpected development which precipitates a crisis, and ensuing developments clearly follow from that event. No one should have much trouble in these circumstances in perceiving that decisions of some sort are being taken and when. Where there is no sudden and obvious emergency, however, both the nature and timing of major decisions are often concealed in closed societies, and sometimes in free societies as well. Thus, it may be some time before there will be indications that any new decisions have been taken at all, let alone when they were taken, or what they might have been. The analyst may often have to work from very fragmentary data in his effort to reconstruct what has been happening up to now and to attempt to determine when the adversary decided to initiate the action. Why bother?

The reason to bother is that the recapitulation of the events or developments in time sequence from the date when the first anomalies become apparent will not only help to fix the decision time but also the nature of the decision. The interrelationship of events as part of a plan may begin to become apparent; they may cease to be isolated, unexplained anomalies when they can be traced back to a common date. Only as they are assembled by the date they were first observed to have occurred (not date they were reported) will the analyst begin to perceive their possible relationships and suspect that some common prior decision may lie behind all or many of them. Once again, the value of keeping chronologies of bits of seeming incidental intelligence is evident. It is only by doing this that the probable times of secret decisions are likely to be suspected at all, or that the analyst can begin to fit the pieces together. Once it becomes apparent (as it probably will only after meticulous research) that a shift in the propaganda line actually coincided with the first secret mobilization of reservists and a variety of other preparations for possible conflict will the possible scope and significance of the early decisions begin to emerge.

Judging that crucial decisions are being made. One of the most important things to know about what the adversary is up to is whether he is making major new decisions at all. That is, even if we have no evidence as yet as to the nature of the decisions, we may gain considerable understanding of the intentions of the adversary if we have some insight into what he is concerned about and whether some particular subject is of priority to him at the moment. This is often not so difficult to ascertain as it might appear, although clearly it will be dependent either on what the adversary chooses to publicize about his concerns, or on our ability to collect some information on political developments and the activities and attitudes of the leadership.

Contrary to what many may think, the preoccupation of the leadership with particular problems and decisions may often be no secret at all. To pick a conspicuous example, it was abundantly evident in the summer of 1968 that the Soviet leadership was obsessed with the problem of what to do about Czechoslovakia, and that it had overriding importance to them. It was evident that the Soviet leadership was making decisions of some kind about Czechoslovakia, even if analysts could not agree what those decisions were. The perception of the crisis thus derived in part from our knowledge that Czechoslovakia, from the Soviet standpoint, was what the whole summer was about.

Contingency, intermediate and final decisions. All analysts should beware the pitfall of oversimplification of the decisionmaking process, which is one of the most common of errors. Crucial national decisions usually involve a series of steps, which may range from preliminary decisions to take certain measures on a contingency basis, subsequent decisions to take further preparations and to "up the ante" in case military action becomes necessary, up to near-final and final decisions to proceed with the action. Or, alternatively, actions may be initiated only for pressure purposes or in an attempt to dissuade by threat of force, with no intention of following through.

It may be noted that a country may make a final or near-final decision as to an objective which it firmly intends to obtain, but will also make a series of decisions on the various means which may be tried to obtain that objective. Often, these will involve both political and military pressure tactics, since presumably all-out force is the means to be employed only if all other measures have failed. In this case, a state's leaders may seem to be indecisive (because a series of measures is tried) when in fact it has the objective clearly in mind and always intends to reach it.

In recent years, we have heard much about options, and to "keep his options open" has become a popular phrase to describe various preliminary steps or contingency preparations which the country may take, presumably when it has not yet decided which course of action it will finally adopt. Indeed the phrase strongly implies "decision deferred," and the more options a nation has, the better off it presumably is and the longer it can defer the crucial decisions. It is well to avoid over-dependence on this idea, which can lead the analyst into cliche-type reasoning where all preparations for military action, no matter how ominous, are written off as inconclusive and indicative of no decisions on the part of the adversary. The important questions are: "What options are left?" and "Does this action indicate that the adversary himself now believes that the options are dwindling and that the chances for a political solution are running out?" Many people seem unable, or unwilling, to carry out this type of analysis, and will fall back time and again on the argument that it was impossible to come to any judgment of the adversary's intentions or decisions since he was "only keeping his options open."

The reader may wish to refer back to the five questions suggested above as basic guidelines to the interpretation of a country's course of action. They are also the crucial factors in the decisionmaking process. If the first question, or premise, is judged to be positive—that the national leadership is committed to the achievement of the objective in question—then this is the operative factor behind the decision, or series of decisions. Only if some other factor effectively prevents or precludes obtaining that objective, will the nation presumably be deterred from a course of action which will fulfill its objective. Some of the means it may use (which we describe as options) may indeed be contingency or preparatory steps initially, in case other more desirable options fail or do not prove viable, but they are means to an end, not just steps taken to have "more options" and hence to postpone coming to any decisions. Indeed, the number of options which the leaders devise, or try out, to secure its objective may be something of a rough measure of how serious they are about obtaining it. As applied to Czechoslovakia in 1968, the mere fact that the USSR tried so many means of bringing the situation under control before it invaded was in itself indicative of the seriousness of its intent and raised the probability that the military option ultimately would be exercised if all else failed.

Interplay of political and military decisions. Another simplistic approach to the decisionmaking question, which also occurs surprisingly frequently, is to assume that political and military decisions are taken by different groups and are somehow not really related to one another. On the one hand, are political leaders making political decisions, and on the other are military leaders undertaking military exercises, carrying out mobilization, deploying troops, and so on, almost on their own without relationship to the political situation. This is highly erroneous, at least in countries where the national leadership exerts effective command and control over the military forces, and it is particularly erroneous in Communist nations in which the political leadership maintains a monopoly on the decisionmaking process and the military undertakes virtually nothing on its own.

Thus, military and political decisions are interrelated and part of the same process, and the military steps are undertaken and insofar as possible timed to achieve specific political objectives. They must not be considered in isolation or as unrelated to the political objective. To consider them in isolation is not only to misunderstand the cause of the military actions, but more importantly to fail to perceive the strategic objective and the interrelationship of the various means that may be used to obtain it.

Chapter 6
SURPRISE AND TIMING

One of the most widespread misconceptions about warning is the belief that, as the hour of attack draws near, there will be more and better evidence that enemy action is both probable and imminent. From this, the idea follows naturally that intelligence will be better able to provide warning in the short term and will, in the few hours or at most days prior to the attack, issue its most definitive and positive warning judgments. Moreover—since there is presumed to be accumulating evidence that the adversary is engaged in his last-minute preparations for the attack—this concept holds that intelligence will likely be able to estimate the approximate if not the exact time of the attack. Therefore, if we can judge at all that the attack is probable, we can also tell when it is coming. This concept of warning—as a judgment of imminence of attack—has affected U.S. thinking on the subject for years.

In many cases experience shows that the reverse will be true, and that there will be fewer indications that the attack is coming and even an apparent lull in enemy preparations. This can be quite deceptive, even for those who know from experience not to relax their vigilance in such circumstances. Those who do not understand this principle are likely to be totally surprised by the timing—or even the occurrence—of the enemy action. They will probably feel aggrieved that their collection has failed them and they will tend to believe that the remedy for the intelligence "failure" is to speed up the collection and reporting process, not appreciating that the earlier collection and analysis were more important and that a judgment of probability of attack could have been reached much earlier and should not have been dependent on highly uncertain and last-minute collection breakthroughs.

PRINCIPAL FACTORS IN TIMING AND SURPRISE

Nearly all countries, except in unfavorable or unusual circumstances, have shown themselves able to achieve tactical surprise in warfare. History is replete with instances in which the adversary was caught unawares by the timing, strength or location of the attack, even when the attack itself had been expected or considered a likelihood. Even democracies with their notoriously lax security in comparison with closed societies have often had striking success in concealing the details (including the timing) of their operations. To cite the most conspicuous example, the greatest military operation in history achieved tactical surprise even though it was fully expected by an adversary who potentially had hours of tactical warning that the massive invasion force was approaching. Deception played a major role in this, the Normandy invasion.

It is not only by deception, however, that tactical surprise is so often achieved and that last-minute preparations for the attack can be concealed. A more important and more usual reason is that the indications of attack which are most obvious and discernible to us are the major deployments of forces and large-scale logistic preparations which are often begun weeks or even months before the attack itself. Once these are completed, or nearly so, the adversary will have attained a capability for attack more or less at the time of his choosing, and the additional preparations that must be accomplished just prior to the attack are much less likely to be discernible to us or may be ambiguous in nature. Staff conferences, inspections, the issuance of basic loads of ammunition and other supplies, and the final orders for the attack all are measures that require little overt activity and are not likely to be detected except by extraordinarily fine collection and rapid reporting—such as a well-placed agent in the enemy's headquarters with access to some rapid means of communications, or the fortuitous arrival of a knowledgeable defector.

Even the final deployments of major ground force units to jumpoff positions for the assault may be successfully concealed by the measures that most states take to ensure tactical surprise, including rigid communications security and night movements. Thus, unlike the major deployments of troops and equipment which almost never can be entirely concealed, the short-term preparations have a good chance of being concealed, and quite often are. And, even if detected, there will often be minimal time in which to alert or redeploy forces for the now imminent attack, still less to issue warning judgments at the national level. Such tactical warning usually is an operational problem for the commander in the field. Ten minutes or even three hours warning does not allow much time for the political leadership to come to new decisions and implement them.

Another facet of the problem of assessing the timing of attack is the difficulty of determining when the enemy's preparations are in fact completed, and when he himself will judge that his military forces are ready. As we have noted elsewhere, it is particularly difficult to make this judgment with regard to logistic preparations. In fact, I can recall no instance in my experience in which it could be clearly determined that the logistic preparations for attack were complete, particularly since heavy supply movements usually continue uninterrupted even after the attack is launched. There has often been a tendency for intelligence to believe that all military preparations are completed earlier than in fact is the case, the discrepancy usually being attributable to the fact that the major and most obvious troop deployments had apparently been completed. Thus, even when intelligence has come to the right judgment on enemy intentions, it has sometimes been too early in its assessment of the possible timing of the attack.

In addition, the enemy command for various reasons may not go through with an attack as soon as the forces are fully prepared, or may change the date of the attack even after it has been set. A student has compiled some data concerning the frequency with which D-Days are not met, and the effects of this on the adversary's judgments. Of 162 cases analyzed where D-Days applied, almost half (about 44 per cent) were delayed, about five per cent went ahead of schedule, and only slightly more than half (about 51 per cent) remained on schedule. The most common reasons for delay were weather and administrative problems, presumably in completing or synchronizing all preparations. Some attacks have had to be postponed repeatedly. For example, the Germans' Verdun offensive of 21 February 1916 was postponed no less than nine times by unfavorable weather.[9]

Of all aspects of operational planning, the easiest to change and most flexible is probably timing. Once troops are in position to go, orders to attack usually need be issued no more than a few hours ahead, and the postponement of even major operations rarely presents great difficulties to the commander. Attacks have been postponed, or advanced, simply because there was reason to believe that the adversary had learned of the scheduled date. Obviously, among the simplest of deception ruses is the planting of false information concerning the date of operations with the enemy's intelligence services.

In addition to general preparedness, tactical factors and surprise, operations may be delayed for doctrinal reasons or to induce enemy forces to extend their lines of communication or to walk into entrapments in which they can be surrounded and annihilated. The delayed counteroffensive, designed to draw enemy forces into untenable advanced positions, is a tactic that has been employed with devastating effect.

Political factors also may weigh heavily or even decisively in the timing of operations. This will be particularly true when (as is often the case) the state in question intends to resort to military operations only as a last resort and hopes that the threat of such action will induce the opponent to capitulate. Obviously, in such cases, the decision of the national leadership that the political options have run out and that only force will succeed will be the determining factor in when the military operation is launched. In this event, operations may be deferred for weeks beyond the date when military preparations are completed, and the assessment of the timing of the attack may be almost exclusively dependent on knowledge of the political situation and insight into the enemy's decisionmaking process.

Still another political variant which may affect the timing of attack is when one nation is attempting to induce the other to strike the first major blow and thus appear as the aggressor. In this case, a series of harassments, border violations and various clandestine tactics may be employed as the conflict gradually escalates until one or the other power decides to make an overt attack. Clearly, the point at which this may happen will be very difficult to predict.

As is well known, many attacks are initiated near dawn, for two reasons: the nighttime cloaks the final deployments of the attacking units, and the hours of daylight are desirable to pursue the operation. Some aggressors have shown a marked favoritism for attacks in the dead of night. This was particularly true of

---

[9]Barton Whaley, *Stratagem: Deception and Surprise in War* (Cambridge, MA: Massachusetts Institute of Technology, Center for International Studies, April 1969), unpublished manuscript, 177-178, A69.

North Vietnamese and Viet Cong forces, which showed themselves highly adept in night penetration operations and assaults. The USSR also often launched attacks or other operations hours before dawn: the operation to crush the Hungarian revolt began between about midnight and 0330 hours; the Berlin sector borders were sealed about 0300; the invasion of Czechoslovakia began shortly before midnight.

EXAMPLES OF ASSESSING TIMING

There is considerable coverage of the problems associated with attack timing in military historical writing. The following cases are truly representative, and are not selected as unusual examples.

The German Attack on Holland, Belgium and France, May 1940. World War II had been under way for eight months before Hitler finally launched his offensive against Western Europe in May 1940, the long delay in the opening of the western front having generated the phrase "phony war." All three victims of the final assault had ample and repeated warnings, and indeed it was the redundancy of warnings which in large part induced the reluctance to accept the final warnings when they were received. The "cry-wolf" phenomenon has rarely been more clearly demonstrated—Hitler is said to have postponed the attack on the West 29 times, often at the last minute.

Owing to their access to one of the best-placed intelligence sources of modern times, the Dutch had been correctly informed of nearly every one of these plans to attack them, from the first date selected by Hitler, 12 November 1939, to the last, 10 May 1940. Their source was Colonel Hans Oster, the Deputy Chief of German Counterintelligence, who regularly apprised the Dutch Military Attaché in Berlin of Hitler's plans and of their postponements. Although in the end Oster provided one week's warning of the 10 May date, and there was much other evidence as well that the German attack was probably imminent, the Dutch ignored the warnings and failed even to alert their forces prior to the German attack. The Belgians, more heedful of the numerous warnings received, did place their forces on a general alert. The French, having also experienced several false alarms of a German attack, seem to have ignored the repeated warnings of their own intelligence in early May, including a firm advisory on 9 May that the attack would occur the following day. These instances clearly demonstrate two fundamental precepts of warning: "more facts" and first-rate sources do not necessarily produce warning, and intelligence warnings are useless unless some action is taken on them.

The Soviet Attack on Japanese forces, August 1945. This is one of the lesser studied World War II examples, but clearly demonstrates the difference between strategic and tactical warning. The Japanese, who were able to follow the Soviet buildup in the Far East from December 1944 through July 1945, correctly judged that the USSR would attack the Japanese Kwantung Army in Manchuria. They had also concluded by July that the Soviet troop and logistic buildup had reached the stage that the USSR would be ready to attack any time after 1 August. Despite this expectation which almost certainly must have resulted in a high degree of alert of the Japanese forces in Manchuria, the Kwantung Army had no immediate warning of the timing of the attack, which occurred about midnight on the night of 8-9 August.

The North Korean attack on South Korea, June 1950. This was a notable example of both strategic and tactical surprise, and indeed one of the few operations of the century which truly may be described as a surprise attack. Neither U.S. intelligence, at least by official admission, nor policy and command levels had expected the attack to occur, as a result of which there had been no military preparations for it. The South Koreans, despite many previously expressed fears of such an attack, also were not prepared and had not alerted their forces. Since strategic warning had been lacking, the short-term final preparations of the North Korean forces (insofar as they were detected) were misinterpreted as "exercises" rather than bona fide combat deployments. In considerable part, the warning failure was attributable to inadequate collection on North Korea—but the failure to have allocated more collection effort in turn was due primarily to the disbelief that the attack would occur. In addition, the "cry-wolf" phenomenon had in part inured the community; for at least a year, there had been about one report per month alleging that North Korea would attack on such-and-such a date. When another was received for June, it was given no more credence than the previous ones—nor, in view of the uncertain reliability and source of all these reports, was there any reason that it should have been given greater weight. Although we can never know, most and perhaps all of these reports may have been planted by the North Korean or Soviet intelligence services in the first place. The attack is a notable example of the importance of correct prior assessments of the likelihood of attack if the short-term tactical intelligence is to be correctly interpreted.

Chinese Intervention in the Korean War, October-November 1950. Among the several problems in judging Chinese intentions in the late summer and fall of 1950 was the question of the timing of their intervention. Based on the premise that the less territory one gives up to the adversary, the less one's own forces will have to recover, the Chinese can be said to have intervened much "too late" in the conflict. And this conception of the optimum time for Chinese intervention strongly influenced U.S. judgments of their intentions. From the time the first direct political warning of the Chinese intention to intervene was issued on 3 October (to the Indian Ambassador in Beijing) until the first contact with Chinese forces in Korea on 26 October, all Communist resistance in Korea was rapidly collapsing as the U.S./UN forces were driving toward the Yalu. As the Chinese failed to react and the communist prospects for recouping their losses appeared increasing unfavorable, the Washington Intelligence Community (and probably the Far East Command as well) became increasingly convinced that the time for effective Chinese Communist intervention had passed. In the week prior to the first contact with Chinese forces, the U.S. warning committee (then known as the Joint Intelligence Indications Committee) actually went on record as stating that there was an increasing probability that a decision against overt intervention had been taken.

Once the Chinese forces had actually been engaged, there was an interval of a month before they became militarily effective and launched their massive attacks in late November. Thus in this period the intelligence process again was confronted with the problem of assessing the timing of any future Chinese operations, as well as of their scope. The four-week period produced many hard indications, both military and political, that the Chinese in fact were preparing for major military action. But there was virtually no available evidence about when such action might be launched, and even those who believed that the coming offensive was a high probability were somewhat perplexed by the delay and were unable to adduce any conclusive indications of when the attack would occur. As is well known, tactical surprise was indeed achieved.

Even in retrospect, we cannot be sure whether the Chinese delayed their intervention and their subsequent offensive because of political indecision, the need for more time to complete their military preparations, or as a tactical device to entrap as many UN forces as possible near the Yalu. I believe that military rather than political factors probably delayed the initial intervention and that both preparedness and tactical considerations accounted for the delay in the offensive, but I cannot prove it. Others may argue—and they cannot be proved wrong—that the Chinese may not have decided inevitably on intervention by 3 October, and/or that negotiations with the USSR and North Korea may have delayed the intervention as much as military factors.

Arab-Israeli Six-Day War, June 1967. There were many indications of the coming of this conflict. From 22 May, when Nasser closed the Gulf of Aqaba to Israeli shipping, tensions had been mounting, and the possibility of war was universally recognized. Both sides had mobilized and taken numerous other military preparedness measures. Before 1 June U.S. intelligence was on record that Israel was capable and ready to launch a preemptive and successful attack with little or no warning, and that there was no indication that the UAR was planning to take the military initiative. The Arabs were surprised by the Israeli attack, although we were not. U.S. intelligence predictions of the likelihood and probable success of an Israeli assault were highly accurate, although the precise timing and tactics of the operation, of course, were not known to us.

The Israelis screened their plans from the Arabs by a combination of rigid security (there was no leak of their decisions or final military preparations) and an exceptionally well-planned and effective deception campaign. There were several facets of the deception plan, one of which was to lead Egypt to believe that the attack, if it occurred, would be in the southern Sinai rather than the north. In addition, numerous measures were taken in the several days prior to the attack to create the impression that attack was not imminent. These included 1) public statements by newly appointed Defense Minister Moshe Dayan that Israel would rely on diplomacy for the present, 2) the issuance of leave to several thousand Israeli soldiers over the weekend of 3-4 June, and 3) public announcements that concurrent Israeli cabinet meetings were concerned only with routine matters, and more.

In addition, the attack was planned for an hour of the morning when most Egyptian officials would be on their way to work and when the chief of the Egyptian Air Force usually took his daily morning flight. The greatest surprise in the Israeli operations was not their occurrence, however, or even their timing, but their devastating effectiveness in virtually wiping out the Egyptian Air Force on the ground. And this success in turn was due on the one hand to the excellent planning of the operation and its meticulous execution by the Israeli pilots, and on the other to the ineptitude of the Egyptian military leadership in having failed to prepare for the possibility of such a strike or to have dispersed or otherwise protected at least a portion of the air force. (It is of interest to note that the USSR, which was providing at least some intelligence assistance to Nasser, was seemingly as surprised as Egypt. One result of this was that the USSR soon began to adopt measures to reduce the vulnerability of its own air forces to surprise attack, including the widespread construction of individual hangarettes to protect aircraft.)

The Invasion of Czechoslovakia, 20-21 August 1968. Obviously, our perception of the USSR's decisionmaking process in this case has major bearing on our understanding of why the attack occurred when it did, rather than sooner or later. And, since our knowledge of the decisions of the Soviet leadership, although considerable, is still incomplete, we must also remain somewhat uncertain as to why the invasion began on 20 August rather than some time earlier that month, or alternatively why the USSR did not wait to see the outcome of the Czechoslovak party congress scheduled for early September, as many people believed that it would.

Regardless of one's views on this point, however, the invasion of Czechoslovakia illustrates some of the pitfalls of trying to assess the timing of military operations. First, we are not sure in retrospect whether the USSR was fully ready to invade on about 1 August when the deployments appeared largely complete and U.S. intelligence concluded that Soviet forces were in a high state of readiness to invade. We do know that logistic activity continued at a high level thereafter and that the conclusion of the so-called rear services "exercise" was not announced until 10 August. Thereafter, other military preparations were continuing, including inspections of forces in the forward area by the high command, which the meticulous Soviet military planners may well have desired to complete before any invasion. Indeed it is possible, on military evidence alone (the political evidence is less persuasive), to argue that the invasion was always scheduled by the military for 20 August, and that it was we who were wrong in our assessment that the military forces were in high readiness to go on 1 August.

It can also be argued that military factors may have prompted the invasion somewhat earlier than the political leadership might have chosen and that it was this which occasioned the leadership meetings and final decisions on 16-17 August. If so, the approaching autumn and the problem of housing Soviet forces in Czechoslovakia into the winter might have been a major factor in determining the timing of invasion.

More important, however, are the lessons to be drawn for our judgments in the future concerning the timing of operations. The Czechoslovak case well demonstrates the psychological effects on intelligence assessments when an operation does not occur as soon as we think it might, and when the community is most ready for such action. When the Soviet Union did not invade in early August but instead reached a tenuous political agreement with Czechoslovakia, a letdown occurred and intelligence assessments almost immediately began placing less stress on the Soviet capability to invade. In fact, of course, that capability was being maintained and actually was increasing. So long as this was so, the possibility was in no way reduced that the USSR sooner or later would exercise its military capability.

Above all, the Czechoslovak case provides an outstanding illustration of the critical importance for warning of the judgment of probability of attack and of the lesser likelihood that intelligence will be able to assess the timing or imminence of attack. U.S. intelligence in this instance, as in others, placed too great weight on short-term or tactical warning, and too little on the excellent strategic intelligence which it already had. Moreover, many persons (including some at the policy level who were aggrieved that they had not been more specifically warned) tended to place the blame on the collection system which in fact had performed outstandingly in reporting a truly impressive amount of military and political evidence, much of it of high quality and validity, bearing on the Soviet intention. The Intelligence Community, while clearly reporting the USSR's capability to invade, deferred a judgment of whether or not it would invade in seeming expectation that some more specific or unequivocal evidence would be received if invasion was imminent. On the basis of historical precedent and the experience derived from numerous warning problems, this was a doubtful expectation; an invasion remained a grave danger, if not probable, so long as the military deployments were maintained, while the timing was far less predictable. The history of warfare, and of warning, demonstrates that tactical evidence of impending attack is dubious at best, that we cannot have confidence that we will receive such evidence, and that judgments of the probable course of enemy action must be made prior to this or it may be too late to make them at all.

North Vietnamese attacks in Laos and South Vietnam, 1969-70, 1971-72.
As a final example of problems in timing, three instances of North Vietnamese

attacks in Laos and South Vietnam provide quite striking evidence of the problems of assessing timing of attacks even when the preparatory steps are quite evident.

Traditionally, in the seesaw war in northern Laos, the Laotian government forces made gains in the Plaine des Jarres area during the rainy season, and the communist forces (almost entirely North Vietnamese invaders) launched offensives during the dry season (November to May) to regain most of the lost territory and sometimes more. In the fall of 1969, evidence began to be received unusually early of North Vietnamese troop movements toward the Plaine des Jarres, including major elements of a division which had not previously been committed in the area. As a result, intelligence assessments beginning the first week of October unequivocally forecast a major communist counteroffensive. After eight consecutive weeks of this conclusion (qualified in later weeks by the proviso "when the communists have solved their logistic problems"), it was decided to drop it not because it was considered wrong, but because consumers were beginning to question repeated forecasts of an enemy offensive which had not materialized yet, and the impact of the warning was beginning to fade. In mid-January, evidence began to become available that preparations for an attack were being intensified, and a forecast of an impending major offensive was renewed. The long-expected offensive finally come off in mid-February, or four months after the troop buildup and the initial prediction of the attacks. The delay was not a surprise to experienced students of the area, who had learned that the North Vietnamese meticulously planned and rehearsed in detail each offensive operation and that their attacks almost always were slow in coming.

Two years later, in the fall of 1971, a very similar repetition of the North Vietnamese buildup in northern Laos began, again in October and again involving the same division, although this time there were indications (such as the introduction of heavy artillery) that an even stronger military effort would be made. Intelligence assessments again forecast major North Vietnamese attacks in the Plaine des Jarres but for the most part avoided any firm judgment that they were necessarily imminent. There was almost no tactical warning of the attacks which this time were launched in mid-December in unprecedented strength and intensity. Within a few days, all Laotian government forces were driven from the Plaine, and within three weeks, the North Vietnamese launched an offensive against government bases southwest of the Plaine. Concurrently, the North Vietnamese were preparing for their major offensive against South Vietnam which finally kicked off on 30 March 1972 after months of buildup and intelligence predictions that an offensive was coming. Initial expectations, however, had been that the attacks most likely would come some time after mid-February, possibly to coincide with President Nixon's visit to China later that month.

Once again, timing proved one of the most uncertain aspects of the offensive, and we remain uncertain whether Hanoi originally intended to launch the attacks earlier and was unable to meet its schedule, or never intended the operation to come off until the end of March. In retrospect, it appears that the forecasts of another "Tet offensive" in mid-February probably were somewhat premature, since the deployments of main force units and other preparations continued through March. Nonetheless, the intelligence forecasts were essentially right, and it could have been dangerous in February to suggest that the attacks would not come off for another six weeks.

WARNING IS NOT A FORECAST OF IMMINENCE

It is from experiences like this that veteran warning analysts have become extremely chary of forecasting the timing of attacks. They have learned from repeated instances, in some of which the timing of operations appeared quite a simple or obvious problem, that this was not the case. In most instances, attacks have come later and sometimes much later than one might have expected, but even this cannot be depended on—sometimes they have come sooner. But except in rare cases, any forecast of the precise timing of attack carries a high probability of being wrong. There are just too many unpredictable factors—military and political—which may influence the enemy's decision on the timing and a multitude of ways in which he may use deception to obscure his decision.

The lesson is clear. Both analysts and supervisors should keep their attention focused on the key problem of whether the adversary is in fact preparing to attack at all, a judgment which they have a good and sometimes excellent chance of making with accuracy. Judgments often can be made, with less confidence in most cases, that all necessary preparations have probably been completed. A little less confidence still should be placed in forecasts as to when in the future all necessary preparations may be completed. At the bottom, and least reliable of all, will be the prediction of when the adversary may plan to strike. As a general rule, analysts will do well to avoid predictions of when precisely an attack may occur, particularly when some preparedness measures have not yet been completed. If pressed, it will normally be best to offer some time range within which the attack appears most likely, rather than attempt too specific a guess (for that is what it is). And some explanation of the uncertainties and perils of forecasting dates, backed up by historical evidence, may be helpful from time to time for the benefit of the policymaker as well.

Strategic warning is not a forecast of imminent attack, but rather a forecast of probable attack and it is this above all which the policy official and commander need to appreciate. If we recognize the uncertainties of timing, we will also be less likely to relax our vigilance or alerts just because the adversary has not yet attacked even as he is seemingly ready to do so.

Chapter 7

THE PROBLEM OF DECEPTION

Confidence that a study of history and of techniques and principles of indications analysis will enable us to come to the right judgment of the adversary's intentions fades as one contemplates the chilling prospect of deception. There is no single facet of the warning problem so unpredictable, and yet so potentially damaging in its effect, as deception. Nor is confidence in our ability to penetrate the sophisticated deception effort in any way restored by a diligent study of examples. On the contrary, such a study will only reinforce a conclusion that the most brilliant analysis may founder in the face of deception and that the most expert and experienced among us on occasion may be as vulnerable as the novice.

THE INFREQUENCY AND NEGLECT OF DECEPTION

There can be no question that, at least until quite recently, deception has been one of the least understood, least researched and least studied aspects of both history and intelligence. Military historians often have not even perceived the role which deception has played in the outcome of some major military operations. Indeed, the revelation in recent years of the part that deception played in World War II has led to a wholly new understanding of the history of that conflict. What accounts for the neglect of such an important subject?

One reason for the scant attention to deception almost certainly is its rarity. If true warning problems are seldom encountered, useful examples of deception are rarer still, and indeed a number of major crises of recent years seemingly have involved relatively little if any deception. A second, and related, factor is that the deception effort is likely to be the most secret and tightly held aspect of any operation and that countries often have been reluctant, even after the fact, to relax security on the deception plan, even when other aspects of the operation are fairly well known. The exceptions, in which the deception operation has been recorded for our benefit and study, usually have been the result of the publication of articles or memoirs by participants in the plan, or the declassification of war records, usually well after the event. Deception tends to be forgotten and neglected between wars because it is usually not an instrument of peace. Few countries have made a practice of extensive or elaborate deception in time of peace. There are some exceptions to this, particularly in the field of counterintelligence and espionage in which deception is routinely practiced.

One reason why active deception is reserved for the exceptional situation involving national security interests is that success in deception is heavily dependent on its rarity and on the prior establishment of credibility. Any country that constantly or even frequently disseminates falsehoods would rapidly lose credibility and acceptance with other nations, and with its own populace. It is one thing to be highly security conscious and not to reveal much, and quite another to engage in an active deception effort to mislead. The most effective deceptions are by those whom we have come to trust, or at least who have been relatively truthful in their dealings with us over a period of years. Thus the true deception operation, at least a major and sophisticated one, usually is reserved only for that critical situation in the life of the nation when it is most essential to conceal one's intent. This will usually be in preparation for or in time of war.

PRINCIPLES, TECHNIQUES AND EFFECTIVENESS OF DECEPTION

The principle of deception, most simply stated, is to induce the adversary to make the wrong choice; or, as General Sherman put it, the trick is to place the victim on the horns of a dilemma and then to impale him on the one of your choosing. If this is left entirely to chance, the probability of the enemy's making the right or wrong choice will be in direct ratio to the number of alternatives which he perceives as equally viable. Although surprise can result from sheer misunderstanding, "the possibility of surprise through misunderstanding diminishes nearly to the vanishing point as one considers the more elaborate strategic operations."[10] Therefore, the planner must develop one or more plausible alternatives as bait for his victim and then employ a range of stratagems to mislead him. "The ultimate goal of stratagem is to make the enemy quite certain, very decisive and wrong."[11] If this ideal cannot be achieved (and this writer believes that it would be a rare situation in which such total deception could be achieved), the mere presenting of alternative solutions nonetheless will serve to confuse the adversary and lead him to disperse his effort or to make at least a partially wrong response.

In other words the best stratagem is the one that generates a set of warning signals susceptible to alternative, or better yet, optional interpretations, where the intended solution is implausible in terms of the victim's prior experience and knowledge while the false solution (or solutions) is plausible. If the victim does not suspect the possibility that deception may be operating he will inevitably be gulled. If he suspects deception, he has only four courses open to him: These are, in summary:

---

[10] Whaley, 133. The most thorough, published exposition on military deception is in *Strategic Military Deception*, eds. Donald C. Daniel and Katherine L. Herbig (New York: Pergamon Press, 1982).

[11] Whaley, 135.

1. To act as if no deception is being used.

2. To give equal weight to all perceived solutions (in violation of the principle of economy of force).

3. To engage in random behavior, risking success or failure on blind guesswork.

4. To panic, which paradoxically may offer as good a chance of success as the "rational" course in 3.[12]

Thus, even a primitive deception effort will, by threatening various alternatives, create enough uncertainty to distract the most wily opponent and force him either to disperse his effort or gamble on being right. Further, Whaley concludes, in a judgment of greatest importance for warning, that even the most masterful deceivers have proved to be easy dupes for more primitive efforts. "Indeed, this is a general finding of my study—that is, the deceiver is almost always successful regardless of the sophistication of his victim in the same art. On the face of it, this seems an intolerable conclusion, one offending common sense. Yet it is the irrefutable conclusion of the historical evidence."[13]

A related, and also unexpected, finding of Whaley's study is that only a small repertoire of stratagems is necessary "to insure surprise after surprise." The fact that the victim may be familiar with specific ruses "does not necessarily reduce much less destroy their efficacy. This can be predicted from the theory, which postulates that it is the misdirection supplied by selective planting of false signals that yields surprise and not the specific communications channels (that is, ruses) used."[14] In other words, the same tricks can be used over and over again, and stratagem can be effective with only a small number of basic ruses or scenarios.

Whaley goes on to note that, as between security and deception, deception is by far the most effective in achieving surprise since the only important security in this case will be the protection of the deception plan itself, which usually needs to be revealed only to a very small number of individuals. If the security on the deception plan is tight enough, security on the rest of the operation can be outright slovenly, and "the most efficient stratagems calculatedly utilize known inefficiencies in general operational security." Whaley cites some examples of the extreme security maintained on deception plans, which the warning analyst should well heed, since it will upset the accepted theory that enemy plans may be learned from full confessions of high-ranking prisoners or defectors, or from interception of valid communications, authentic war plans, and the like. Thus, in preparation for the Pearl Harbor attack, the Japanese Navy

[12] Whaley, 142-143.

[13] Whaley, 146.

[14] Whaley, 228.

issued a war plan on 5 November which gave full and accurate details of the planned attacks on the Philippines and Southeast Asia but which omitted any reference to the Pearl Harbor missions of the Navy, this portion of the order having been communicated only verbally. In the Suez attack in 1956, the entire British military staff from the Allied CinC on down were not informed on the collusion of the UK and France with Israel, so tightly was this held. In the Korean war, the U.S. planned an amphibious feint (the so-called Kojo feint) which only the most senior commanders knew to be a bluff; even the planners and commanders of the naval bombardment and carrier strike forces thought the operation was real and behaved accordingly. Thus, the misleading of one's own people has been an important feature in many deceptions, with the unwitting participants in the plan convincingly carrying out their roles in good faith, thus contributing materially to the success of the operation. So effective has security been on deception operations, that Whaley concludes that there have been almost no cases in which the deception plan itself was prematurely disclosed to the victim.

TYPES OF DECEPTION

This subject may be approached in a number of ways. Whaley identifies five specific varieties of military deception: intention (whether an attack or operation will occur at all), time, place, strength, style (the form the operation takes, weapons used, and so forth).

For strategic warning, the subject of this book, it will be obvious that the first of these (intention) is the most important. Indeed, some might say that this is the only variety of deception which should properly be defined as strategic, the other types above being essentially tactical problems. In fact, however, strategic warning or the perception of the adversary's intention often does fall victim to one or more of the other foregoing varieties of deception as well. Thus, in the Tet offensive of 1968, we were less the victims of misperception of the enemy's intention as such (it was obvious that attacks of some type and scope were in preparation) than of the other factors. We greatly underestimated the strength of the attacks; we were astounded at some of the places (particularly cities) in which the attacks occurred; we misperceived the style of the offensive in some degree (that is, the extent of covert infiltration of saboteurs and troop units, again particularly into the major cities); and there was something of a misestimate of the timing of the attacks in that it was generally assumed that they would be launched before or after the holidays rather than during them (a factor which accounted for so many South Vietnamese troops being on leave and for the lax security). Thus, it was all these misperceptions of the enemy's planning and intentions which contributed to the surprise—and initial success—of the Tet offensive. We were the victims of a combination of effective security, enemy deception and self-deception.

The history of warfare is filled with examples of the achievement of surprise in time, place or strength, or a combination of them. Whaley finds that, of the examples which he studied in which surprise was achieved, the most common mode was place (72 percent), followed by time (66 percent), and strength (57 percent). The least frequent type of surprise which he found was style, which prevailed in 25 percent of the cases he analyzed. There are nonetheless some very famous examples, including the dropping of the first atomic weapon on Hiroshima, and the introduction of Soviet strategic missiles into Cuba.

We may close this very inadequate discussion of this approach to types of surprise and deception by observing that one of the greatest and most successful military surprises in history, the Pearl Harbor attack, involved at least four of these modes. The United States had not correctly perceived the Japanese intention to attack U.S. territory at all and thus to bring the U.S. into the war—a step which logically appeared to be a gross strategic miscalculation, as indeed it was. The place of attack was not perceived, since the great bulk of the evidence pointed to Japanese attacks in Southeast Asia (which were in fact initiated almost simultaneously). The time of the attack contributed greatly to its success, Sunday morning having been deliberately chosen because the bulk of the U.S. warships would then normally be in port. The strength of the attack of course was not anticipated (since it was not expected at all where it occurred), security and deception having effectively screened the movements of the Japanese task force.

A second approach to types of surprise and deception, which is somewhat broader and perhaps more pertinent to strategic warning, is to examine the various methods or measures which may be used to achieve one or more of the foregoing types of surprise. We may identify roughly five of these: *security, political deception, cover, active military deception, confusion and disinformation.*

1. *Security* in itself is not strictly speaking a type of deception, in that it involves no active measures to mislead the adversary to a false conclusion, but is designed only to conceal preparations for attack. Thus the sophisticated analyst should take care to distinguish normal or routine security measures from true deception. Nonetheless, the line between deception and security is narrow and the two are very often confused. Moreover, an effective security program often can do much to mislead or deceive the intended victim of attack even if no more sophisticated measures are undertaken. Although security alone will not normally lead the adversary to undertake the wrong preparations or to deploy forces incorrectly, it may lead him to undertake very inadequate countermeasures or even to fail to alert his forces at all if security is totally effective.

In general, the greater the number of military measures which must be undertaken for the operation, and the larger the mobilization and deployment of forces required, the less likely it is that security alone can mislead. Whaley cites the views of Clausewitz that the high visibility of large-scale operations makes their concealment unlikely, and that true surprise is therefore more likely to be achieved in the realm of tactics than in strategy. This in fact has been borne out in recent examples. Although it was possible in large measure to conceal the military deployments required for the closure of the Berlin sector borders, it was not possible to conceal those for the invasion of Czechoslovakia, and in fact the USSR made no particularly great effort to do so. Some writers have argued that modern collection systems and communications will make security measures even less effective in the future—and this would appear likely to be the case. Thus, the prospects are that various forms of active or deliberate deception will assume even more importance if surprise is to be achieved.

2. Preeminent among such methods is *political deception*—probably the easiest of all deception measures and possibly the most common. While political means may be used to promote tactical surprise, this method is of particular value as a strategic measure to conceal intent. Moreover it is one of the most economical means of deception and one in which the likelihood of disclosure is remote, since so few people need be involved in the plan. There are a variety of political deception tactics, of which we will note a few:

The direct or indirect falsehood may be put forth through diplomatic channels, official statements, the press or other media. In its simplest and most crude form, the state simply denies that it has any intent whatever of doing what it is preparing to do and asserts that all such charges are false—a method sometimes used, particularly if the stakes are very high. The more subtle method of the indirect falsehood is often preferred, however, and permits the leadership to maintain some degree of credibility after the event, or at least to deny charges of outright prevarication. This tactic was used by the USSR in a number of its public statements prior to the Cuban missile crisis, for example in the celebrated TASS statement of 11 September 1962 in which the USSR stated that all weapons being sent to Cuba were "designed exclusively for defensive purposes," and that there was "no need" for the USSR to deploy its missiles to any other country.

Another method of political deception which has often been used, particularly to lull suspicions in the relatively short term as final preparations for the attack are being made, is to offer to enter into "negotiations" to discuss the matter at issue when in fact there is no intention of reaching any sort of agreement. This tactic was used by the USSR on the eve of the counterattack to suppress the Hungarian revolt in November 1956, when Soviet officers opened negotiations with the Hungarians on Soviet "troop withdrawal." A form of this ruse was also used by the North Koreans for about two weeks before the attack on South Korea in 1950 when they issued "peace proposals" calling for a single national election.

Whaley identifies a slightly different form of this deception tactic, which is to lead the adversary to believe that the firm decision to attack is actually bluff. "This is a fairly common type of ruse, one intended to restore the initiative and insure surprise by implying that options other than war are still open, thereby concealing the full urgency of a crisis and encouraging the intended victim in the belief that he has more time and more options than is, in fact, the case."[15] He notes that this ruse was used at Port Arthur, at Pearl Harbor, in the German attack on the USSR in 1941, by the British in the attack at Alamein in 1942, and in the Israeli attack on Egypt in 1967.

A somewhat similar and relatively subtle form of political deception is to downplay the seriousness of the situation in diplomacy and in public statements in an effort to create the impression that the nation does not consider its vital interests at stake, or that its relations with the intended victim are pretty good or even improving. This may result in a quite sudden shift in propaganda to a more conciliatory tone, and friendly gestures to the adversary, after the decision or at least contingency decision to attack has already been reached. This is a quite common tactic, and one in which dictatorships are usually masters, particularly since their complete control of the press makes a shift in the propaganda line so easy. The USSR employed this tactic for weeks and even months prior to its attack on Japanese forces in Manchuria in August 1945, when it undertook an ostensible easing of tensions with Japan and began to be "almost cordial" to the Japanese Ambassador in Moscow, while the buildup of forces for the attack was under way in the Far East. The effort to deceive by political means will often entail not only the deception of many of one's own people, but may extend on occasion even to the leadership of allied nations, if the issue is of sufficient importance. And true practitioners of the art of deception even have been known to deceive their superiors (by failing to inform them of their plans)—although clearly this is a risky business undertaken only in the interests of tactical surprise for a specific military operation when war already is in progress.

3. *Cover* (here meaning the "cover plan" or "cover story") is a form of military deception which should be distinguished from active military deception, although it may often be used in conjunction with it. Cover will be used when it may be presumed that the military buildup itself cannot be concealed from the adversary, and its purpose therefore is to offer some seemingly plausible explanation (other than planned aggression) for the observable military activity. It may involve simply the putting out of false statements about the scale or purpose of the military buildup in order to conceal the real intention by attributing the military preparations to some-thing else. Throughout history, the most usual explanation offered has been that the troops are "on maneuvers," although it is possible to think of other pretexts which might sometimes be used to explain troop move-ments, such as an alleged civil disturbance or disaster in a border area. The likelihood that the pretext of maneuvers would be used by the USSR to mask preparations for aggression was long recognized by Western

---

[15]Whaley, A548.

intelligence, and the USSR and its Warsaw Pact allies also professed to believe that NATO exercises could serve as a cover for attack.

Despite our presumed understanding of this tactic, the USSR achieved at least partial success with its several announcements during July and August of 1968 that its troops were engaged in various "exercises" in the western USSR and Eastern Europe. In fact, there were no bona fide exercises and the sole activity under way was the mobilization and deployment of Soviet and Warsaw Pact forces for the invasion of Czechoslovakia.

4. *Active military deception* is at once the most difficult form of deception to carry out, at least on any large scale, and also one of the most effective and successful. If security and political deception measures are most effective in lulling suspicions as to intent, active military deception is the primary means whereby the adversary is led to misdeploy his forces and to prepare for an attack at the wrong place and the wrong time. Even when strategic deception has failed, or was never possible in the first place, positive military deception has proved enormously effective in achieving tactical surprise, and hence in gaining victory and/or greatly reducing the attacker's casualties in the operation. Whaley in his treatise has compiled some impressive statistics on the effectiveness and rewards of positive deception operations, some of which have been so valuable and successful as literally to affect the course of history (as in the Normandy invasion).

The successful military deception operation may range from a relatively simple hoax or feint to a highly complex series of interrelated and mutually consistent measures all designed to create the wrong impression in the mind of the adversary (or to support his original but false conceptions) as to timing, nature, strength and place of the attack. Among the recognized techniques of active military deception are:

- Camouflage of military movements and of new military installations
- Maintenance of dummy equipment at vacated installations or in areas of the front where the attack is not to occur
- The simulation of a great deal of activity using only a few pieces of military equipment moving about
- The use of noisemakers or recordings to simulate a lot of activity
- The planting of seemingly valid, but actually false, military orders in the hands of the adversary
- The sending out of "defectors" with seemingly plausible but false stories
- The use of doubled agents for the same purpose
- The sending of invalid military messages by radio in the clear or in ciphers which the adversary is known to be reading

- The maintenance of normal garrison communications while the units themselves deploy under radio silence
- The establishment of entirely spurious radio nets to simulate the presence of forces which do not exist at all or to convey an impression of a buildup of forces in some area other than the planned attack
- A concentration of reconnaissance, bombing or artillery fire in an area other than the area of attack, or at least the equalization of such activity over a wide area so that the actual area of attack is not discernible from such preparatory measures
- False announcements or other deception as to the whereabouts of leading commanders
- Obvious training exercises for a type of attack (such as amphibious) which is not planned
- False designations for military units
- Actual deployments or feints by ground or naval units to simulate attack in the wrong area
- The use of enemy uniforms and other insignia
- Announcements that leaves are being granted on the eve of attack, or even the actual issuance of numerous passes for a day or so just prior to attack

The above list does not exhaust the tricks and ruses which have been devised and successfully used in military operations. Such active deception measures of course are often supplemented by political and propaganda deception measures, cover stories and extremely tight security on the real military operation. Thus the effect of the measures collectively can be the total misleading of the adversary as to the coming attack, even sometimes when he has accepted its likelihood and indeed may be well prepared for it in other respects.

It is obvious that a number of ruses cited above would be of limited use, and indeed could be counterproductive, in a strategic deception designed to conceal that an attack is planned at all, or in any area. In such cases, one does not wish to stir up a lot of military activity, or plant false documents about impending attacks, which will only arouse suspicions and stir the enemy's intelligence services into greater collection efforts. Some measures, such as bombing and artillery fire or even highly obvious and unusual reconnaissance, cannot be undertaken at all before hostilities have begun. For these reasons, some of the time-honored devices of military deception would not be used prior to an initial surprise attack which opens a war, the attack with which strategic warning is particularly concerned. At the same time, the reader can easily see that a substantial number of the tactics cited above could be most effectively applied to deceive us in a period prior to the initial attack. Among the ruses which should particularly concern us are: communications deception, especially the maintenance of normal communications accompanied by radio silence on deployments; planted military orders and other documents; the use of false defectors and doubled agents; and any of the other measures which might be used effectively to distract us from concentrating on the preparations for the real attack. For we may be reasonably certain that the greater and more important the operation, the greater and more sophisticated will be the positive deception effort. The fact that we have encountered relatively few cases of active military deception since World War II should not reassure us—in fact, it only increases our vulnerability.

5. *Confusion and disinformation* probably rank second only to political deception in the ease with which they can be used to mislead and distract the opposition. Confusion and disinformation tactics do not have to be highly sophisticated to be successful, although of course they may be. Even an elementary program to flood the market with a mass of conflicting stories and reports can be highly effective in distracting the time and attention of analysts and their superiors from the reliable intelligence on which they should be concentrating their efforts. Particularly if a crisis atmosphere already exists, as is highly likely, and some of the reports are sensational but have some degree of plausibility, they can prove to be a tremendous distraction. If the volume of such planted information is large enough, the analytical system can literally be overwhelmed to a degree that some important and valid facts become lost in the mill, and others are not accorded their proper weight.

Moreover, such a mass of material compounds immeasurably the problem of analyst fatigue, always a factor in crisis situations, and may tend to generate a series of "cry wolf" alarms which will reduce the credibility of the authentic warning when or if it is received.

A conspicuous example of the damage that can be done by a large volume of false or unevaluated information was in the Chinese intervention in Korea in October-November 1950. This is not to say that the Chinese themselves necessarily had devised a sophisticated or extensive disinformation program. It is probable that a high percentage of the mass of spurious and contradictory reports which so confused the situation that summer and fall was never planted by the communists at all but was rather the product of the several highly productive paper mills in the Far East.

Most of those who have examined the intelligence failure that year have given altogether too little, if indeed any, attention to the adverse effects of the volume of this spurious material on the analytical process. Regardless of the origins of the material in this case, something of the same problem could surely arise again in another crisis should our adversaries choose to exercise their full capabilities to employ such tactics.

WHAT CAN WE DO ABOUT IT?

All states are vulnerable to deception, including even those whose officials are sophisticated practitioners of the art themselves. Logic also suggests that, in some respects at least, democracies are likely to be more vulnerable to deception than are dictatorships and closed societies and it is undeniably more difficult for open societies to practice it.

What, if anything, can we do to make ourselves less vulnerable? Is it hopeless? Some writers believe that it is, or nearly so. They observe that deception is almost always successful in achieving surprise, regardless of the experience of the adversary. Particularly if the victim is seeking to avoid war, ambiguity-producing tactics (one of the simplest forms of deception) are virtually always successful in producing procrastination—that is, in deferring appropriate decisions. Or if the victim does recognize that deception is being practiced, he may still make the wrong decision; that is, reject the right rather than the false information. Moreover, even without significant deception, the initiator of the attack has an inherent advantage over his victim. Thus, some maintain, surprise is inevitable. Others have sought to devise counter-deception techniques as the most effective way of avoiding surprise. A variety of methods—from planting false information in known feedback channels to complex tests of the reliability and consistency of the data—have been suggested. Most of these seem either to assume more access to the enemy's intelligence apparatus than is likely to prevail or to be so impractical or time-consuming that they would not be very feasible in a real crisis.

Perhaps the pessimists are correct and there is little if anything we can do to detect, let alone counter, a sophisticated strategic deception plan. But there have been many crises in which deception has been far less complex, even transparent. One is struck by the fact that even elementary deception tactics, to which all intelligence personnel should be alert, have often been very effective. Thus, the suggestions offered below would, I believe, be of some help in real situations.

The first thing that is necessary, if we are to have any hope of coping with deception, is to learn something about it, and to study some case histories. While we may all be vulnerable in some measure to old ruses, we need to know what some of these ruses are if we are to have much chance of recognizing them. Secondly, both the intelligence services and perhaps even more the policy and command levels need to understand that deception is likely to be practiced in certain situations, not only by our enemies, but sometimes even by our friends. It is essential to the recognition of deception that the probability or at least the possibility of its occurrence be anticipated or else we will almost inevitably be gullible victims of even a simple deception plan. And how can we recognize such situations? It is when great national objectives are at stake, when military forces are mobilizing and deploying, when it is clear that the adversary is "up to something." In such situations, it is the height of folly to presume that he will not also employ deception. We must be continually alert in such situations for the possibility of deception and assume its likelihood—rather than its improbability. Rather than wax indignant over the enemy's "perfidy," as is our usual wont, we should be indignant at ourselves for failing to perceive in advance such a possibility. Bluntly, we need to be less trusting and more suspicious and realistic.

To recognize that deception is being practiced at all may be half the battle. For the recognition of this in turn will alert us: 1) that the adversary is very likely preparing for some unpleasant surprises—else why bother to deceive us?—and 2) to start attempting to figure out what his real plans or intentions may be behind the smoke screen of the deception effort. The easiest (or more accurately least difficult) of smoke screens to see through should usually be the political deception effort, and its accompanying military "cover story," during a period of massive military buildup. When the political conduct of the adversary is out of consonance with his military preparations, when he is talking softly but carrying a bigger and bigger stick, beware. This is the simplest and least sophisticated of deception methods. No country should be so gullible as to fall for such tactics, without at least asking some searching questions. While the recognition that such deception is being practiced, or possibly is, will not in itself necessarily lead to a clear understanding of what the adversary is going to do, it will at least alert us that what he is going to do is probably not the same as what he says. And for strategic as opposed to tactical warning this recognition may be the most important factor of all.

It is virtually impossible to conceal the preparations for great military operations. The adversary, despite the most elaborate security precautions, is not going to be able to build up his forces for a major attack in total secrecy. If we are deceived or surprised in such circumstances, it will be because we either fell for his cover story or offers to enter into peaceful negotiations, allowed our preconceptions to override our analysis of the evidence, or because we were grossly misled as to the time, place or strength of the attack and thus failed to take the right military countermeasures at the right time.

As opposed to strategic warning or the recognition that the adversary is preparing to attack at all, tactical warning may be highly dependent on our ability to see through the enemy's active military deception plan. And on this score—which is largely the type of stratagem and deception which Whaley addresses in his book—experience teaches us that the chances of successful enemy deception are indeed high. Even when it is recognized that deception is being practiced—for example, if camouflaged equipment is detected—this will not necessarily lead to the right conclusions as to the strength, place or date of attack. The military commander, in other words, will still have the problem of penetrating the specifics of the enemy's deception plan and preparing his defenses against it, even though the likelihood of attack itself has been generally accepted. Thus the tactical warning problem will remain even though the strategic warning problem may in large part have been resolved.

For both strategic and tactical warning, confusion and disinformation tactics present an enormous problem. The prospect that we could, in time of great national emergency, be confronted by such tactics should be a cause for grave concern. The releasing of the full disinformation capabilities of the counterintelligence systems of other countries, together with the use of other deception techniques, could place an unprecedented requirement for sophisticated analysis and reporting on our collection mechanism, on which in turn the substantive analyst would be heavily dependent for evaluation of the accuracy and potential motivation for deception by the informant. It is critically important in such circumstances that the collector provide as much information as possible on the origins of the report and the channels by which it was received, since the analyst who receives it will be almost completely dependent on such evaluations and comments in making his assessment. At best, it will be extremely difficult in time of emergency to distinguish even a portion of the reports which have originated with the enemy's intelligence services from those that have other origins. The tracing of the origins of rumors, for example, is often virtually impossible, yet in many cases rumors are valuable indications of authentic developments which the analyst cannot afford entirely to ignore.

Additionally, there are two general guidelines that will usually assist the analyst in perceiving the enemy's most likely course of action through a fog of deception:

Separate the wheat from the chaff. Weed out from the mass of incoming material all information of doubtful reliability or origin and assemble that information which is either known to be true (the "facts") or which has come from reliable sources which would have no personal axes to grind or reasons to deceive. This will allow you to establish your reliable data base which, limited though it may be, will serve as the yardstick against which the reliability or consistency of other data and sources may be judged. It sounds simple and obvious; it is usually not done.

Keep your eyes on the hardware. In the end, the adversary must launch operations with his military forces and what they do will be the ultimate determinant of his intent. Warning has failed in some cases primarily for lack of this concentration on the hardware. There are all kinds of ruses and red herrings, both political and military, which the adversary may devise, and they have often been highly successful in distracting attention from the all-important factor of the military capability. So long as that capability is being maintained, or is increasing, the analyst and military commander who concentrate on it are likely to have a much more accurate perception of the enemy's intention than are those who have permitted their judgments to waver with each new piece of propaganda or rumor of the enemy's plans.

Finally—more for policymakers and commanders—the best defense of all against the enemy's deception plan may be the alerting and preparedness of one's own forces, If these are ready for the possibility of attack, no matter how unlikely that may seem, the enemy's efforts may be largely foiled even though his operation itself is really not anticipated. In other words, it is possible to be politically or psychologically surprised, and at the same time be militarily prepared. The dispersal of the U.S. fleet from Pearl Harbor as a routine readiness measure against the possibility of attack, however remote that might have appeared, would have saved the fleet even though all other assessments of Japanese intentions were wrong.

Chapter 8

JUDGMENTS AND POLICY

The ultimate function of warning intelligence is to come to an assessment of the enemy's most probable course of action, to provide a judgment for the policymaker of the intentions of the adversary. It is this which distinguishes warning intelligence from order-of-battle and military capabilities assessments, that normally shun judgments about what may happen; current intelligence, which is preoccupied with a vast amount of day-to-day requirements and reporting, only a portion of which is likely to relate to indications and warning; and estimative intelligence, which is probably closest to warning, but which normally takes a longer term and somewhat more general approach to an adversary's courses of action than does warning intelligence.

Why is it not enough to give the "facts" or a statement of capabilities and to stop there? An obvious answer, of course, is that warning intelligence is both expected and explicitly directed to come to an assessment of intent. In reaching a judgment, it is only carrying out its charter and responding to the wishes of consumers. It really has no choice in the matter. This, however, does not explain why this state of affairs has come to exist.

FACTS DON'T "SPEAK FOR THEMSELVES"

Intelligence is made up of many facets and types of information, some simple, some complex, some readily understood by non-experts, and some that require detailed research and analysis before they come to have meaning to users. If the sole function of intelligence was to compile "facts," there would be little need for analysts of any type. The intelligence process would consist almost entirely of collection of raw data which would be evaluated for accuracy but then passed on without further comment or analysis to the policy official.

Of course, intelligence practitioners at all levels are continually coming to judgments, acting on these judgments, or reporting judgments in various publications or briefings. The collector in the field who elects to forward, or not forward, some fragment of information to his home office is making a judgment. The current analyst who decides to write up a given piece of information, or not do so, is making a judgment about it. The manner in which he writes it up, the emphasis he gives to this or that aspect of it, constitutes another judgment. The items that his immediate superior selects to include in a briefing for the senior officials of his agency or department are the result of another judgment.

In short, it would be impossible for the intelligence system to function, and it would be virtually useless to the consumer, if judgments were not an integral part of the process at all times. The sheer volume of material collected today not only makes it impossible for it to function in any other manner, but it also places a greater responsibility for intelligent and perceptive judgments on many relatively low-ranking and obscure members of the system—not the least of them the collectors of raw data in the field.

Value of Judgments for the Intelligence Process Itself

Quite apart from the end result—serving the needs of policy officials—the process of coming to judgments is extremely valuable in itself for the intelligence system, and particularly its warning elements. This aspect often has been overlooked.

If facts do not speak for themselves to policy officials, neither do they necessarily do so to intelligence analysts and their supervisors. Or, if they seem to be doing so, it will often be found on further analysis that not all are hearing the same oracle, not by any means. Those not initiated into the system might be amazed at the variations in interpretation—sometimes almost diametrically opposed—that a group of people can draw from the same set of "facts," even when the facts are relatively simple and non-controversial in themselves. This problem of varying interpretations, and its implications for warning, has been considered at length in other portions of this work. It is a most crucial aspect of the warning problem.

In general, the farther one proceeds in the indications process from the collection of raw data to the final judgment of the adversary's course of action, the greater the spread of opinion or interpretation is likely to be. That is, it will usually be easier to reach agreement that certain pieces of incoming information constitute indications or possible indications than it will be to reach agreement as to what these indications individually signify. And it will be still more difficult to reach agreement that the facts or indications collectively mean that the adversary is about to embark on hostilities or other actions inimical to our interests. Or, to cite a specific and rather simple example:

There will be a large measure of agreement that a high level of military activity in the border area of Country X is potentially significant as an indication and should be closely watched and reported by the Intelligence Community; there will probably be a lesser degree of agreement, in the absence of better information than is likely to be obtainable on a current basis, as to whether the observed activity constitutes a bona fide mobilization or buildup of combat forces rather than an exercise; there will usually be least agreement that this activity, even if it appears to be of a very large scale, indicates an intention by Country X to attack its neighbor, Country Y, or whether X is only: putting pressure on Y, carrying out an unusually realistic war game, or "keeping its options open." Now, of these three questions or judgments, the last of course is by far the most important, and is what the policymaker most needs to know.

Let us suppose, however, that the group responsible for warning, or which turns out watch reports, does not go through the analytic process of examining the indications, attempting to determine their significance, and coming finally to some judgment of whether hostile action is or is not impending. Instead, it goes through only a portion of this process. It discusses only some of the indications or possible indications without coming to any agreement, or in fact ever really discussing, whether there is a mobilization or an exercise. By tacit or unspoken agreement, perhaps because the issue is so "hot," it does not really come to grips with the crucial question of intent. The end product is a non-controversial, wishy-washy statement such as: "A high level of military activity continues along the X-Y border, and the situation remains very tense." Naturally, everyone can agree on this—it cannot be said to be "wrong." But not only is this unhelpful to the policy official, it also means that intelligence has not really gone through the rigorous intellectual process of analyzing the meaning of the available data and attempting to interpret its true meaning. Yet agreement might have been reached on a meaningful judgment if enough time and effort had been applied. In the process, intelligence personnel would come to a much better understanding of the facts and the issues involved, and the policymaker would be given a much more explicit analysis of the evidence and the alternative courses of action open to him.

Value of Judgments for the Policy Official

> *"Another consequence of the failure to reach an intelligence judgment may be that the policy official will also fail to come to judgments, or will make judgments on the basis of inadequate information."*

Another equally dangerous consequence of the failure to reach an intelligence judgment may be that the policy official will also fail to come to judgments, even though it may be critically important to do so. In the absence of some positive intelligence judgment—some warning—the policy official can hardly be blamed if he tends to minimize the danger or to believe that he will have time later to make decisions, or that the threat is not yet imminent. There are many reasons why policy officials have been dissatisfied over the years with their intelligence. But unquestionably one of the causes of most bitter complaint has been inadequate warning, which in the end comes down to the judgment of what some other country is going to do.

Moreover, it is this type of intelligence failure which is most likely to provoke investigations by special boards or even Congress. Intelligence can afford to be wrong on many minor matters, some of which will go totally unnoticed in fact by the consumer. But it cannot afford to be wrong on great issues of national security, including warning of attack. Such errors never go unnoticed. In this arena, errors of omission—the failure to come to judgments at all—can be as serious as errors of commission, coming to wrong judgments. The intelligence office which seeks to be "safe" by being noncommittal may find in the end that it served the nation as ill as if it had predicted that there was no danger.

One of the most difficult things for analysts to find out is what people higher in the chain of command actually know in the way of facts and how they have interpreted them. As intelligence has evolved from the rather small, informal shops which prevailed after World War II to a large and highly organized bureaucracy, these problems have been compounded. It is safe to say that most analysts never get to talk with anyone at the policy level, and that their understanding of what these officials know, and need to know, is likely to be extremely limited.

One result of the failure of intelligence to provide the policymaker with judgments therefore is likely to be that the official will make his own judgments, but will make them on the basis of inadequate information—or at least without benefit of interpretation which might have assisted him[16] These difficulties of course are compounded in warning situations when the volume of information is both much greater than normal and its interpretation more complex.

WHAT DO TOP CONSUMERS NEED, AND WANT, TO KNOW?

If what policymakers want to know could be set forth in hard and fast, and readily understandable terms—and the requirements were more or less immutable—then it is likely that we should all know them. In fact, this problem is very complex, and it is doubtful that even the most experienced policy officials could come up with ready answers as to what they would need to know in a variety of hypothetical situations, the most dangerous and important of which we have yet to experience.

---

[16]This is precisely what happened in the case of the shootdown of the Korean Airlines flight 007 in 1983, as presented in Seymour Hersh, *The Target Is Destroyed* (New York, Random House, 1986). An accurate, intelligence-based report of the shootdown was presented to the Secretary of State, but only after he had come to biased conclusions about the intentions of the Soviets.

Many policymakers themselves have written memoirs and other works which reveal a considerable amount about how high-level decisionmakers think and act in real situations. These works often are fascinating as well as educational, such as the numerous memoirs and studies of the Cuban missile crisis. They provide an insight into policy as it really operates that is more interesting, and probably more valuable, than any amount of theory or pseudo-science on the subject.

Anyone who has been in the intelligence business for any length of time has long since learned that the guidance and directives on what the higher levels want to receive are likely to be transitory. The requirements levied on intelligence will vary from month to month, even sometimes from day to day. And these changes do not derive entirely, or sometimes even primarily, from changes in the international situation or from the unpredictability of events; obviously a critical situation in some area will generate a demand for more intelligence on that particular subject. They derive also from the unpredictability of individuals and how they operate, how much they want to know and how they want it presented. The first thing that intelligence analysts are likely to learn about policy officials and military planners is that:

Policymakers are Highly Individualistic

One does not need to have served in the government to know this. Nearly everyone knows that U.S. presidents have varied markedly with respect to the amount of information they wished to receive and how they wanted it presented, that some (for example, Truman and Kennedy) were ardent readers of intelligence, while others (such as Eisenhower) relied heavily on their staffs and wished to hear only the essentials. Some read three or four newspapers before breakfast, others purportedly rarely looked at the press. In recent years, the national security advisor to the President has become the principal and sometimes almost the sole channel through which foreign intelligence and foreign policy matters are conveyed to the chief executive. Thus, intelligence becomes tailored to the needs and requirements of that individual rather than directly to the President himself.

The National Security Council and the various committees or special groups that are affiliated with it also have numerous intelligence requirements in support of national policy. The attitudes and working habits of individual Secretaries of State and Defense (and to a lesser extent some other cabinet members), the Joint Chiefs of Staff, the chiefs of the major intelligence organizations and of their staffs can also strongly influence what intelligence produces and in what detail and how it is presented. A change in administration nearly always brings with it a rash of requirements for new intelligence and policy studies or for a review and refurbishing of old studies, for changes in scope or format of intelligence documents, and new directives concerning the amount of detail or factual evidence that should be presented.

Requirements Differ for Special versus Routine Situations

The U.S. and its leaders clearly have continuing requirements for all types of intelligence—basic, current, and analytic or estimative—relating to the current activities, policies and objectives of innumerable nations, both friendly and potentially hostile, with whom the policymaker needs to deal. There is almost no country whose policies and attitudes do not affect us in some way. Even the smallest may have a crucial vote in the United Nations or produce some vital raw material. The potential need of the policymaker for some type of information or other is thus virtually endless. Of course, not all the information which the decisionmaker may require will be supplied by intelligence. Indeed, in many instances, foreign intelligence may play a relatively small role in providing either the information or influencing the policymaker's course of action.

As a general rule, foreign intelligence is likely to have its greatest impact on policy when it is apparent that a foreign government is adopting a course which could gravely affect our national security interest in the relatively near future. In such situations the Intelligence Community usually is in a strong position to provide vital information needed for the formulation of policy.

The policymaker and military commander alike will have a great requirement for intelligence on matters which may require a military action or response by our side, both in war and peace. In recent years, there has been a growing tendency for the highest authorities to take over supervision of what may appear to be the most minor actions or decisions, on both political and military matters. Many general officers, as well as lesser ranks, have been known to complain that they had more responsibility and decision-making authority as field or even company grade officers in World War II than as senior officers in more recent conflicts or threatened conflicts. It is no secret that President Kennedy personally reviewed the progress of U.S. convoys on the Berlin Autobahns during the crisis of 1961, and that even the most minor decisions on the Berlin issue were made at the White House. Similarly, during the Vietnam war, U.S. bombing missions were reviewed in advance at the highest governmental levels—not just general policy on targeting but the selection of specific targets. Obviously, this requires more detailed military intelligence at the national level than would otherwise usually be necessary.

Finally, there is the requirement of the policymaker for intelligence in all kinds of crisis situations, particularly sudden or fast-moving situations in which reliable and up-to-date intelligence may be vital to the decisionmaker. These critical situations are likely to place the greatest of all demands on the Intelligence Community at least in the short term. It is probably true that, the greater the crisis and the more critical and immediate the requirement for decisions, the greater is the decisionmaker's need for information. And the more is the prestige and reputation of intelligence at stake. Fairly or unfairly, the intelligence system is likely to be judged in large part by its performance in expectation of and during crises.

As we have noted before, intelligence can afford to be wrong on many subjects (and few will notice it) if it provides the policymaker the kind of support he needs, and if he is satisfied with it, when grave national issues are at stake.

Policymakers Need Evidence On Which They Can Act

Sherman Kent has discussed the kinds of intelligence which policy officials generally have found most credible and useful. His conclusions derived not only from his own long experience as Chairman of the Board of National Estimates but also from a separate inquiry into this subject made by Roger Hilsman who later became the director of intelligence for the Department of State. Their conclusions concerning the policymaker's views on three types of intelligence—basic, current, and estimative—were:

- Policy officials placed highest credibility in basic intelligence, and were particularly grateful for the breadth and depth of factual information which intelligence was able to produce on numerous subjects, often on very short notice.
- They were somewhat less enthusiastic about current intelligence, tending to compare it unfavorably to the daily press.
- They placed least credibility in estimates, probably because they recognized that estimates are at least in part speculative and therefore lack the authority and reliability of basic intelligence, which is essentially factual and deemed to be highly reliable. Also, they were inclined to feel that they could speculate just as well or better than their colleagues in intelligence.[17]

These gentlemen evidently did not address the question of how often the policymaker may have been misled by basic intelligence which proved to be erroneous, such as order-of-battle "facts" which were inadequate or out-of-date. It is not true that basic intelligence always is more accurate or factual than estimative intelligence, although in its form of presentation it may seem to be.

Why should this be the reaction of policy officials, particularly when the Intelligence Community tends to look on the national estimate as its highest level creation, and certainly the one on which it lavishes the greatest care and most extensive coordination by its most expert authorities? Does not every low-level basic intelligence analyst look forward to the day when he will be promoted to being an estimator, with the rewards which this brings both in money and prestige?

This issue cannot be better illustrated than by the Cuban missile crisis. In retrospect, some have been critical of the national intelligence estimate of 19 September 1962 which concluded, in effect, that the Soviet Union was unlikely to introduce strategic missiles in Cuba. There is no question that the intelligence

---

[17] Sherman Kent, "Estimates and Influence," in Donald P. Steury, ed., *Sherman Kent and the Board of National Estimates* (Washington, DC: Center for the Study of Intelligence, 1994), 34-35.

effort, up until the discovery of the missiles, must be rated something of a "failure" (however logical its conclusions may have been) in that it did not predict that the USSR would do what in fact it did. But what if intelligence had been "right"? What if the September estimate had concluded that the introduction of strategic missiles into Cuba was a better than even chance, or highly likely, or nearly certain? Even assuming that the President had believed it also, what could he have done about it in the absence of proof? The fact is, of course, that he could not have acted without hard and convincing evidence that strategic missiles either were in Cuba or on their way. It really did not matter what intelligence "thought" about it. But it did matter, imperatively, that it collect the data which would permit a firm judgment whether or not the missiles were there, and hence provide the basis on which the President could confront the Soviet Union and justify his actions to the people of the United States and the rest of the world.[18]

INTELLIGENCE IN SUPPORT OF POLICY?

Strategic intelligence must actively support higher level officials—policymakers and military commanders—not just collect and analyze information, however desirable that may be in itself. The U.S. Congress confirms this requirement. It does not follow, however, that intelligence is the slave of policy, or that its function is to produce only what policymakers think they need or what they wish to hear. The independence and intellectual integrity of the intelligence system are essential, both in the long and short term, to the production of high-quality information which will truly serve the national interest. Many have learned, to their ultimate misfortune, the dangers of tailoring intelligence to fit the views of policy officials.

Few indeed would probably disagree in theory with the need for an independent, unbiased intelligence service, not subject to the whims of higher officials, and removed from politics. More subtle and less widely recognized is the problem of insuring that intelligence is not unintentionally distorted in the process of genuinely seeking to serve the policy official.

It is common practice for officials considering a given course of action to request from intelligence an analysis of the feasibility of this action and a review of its possible consequences. Or the military commander reviews his options and asks his intelligence officers to summarize the information they have available which would support one or another course of action. With no intent perhaps by anyone to distort the picture, intelligence nonetheless finds itself selecting the information—from the great mass probably available—that is consistent with the proposed course of action or that tends to make it look desirable. Perhaps because it has not been asked for any negative data or contrary information which

---

[18]A thorough review of the Cuban intelligence estimate is presented in Gil Merom, "The 1962 Cuban Intelligence Estimate: A Methodological Perspective," *Intelligence and National Security* 14, no. 3 (Autumn 1999): 48-80.

might suggest another course of action to be more feasible or desirable, the intelligence system does not volunteer it. Or, the potential costs of failure are not assessed because no one asks for such an estimate. Thus, unintentionally, the facts are selected in large part to support an already-favored policy and the potential disadvantages never are really quite conveyed to the policy official.

One historian and student of the intelligence system, Thomas Belden, has called this process adduction from the verb adduce (the act of offering facts, evidence, instances, and the like, as proof or in support of something stated). He regards this type of analysis or reasoning as one of the dangers to which the intelligence process is subject and which can lead both it and the policy official to erroneous conclusions, even though both were honestly seeking to be objective and to select the most desirable policy.[19]

Another well-known writer on the problems of warning and decisionmaking has also reached this conclusion: "For when an official policy or hypothesis is laid down, it tends to obscure alternative hypotheses, and to lead to overemphasis of the data that support it, particularly in a situation of increasing tension, when it is important not to 'rock the boat'."[20]

Now clearly the dangers of this type of error are greatest when the facts are not simple or easily interpretable, when there is room for genuine differences of opinion, or when the policy level is seeking to justify a course of action to which it is already committed. A prime example has been the continuing controversy over who was right in interpreting the course of the Vietnam war, and whether statistics were misused to justify the U.S. course of action and to "prove" that we were winning the war. Setting aside what bias there was in interpretation, the problem arose in large part from the fact that the "statistics" themselves were too tenuous to be of much value in proving a case either way, and that even if North Vietnamese military casualties and supply losses could have been accurately known, they were perhaps meaningless in the face of Hanoi's absolute commitment to continue the war despite the most staggering losses. Nonetheless, as the data moved on up through the intelligence system to the president, it is probably true that statistics or facts which were considered extremely tenuous at the collection level took on solidity and credibility in proportion to the extent to which they confirmed the rightness of U.S. policy. So, at least, a number of observers and critics of the process have claimed. Yet few in either the intelligence or policy process were probably intentionally distorting the evidence. It was a combination of inadequate or irrelevant evidence to begin with, oversimplification in its interpretation, and some propensity for telling

---

[19]One of his contributions to the literature of warning intelligence is Thomas G. Belden, "Indications, Warning, and Crisis Operations," *International Studies Quarterly* 21, no. 1 (March 1977): 181-198.

[20]Roberta Wohlstetter, "Cuba and Pearl Harbor: Hindsight and Foresight," *Foreign Affairs* 43, no. 4 (July 1965): 701.

the boss what he wants to hear—or, more likely, not telling him what he does not want to hear.

One student of the Cuban missile crisis has observed, again apropos of the famous September estimate:

> What the President least wanted to hear, the CIA was most hesitant to say plainly. On August 22 John McCone met privately with the President and voiced suspicions that the Soviets were preparing to introduce offensive missiles into Cuba. Kennedy heard this as what it was: the suspicion of a hawk .... USIB's unanimous approval of the September estimate reflects similar sensitivities. On September 13 the President asserted that there were no Soviet offensive missiles in Cuba and committed his Administration to act if offensive missiles were discovered. Before Congressional committees, Administration officials were denying that there was any evidence whatever of offensive missiles in Cuba. The implications of a National Intelligence Estimate which concluded that the Soviets were introducing offensive missiles into Cuba were not lost on the men who constituted America's highest intelligence assembly.[21]

Reporting the Unpleasant Facts or Judgments

One of the most difficult things for intelligence is to come to judgments which the policymaker does not want to hear, particularly when the judgment may contravene or bring into question the wisdom of some ongoing policy. There may also be grave reluctance, and understandably so, to present evidence or indications that may require the policy official to make a difficult or dangerous decision, particularly so long as there is doubt whether it may be necessary to make the decision at all. There is a natural reluctance to cause alarm when it may be unnecessary.

One potential result of adequate early warning always may be that the policymaker will be able to take action in time to forestall the impending military attack or other threatened action. In this event, intelligence will have performed its greatest service to the nation—it has not only produced accurate information but been instrumental in forestalling disaster. But, ironically, this will probably never be provable, or at least not in the professional lifetime of participants. Thus, in its finest hour, the service rendered by the Intelligence Community not only is unrecognized and unrewarded, but some may even say the alarm was totally unnecessary and there never was a threat. Such are the hazards, and fascination, of intelligence.

---

[21]Graham T. Allison, "Conceptual Models and the Cuban Missile Crisis," *American Political Science Review* 63, no. 3 (September 1969): 712-713.

How Early is "Early Warning"?

A review of crises over a period of years would probably show that, in a substantial number of cases, some warning could have been issued earlier than it was, and in some cases much earlier. The nature of this warning in most instances, however, would of necessity have been tenuous and, at least in some cases, little more than an uneasy feeling of knowledgeable and perceptive analysts that all was not right or normal. This sense of unease that the Soviet Union was up to something certainly was present in the minds of some analysts in the spring of 1962 before there was any tangible indication that the USSR was planning anything unusual in Cuba. Such unease perhaps was still more prevalent in the spring of 1950 in the weeks prior to the outbreak of the Korean war. Is the policymaker or commander interested in this kind of early warning? Does he want to know when astute, experienced and imaginative minds in intelligence begin to feel edgy, but can't really produce factual documentation to support their hunches? It is very hard to say, and policy officials possibly would differ more on this question than almost any other. Their individual interests in particular subjects or areas might dictate their answers more than generalities.

On the whole, the Intelligence Community has tended to be chary of this type of speculative reporting, for at least two reasons. The first is that tenuous "think pieces" are often wrong, and there really is not enough information to issue any kind of meaningful warning. The second reason is that the Intelligence Community knows, or fears, that the policymaker will ask for "proof" or at least some kind of supporting evidence other than apprehension or intuitive feelings.

Nonetheless, such early and speculative pieces may be very useful, even if they do not reach policy officials. They can at least encourage more imaginative analysis within the Intelligence Community itself, they may generate very useful collection efforts, and they may lead to the surfacing of relevant information which would otherwise have been ignored.

In general—if it is possible to generalize on this—the policy official is probably most receptive to early, albeit tenuous, warning in cases where he can take some preliminary action, such as some diplomatic initiative, without incurring any significant risk or major commitment of resources. He is not likely to be so responsive if he has to undertake a redeployment of military forces or a call-up of reservists, particularly if he believes that the threat is not imminent or that action on our part could lead to a military reaction by the adversary and an escalation of the situation. And he probably will not wish to be "warned" about potential dangers which still appear remote and which might require a major change of recently established national policy.

Unanimity or Footnotes?

This also has proved to be a controversial subject. In theory, all intelligence agency chiefs are free to take footnotes, or otherwise to express differing opinions from those of the majority, on all national estimates and other interagency papers. Also in theory, policy officials generally are said to want the frankest and fullest views of the Intelligence Community—including dissenting views—on important issues. In actuality, however, the Intelligence Community often has felt a strong inclination to seek unanimity on critical warning issues, and in many cases this tendency has been encouraged by the policy level, which has asked for an agreed intelligence position.

The arguments in support of unanimity are not inconsiderable. The assumption seems to be that, if all the available facts are set forth and thoroughly reviewed by reasonable people, all of them willing to listen to other points of view, then the differences truly can be resolved and a real agreement achieved. Thus, the unanimous opinion that is finally reached is considered actually to be the best and most accurate obtainable, and one to which all can subscribe. Further, it is argued, conflicting or unresolved differences of opinion do not really help the policymaker in his hour of need. A split opinion on a critical issue on which national action is required does not assist the planner to select the best course of action. If the Intelligence Community cannot make up its mind what the evidence means, how can the decisionmaker make a meaningful decision? If he has asked the Intelligence Community for its "best judgment," then that is what he is entitled to get.

These arguments are, of course, both persuasive and valid when in fact the unanimously agreed position proves to be correct and the chosen course of policy action is successful. And this is probably true more often than not, perhaps far more often than not. Rarely is the intelligence judgment totally wrong, and even when partially wrong, its conclusions may not really greatly affect policy decisions or courses of action. Obviously, it is in cases where the agreed or majority intelligence position does prove to have been wrong, and it contributed to major errors in policy, that the fallacies or disadvantages of unanimity become apparent—often to the anguish of those who really did not agree but felt pushed into going along with the majority, and in retrospect gravely regret that they did not argue their positions more forcefully or insist on their rights to disagree. And in these cases, obviously, the policymaker also will wish that he had asked for minority opinions, particularly for dissents and the reasons for them which might have saved him from an erroneous decision.

Despite the desirability, when possible, of intelligence coming to a single agreed position, the dangers of doing so, where real disagreements exist, almost certainly outweigh the advantages. Unanimous judgments all too often have served only to paper over real and serious differences of opinion, of which the policymaker might be totally unaware if they are not spelled out. Further, when such compromise unanimous judgments are reached, they tend to be wishy-washy or to use ambiguous or qualified statements which may fail altogether to convey how serious the situation may be. Phrases such as, "It is possible that the adversary is considering an attack," or "These forces have a high capability to intervene in force, if necessary," may actually have been chosen only as neutral language to which both those who regard the attack as unlikely and those who believe it likely can agree. In these cases, the policymaker would have been better informed and better served if the real differences of opinion, and the reasons for them, had been spelled out rather than suppressed.

Communication is a Two-way Street

This section has looked at this problem almost exclusively from the standpoint of the Intelligence Community. It has attempted, almost certainly inadequately, to give the intelligence analyst some understanding of what the policymaker wants and how to serve his interests. But this is only half the problem. It is equally and perhaps even more important that the policy official understand what it is that the Intelligence Community can and cannot reasonably be expected to provide him, and that he communicate with intelligence on a continuing basis. The managerial and policy levels must have a meaningful exchange with the so-called working levels of the Intelligence Community or there will inevitably be misunderstandings between them. To insure that he will receive the fullest and most accurate support from the Intelligence Community, the policymaker should, among other things:

- ask for minority and dissenting opinions and for a presentation of the facts supporting such dissents;
- provide, insofar as possible, some explanation of why the information is wanted and for what purposes it will be used;
- insure that information, including both intelligence and operational material, is not being unnecessarily compartmentalized or withheld from intelligence personnel;
- ask the right questions.

ASSESSING PROBABILITES

The Intelligence Community for years has been concerned with making its judgments more precise and meaningful to the policymaker. One method that has received considerable attention is to assess likely courses of action by foreign states in terms of probabilities, expressed in either verbal or numerical terms.

Words of Estimative Probability

This phrase is taken from Sherman Kent, who began an inquiry years ago into what various words such as *possible, probable, conceivable, unlikely,* and so forth actually meant to different people in terms of mathematical probabilities. To his surprise, and consternation, he found that these and other similar words (including various embellishments of possible, such as *just possible or distinctly possible*) were interpreted quite differently, even by people who had worked together in the preparation of national estimates.[22] As a result, he attempted to assign some specific degree of likelihood to a series of words and phrases, grouping a number of them together as generally synonymous. As he himself has noted, these initial efforts met with something less than universal approbation, particularly from those whom he describes as the "poets," and his proposals have not been formally accepted in national estimates. The following is one interpretation in percentages of terms frequently used in estimates:

Estimative Term	Percentage Likelihood
Near certainty (and equivalent terms)	90–99
Probable (and equivalent terms)	60–90
Even chance	40–60
Improbable (and equivalent terms)	10–40
Near impossibility (and equivalents)	1–10

In this usage, words such as *perhaps, may* and *might* would be used to describe situations in the lower ranges of likelihood, and the word *possible*, when used without further modification, would generally be used only when a judgment was important but could not be given an order of likelihood with any degree of precision.

The terms most frequently used in warning documents to express the higher and lower ranges of likelihood are:

Higher	Low
We believe	We believe...will not
We conclude	We do not believe that
It is probable that	It is unlikely
It probably will	It probably will not
It is likely	

Indications analysts have never shown much partiality to giving odds of about 50-50 by the use of phrases like "even chance" or "odds are about even," perhaps in the belief that warning documents are supposed to come to judgments and not toss a coin. Finally, indications analysts also make use of *possible, may,* and *could* and also of the conditionals *might* and *would*, with little attempt at defining what degree of likelihood or unlikelihood is intended.

---

[22]Sherman Kent, "Words of Estimated Probability," in *Sherman Kent and the Board of National Estimates: Collected Essays*, ed. Donald P. Steury (Washington, DC: Center for the Study of Intelligence, 1994), 132-139. These terms were also discussed in *Psychology of Intelligence Analysis*, ed. Richards J. Heuer, Jr. (Washington, DC: Center for the Study of Intelligence, 1999), 154-156.

Probabilistic Information Processing

The attempt to translate verbal statements of probabilities directly into percentages on the basis of what the words really mean to different people has been more widely understood and accepted than the second approach to probability assessments. The second method is considerably more complicated (some would say scientific) and involves specific methodology and the application of certain techniques to the analysis of information, with the objective of coming to more valid and dependable probability judgments. These techniques, particularly one called probabilistic information processing, have been the subject of considerable research and experimentation in recent years. At the outset, it is necessary to emphasize that this discussion will not be concerned with the mathematical aspects of probability theory, even in their most elementary form. Nor will it be concerned with constructing probability and decision "trees" or other specific methodology. Those interested in this aspect of assessing probabilities can find considerable literature which will provide a much more comprehensive and expert description of the techniques than I could attempt to present. We will be concerned with a more general explanation of the techniques, and particularly their apparent advantages and limitations as applied specifically to warning intelligence. Like other techniques, the application of probability theory to intelligence analysis is a tool theoretically capable of assisting both the analyst and the consumer by:

- Assisting the analyst in coming to more accurate or valid judgments, by applying certain probabilistic techniques to the information which he has at hand; and
- Allowing analysts to convey these judgments to consumers in terms which are more precise, less ambiguous and more readily understood.

Complexities of Probability Assessments in Intelligence

It is clear that there are many differences between intelligence problems and the types of problems usually subjected to probability analysis. What is true of most intelligence problems is even more true of warning problems. Although most of these differences are rather obvious, it may be well to list some of them here:

- Most estimates of probability are made on relatively simple occurrences for which there is, usually, a considerable data base, such as weather forecasts, actuarial tables, or even records of race horses. Intelligence forecasts, particularly on topics like warning, are dependent on many types of data, much of it complex, and each occurrence is to some degree unique.
- Probability estimates based on simple or statistical data are in large measure objective, or not subject to personal bias, whereas intelligence judgments are highly subjective. Although it might be possible to prepare

some statistical or historical records which would give us some more objective basis for making warning judgments, analysts usually are dependent on imprecise recollections or subjective feelings about historical precedent.

- In intelligence, again particularly in warning, judgments must be made on incomplete data and on information of unknown or varying degrees of reliability.
- Intelligence forecasts—again, particularly warning judgments—are dependent in large part on our assessment of human decisions, which may or may not yet have been taken, and which, in any case, are enormously complex, variable and to some degree unpredictable.

Probability theorists recognize the subjective nature of intelligence judgments and they do not attempt to apply the science of objective probabilities to what is essentially an opinion as to the likelihood of an occurrence. Rather they apply the theory of subjective probabilities, which apparently dates from the beginning of probability theory in the early eighteenth century. Subjective probability is the degree of belief which an individual holds about something, or how convinced he is that something is true. It is in this meaning that probability theory can be applied to the judgments made by intelligence analysts.

Advantages of Probability Assessments

There are several reasons why an attempt to come to a judgment of probabilities is useful to intelligence analysis, regardless of the techniques used or even how the result is finally expressed. Some of the benefits of probability assessments may be obtained whether or not the probability or likelihood of the occurrence is ultimately expressed as a numerical or percentage factor or in verbal terms. Most proponents of the values of probabilistic analysis, however, are advocates of numerical assessments. Among the advantages which I see, or which proponents have claimed for these methods, are:

- The analysts, or writers of the intelligence forecast, are required to come to some judgment of likelihood—specifically, in the case of warning intelligence, to some assessment of intentions. They are thus precluded from committing one of the most common of warning "crimes," which is to set forth several possible alternatives or courses of action without indicating which is most likely, or simply to report the "facts" or state the capabilities of the adversary without any judgment as to what may occur.
- The policymaker or commander in turn is given some assessment of relative likelihoods to assist him in determining the best course of action. Communication between analysts and policy officials is improved because conclusions are less ambiguous.
- The technique helps to insure that important information is not overlooked, or swept under the carpet by someone because it is inconsistent with an hypothesis. It permits analysts to check the consistency of their

evaluations, to explain or demonstrate how conclusions were reached, and it produces increased confidence in the validity of conclusions.

- It makes for better and more clearly defined hypotheses, so that everyone can debate the same postulated contingencies.

- Since the analyst must consider the relevance of the information to all hypotheses (not just the one he favors), he is less biased, and the technique tends to separate the analysis of new data from preconceptions.

- Analysts are inclined to consider more data as potentially relevant than they otherwise might.

- Studies have shown that the technique overcomes conservatism in assessing odds or probabilities, and leads analysts to a better revision of probabilities when strong positive or negative (diagnostic) evidence is received. They will thus come to higher odds, sometimes much higher odds, than they would directly or intuitively. This is obviously very applicable to warning.

- The technique will expose those who are logically inconsistent or who are giving negative interpretations to data which others consider positive, or vice versa.

- The process of coming to judgments of probabilities serves to bring forth and highlight the differences of opinion that may otherwise not be uncovered or recognized at all, or which, if they are discerned, may be papered over with imprecise or fuzzy language in the interests of seeming "unanimity."

- When such differences become apparent, the group will hopefully attempt to isolate the reasons for the differences, to find out why one individual regards a given course of action as likely (say 60 to 80 percent probability) while another regards it as a less than even possibility (perhaps 35 to 45 percent probability), and still another regards it as quite unlikely (10 to 20 percent). Incidentally, such a spread of opinion is not unusual in indications and warning problems.

- The process of attempting to reconcile these differences will force people to try to explain why they think as they do, or on what evidence, precedent, preconception or "hunch" they have come to their opinions.

- This process of reexamination of the basis of our opinions also should lead to a reexamination of the evidence. As we have also noted, the meticulous examination of the available information is essential to warning, and the failure to have examined all the evidence is one of the primary causes of warning failures. It may develop, in the process of the discussion, that some people have reached their judgments in total ignorance of certain information which others considered absolutely vital evidence (which also is not unusual).

Potential Disadvantages of Probability Assessments

Lest the reader begin to believe that probability assessments are the answer to our prayers in intelligence and will provide us the proverbial crystal ball, it will be well to note also the limitations or even positive disadvantages of such methodology:

- No methodology is a substitute for adequate information and its analysis by competent specialists in the field. The solution is not to turn the raw information over to experts in probabilistic theory for analysis. The analysis must be done by individuals who are substantive experts in the field.
- Undue attention to the mathematical aspects of probability theory and analysis is largely counterproductive. Assessments are not improved by more mathematical refinement when the information was inadequate or imprecise to begin with. The application of statistical techniques only makes the data seem more accurate than they really were.
- It has been shown, as the above would suggest, that the technique works only when there are enough discrete pieces of evidence.
- The application of probability theory to intelligence analysis does not remove the subjectivity from the assessment. Although the procedure may assist in making assessments less subjective, or more objective, at all stages the analyst is making judgments which are not empirically verifiable, but which are the product of his experience, attitudes and expertise in the subject.
- The adequate selection of data for consideration—or, ideally, the inclusion of all available data potentially relevant to the problem—is essential to honest and meaningful results. School problems in probabilistic theory or retrospective analyses that fail to incorporate all the data, including all the spurious or irrelevant data, which the intelligence analyst actually had to consider, can lead to results very wide of the mark, or create an impression radically different from the situation as it actually was.
- The work should be done on a real-time basis and applied to a live crisis if a valid comparison is to be made with more conventional techniques of analysis. The post mortem or retrospective reanalysis of the data often will seem to reach a considerably more accurate assessment of probabilities than was true in the live case. This apparent demonstration of the superiority of the probabilistic method over the intuitive judgment of the analyst may be fallacious since the atmosphere, uncertainties and pressures on the analyst never can be truly recaptured. Retrospective studies also are sometimes the product of simplistic rather than sophisticated understanding of the problem.
- In live crises, time may not permit analysts to undertake any additional tasks beyond keeping up with the incoming flow of traffic and meeting ad hoc requirements. If time allowed, analysts themselves might achieve better results, even without benefit of training in probability techniques.

■ The use of these techniques by themselves would not do much to over-come the problem of inadequate communication between intelligence agencies or between different offices in the same agency, which is a pri-mary cause of inadequate or incomplete analysis in crises. The method may tend to neglect the importance (for warning) of true negative indica-tions (of the developments which have not happened). Perhaps closely related, it seems uncertain whether the application of probabilistic theory to intelligence data will reduce our vulnerability to deception, and indeed it might increase it since the countering of deception involves the rejec-tion of a whole body of seemingly reliable indications as irrelevant to the problem or as having a diametrically opposite meaning.

Breaking Down the Problem

It appears that the application of probabilistic techniques to intelligence and warning analysis is likely to be most useful when the method breaks the prob-lem(s) down into the component parts, which are in fact the indications. I believe that what is important here is that the method simply encourages this type of analysis; the value does not lie in the application of the statistical techniques. Moreover, it does not really matter whether the end result shows a probability of 75 percent versus 65 percent. What does matter is that there has been a more methodical effort to examine the evidence and to interpret it, a more thorough exchange of views concerning the significance of the information, a clearer understanding of where the real differences lie, and a final conclusion which should be both logical and reliable. It is probably not necessary to know or to use any of the modern techniques of probability or decision analysis to go through these processes and to arrive at essentially the same result. The procedures do seem to have some merit, however, as a tool for the analysts, and, since greater attention is being devoted to these methods, it is probably desirable for analysts to have some understanding of them.

Bayes' Theorem

One method which has been frequently applied to intelligence problems is Bayes' Theorem. Most simply stated, this is a procedure whereby the analyst continually is arriving at new odds or probabilities as to the likelihood of an event occurring, based on his assessment of the significance or relevance of new items of information as they are received. The method requires the initial definition of two or more hypotheses, such as: Nation X will attack Nation Y in force; will conduct a limited attack on Nation Y; will not attack Nation Y. (These are often exactly the contingencies with which warning intelligence has to deal.) Some time limit also should be stated (six weeks, six months, a year).

The procedure further requires the assignment of some initial odds to each of the hypotheses, such as: will attack in force (20 percent) will conduct a limited attack (30 percent); will not attack (50 percent). Presumably, some consensus can be reached for these percentages without great difficulty, but in practice this may not be the case. If different individuals start with differing initial odds, their later odds will tend to show a corresponding difference, even though their evaluations of the later evidence are generally similar.

Thereafter, the method consists of examining individual incoming items of information and assessing (1) their reliability (if the information is not established fact) and (2) the relative likelihood that they would or would not occur if one or another hypothesis is true. The likelihood ratio which the analyst comes to is then applied, using a simple mathematical formula, to the previous probability, thereby continually altering the odds as new information comes in. According to its advocates, this procedure has two primary advantages over traditional techniques of evaluation: the analyst is better able to assess the significance or relevance of individual pieces of information than he is of making an assessment of the overall significance of a large body of information; and the method reduces (although it does not eliminate) personal bias by permitting the analyst or the group to separate the evaluation of new evidence from prior opinion about the hypotheses and to make judgments of relative rather than absolute probabilities, leaving the final odds to mathematical logic. Presumably, the result may be a probability assessment either considerably higher, or lower, than might be reached by other or more direct means. A key step in the method is that the analyst must evaluate each piece of information in a systematic manner and weigh its diagnostic or persuasive value—in short, as applied to warning, to assess the indications realistically.

Obviously, the application of Bayes' Theorem to complicated warning problems is by no means as simple as the above suggests. First, there are likely to be major differences of opinion concerning the reliability of given pieces of information and, therefore, the weight, if any, which should be accorded to them. This is apt to be the case with respect to crucial order-of-battle information, in which traditional methods of evaluation are usually far more conservative than the indications method in a period of mounting tensions and troop movements. Thus, information which a warning analyst would wish to include as relevant and important even though not yet "confirmed," might be rejected by an order-of-battle analyst as not worth consideration since it does not meet his standards of "acceptance." There are many other problems in the selection and evaluation of the incoming information which no methodology is going to solve, so long as subjective judgments must be introduced. In the end, the application of the theorem independently by two different analysts, or groups of analysts (one traditional or conservative in their approach, and the other more imaginative or "indications-oriented") might only confirm statistically what was already apparent—that there is a wide spread in their opinions. It has been pointed out that, if the analyst finds he is applying probability ratios to certain developments which are bringing him to higher odds than he is comfortable with, he is simply going to lower his assessments so that he obtains a figure more compatible with how he really "feels" about it.

Since the business of warning analysts is to examine and evaluate indications, it would seem likely that they will tend to reach odds at least as high by their own methods of indications compilation and analysis as they would by the application of Bayes' Theorem, provided they tended to think in numerical probabilities at all. A retrospective application of Bayes' techniques to the information related to the Chinese intervention in the Korean war came to a 3:1 probability of major intervention as of mid-November. Since the method was not applied to the live situation, nor was any attempt made in 1950 to come to any statement of numerical odds, it is impossible to say what the range of individual opinions or a consensus or "average" might have been at the time. It is certain, however, that the range would have been considerable (since many people were convinced that the Chinese would not intervene), and it is my opinion that the warning analysts who had done the most exhaustive indications research would have given odds higher than 3 to 1—perhaps as high as 5 to 1 in favor of major intervention as of mid-November 1950.

University experiments on non-intelligence problems have shown that analysts usually will come to higher probabilities of an event occurring, after receiving and assessing a number of pieces of positive information, if they used Bayes' Theorem than if they made an intuitive judgment of the new odds. In other words, the use of the method tended to make them less conservative in their assessments. Applying the same rationale to intelligence problems, one comes to a logical and simple conclusion. The application of Bayes' Theorem clearly should yield the highest probabilities in those cases in which there is the greatest amount of highly reliable and positive evidence concerning both a large-scale buildup of military capabilities and an abundance of positive political and propaganda indications. The method thus seemingly favors factual and cumulative indications analysis as opposed to other approaches to warning, which place greater weight on such factors as past performance of the nation in question, assessments of the views of its leaders and the risks they will take, and the possibility that the numerous "positive indications" are only bluff, contingency preparations or a show of force.

The Delphi Procedure

This is another technique designed to promote more objective or scientific analysis. It uses a group method but attempts to overcome the tendency in nearly all groups for one or more individuals to dominate the discussion by virtue of rank, official position, presumed expertise, overbearing personality or tendency to talk too much. Thus, it initially seeks anonymous opinions from the participants—an obvious advantage in encouraging independent judgments from those who are fearful of their superiors or timid in the expression of their views. The anonymous responses are then fed back to the participants, or the anonymous opinions of others may be sought, and the initial members may then modify their estimates based on further consideration. The technique probably does bring individual opinions closer together—toward a norm—and tends to prevent conclusions from being based on the wishes of authority. To this extent it may be helpful in indications analysis. At the same time, it does not eliminate the tendencies of groups toward conformity, and it may encourage too many people to cast votes on subjects which they have not analyzed in depth. Since off-the-cuff judgments by those who have not examined all the evidence are one of our major problems in warning, it is obvious that the technique should be applied with care in this forum. Often, the independent view of an individual warning analyst proves to be more accurate than any amount of consensus or examination of others' views.

Low Probabilities and Critical Dangers

In warning, we are dealing with a range of potential dangers to ourselves and our allies, some of which can result in minimal damage to our interests and some of which are potentially disastrous. An example of a threat involving relatively little danger to our interests—even though it would be desirable if possible to warn of it—would be the sabotage of a military depot. Obviously, the greatest of all potential disasters would be the all-out nuclear attack on the U.S. and our allies.

Viewed in the abstract, the probabilities we estimate for any given occurrence—whether expressed as a percentage figure or in some descriptive phrase—would seem to carry about the same weight or importance as the identical probabilities for another occurrence. Thus, if we say that we think that the odds are about even that some country will complete a new road to the border within the next year, it presumably carries the same degree of conviction, and will have the same impact on the policymaker, as if we said that the odds are about even that it would attack in the same time period. Of course, merely to state the problem this way is to demonstrate that the two statements of likelihood, although identical, carry far different messages to the policymaker. And the difference obviously derives from the importance and potential dangers of the two courses of action.

In some instances, even to raise the possibility of an occurrence in positive terms, however qualified, could constitute a most serious warning. One type of intelligence assessment, frowned on by many, is that which sets forth the evidence and logic against a hostile action by an adversary, but then adds, "Nonetheless, we cannot totally discount that he may attack." Objections to such assessments, which are probably well taken in most cases, often are based on the grounds that the writers are attempting to take out insurance against all contingencies so that they will be able to claim, no matter what happens, that they predicted it—if only as an outside chance. The statistician would probably shun this phraseology because it is imprecise—what probabilities do you mean by "cannot totally discount"? And many would say that the phrase is valueless because it tells the reader nothing, and that there is no contingency which we can totally discount. But suppose we were to say, "A nuclear attack on the United States cannot be totally discounted" (within the next month, or six months, or year, or any time frame)? The mere reference to such a possibility clearly would carry the most portentous warning that the gravest apprehensions existed in the Intelligence Community. Even during the Cuban missile crisis, no such intelligence judgment was ever reached (as "insurance" or for any other reason).

In short, it is not the odds in themselves which determine the importance of the warning judgment to the policymaker, but the potential consequences of the action if it should occur. There are dangers which, even though remote in any scale of probabilities, will still warrant the most serious consideration and probable action by the policymaker. For these reasons, the Intelligence Community— and correctly so—gives far greater care to weighing evidence and the phrasing of its warning or conclusions in such circumstances than it does in less dangerous situations. It usually will also be inclined to be more cautious in these circumstances than when the potential consequences are less serious.

Other Factors Affecting the Warning Odds

Some of the seeming disadvantages or limitations of probability assessments for warning might, it seems to me, be overcome by a combination of these techniques with some other techniques for indications analysis which have been suggested elsewhere in this work. Some guidelines were suggested for assessing the meaning of evidence in a warning situation. Somewhat condensed, the five basic guidelines were:

1. Is the national leadership committed to the achievement of the objective in question?

2. Is the objective potentially attainable, or the situation potentially soluble, by military means?

3. Does the military capability exist, and/or does the scale of the military buildup meet doctrinal criteria for offensive action?

4. Have the political options run out?

5. Is the risk factor low, or at least tolerable?

If the leadership of the state in question is following a rational course of action, the answers to the above questions should determine whether or not it opts for military action. As noted, if the answer to all the above is yes, the probabilities should be high that military action will be undertaken. Probabilistic methodology, as applied to decisionmaking problems, takes account of potential losses or risks attendant on various courses of action, as do the above key questions. Thus, a high risk factor will tend to lower the likelihood that a military course of action will be adopted, even if the answer to all other questions is positive, unless of course the leadership is so desperate for a solution of the issue that it will take the risks involved. Or, unless it has perhaps underestimated the risks, as did Khrushchev in 1962.

It might be useful, at least on an experimental basis, in applying Bayesian or other probabilistic methods to specific indications, also to apply the foregoing questions to each relevant piece of information. That is, each pertinent military indication would be assessed as to whether or not it brought the military forces closer to the strength and deployments required for offensive action. Each relevant political development would be evaluated as raising or lowering the probabilities that the leadership a) is committed to attainment of the objective, and b) believes that its political options have run out.

Conclusion

The greatest utility of probabilistic techniques is in requiring the analyst or the group to examine evidence more thoroughly and more objectively, and in assisting them to distinguish more clearly between the evidence that is truly relevant or pertinent to various hypotheses and that which is not. It is less important what precise numerical probabilities are finally reached than that the analytic process be thorough and as divorced from preconceptions and subjective opinions as possible. The expression of the final judgment in terms of numerical probabilities may be helpful, but it is better not to have precise percentage judgments if the process of reaching them is slipshod or inexact, or based on too little information to be meaningful.

Logic, backed by some post-mortem probability studies, leads to a conclusion that probabilistic techniques would have improved intelligence judgments in cases in which we had large amounts of positive evidence but in which no firm judgments of probability were reached. Two conspicuous examples are the Chinese intervention in Korea and the invasion of Czechoslovakia. It is uncertain that these techniques would improve our odds or judgments when the evidence is insufficient and we are lacking specific critical data. One study of the application of Bayes' Theorem to the evidence that was available prior to the Cuban crisis found, for example, that the technique did not result in a positive assessment that strategic missiles were being introduced into the country. It did, however, bring the chances to even money by the end of the first week of October (a week before the missiles were discovered) and furthermore showed steadily mounting odds during the preceding weeks. The odds in mid-September by this method were more than 3 to 1 against the strategic missile hypothesis (which was consistent with the national estimate reached at the time), thus reflecting a dramatic change in odds in about three weeks. It would seem doubtful that probabilistic techniques would be of much help to us in assessing the timing of operations, or that they would help guard against deception.

Chapter 9

IMPROVING WARNING ASSESSMENTS: SOME CONCLUSIONS

FACTORS INFLUENCING JUDGMENTS AND REPORTING

Warning intelligence of course is not produced in a vacuum, divorced from the rest of the intelligence process or from any number of other influences. These other factors, at least in some instances, will determine what is made of "facts" and even sometimes what facts may be reported at all. The following set of concepts, although far from being an exhaustive list, highlight some of the more important factors that influence judgments.

The "Climate of Opinion"

By "climate of opinion" is meant the prevailing attitudes in any country on any major subject and specifically, for our purposes, attitudes about other states and particular international problems. The climate of opinion on such matters is not necessarily the same within the government as in public opinion polls. Although the two over any period of time will tend to run parallel, the policy and intelligence elements of the government may on occasion be well ahead of public opinion in their perception of the attitudes or intentions of foreign powers, whether these intentions be hostile or accommodating. Further, the executive branch of the government of course is in a strong position to influence or change the attitudes of other countries toward us through its conduct of foreign affairs. Although the national leadership in the end is responsive to public opinion, it can also do much to shape it, and in the short term may even run counter to it on international issues. This point is made here only to emphasize that the government, and its intelligence services, are not just captives of a prevailing popular "climate of opinion" as is sometimes implied in discussions of this question. In large measure, they can have an independent "climate of opinion" and they can do much to shape the public climate. At the same time, governmental and public opinion on major international issues are not likely in a democracy to be very divergent over an extended period. Nor are members of the intelligence services likely to have a view of other states, and of their leaders' intentions, that differs substantially from that which is expressed by the public media or other educated and informed public opinion.

It is very difficult, even with the best intentions of maintaining an open mind and evaluating the evidence objectively, to set aside such preconceptions of how the other fellow will behave. And even the individual who is able to do so will probably have the greatest difficulty in persuading others. The atmosphere will probably be slow to change, and it may require some dramatic event, even a national catastrophe, for a revised "climate of opinion" to gain general acceptance. Pending that acceptance, indications of it are likely to have tough going even when they are substantial in quantity and quality.

There is no doubt that there was an atmosphere or climate in both intelligence and policy circles in 1950 which was hostile to acceptance of the idea that North Korea would attack South Korea and that the Chinese would intervene. I believe that it is erroneous, however, to attribute this atmosphere to any illusions about the good intentions or non-hostile attitudes of North Korea, China, or the Soviet Union. The climate was more a product of a number of other things, including: the lack of recognition at that time of the concept of limited war; the lack of experience in U.S. intelligence in indications analysis and the deficiencies in interagency collaboration and analysis; widespread preconceptions by Chinese analysts that the Chinese would attack Taiwan rather than intervene in Korea; a reluctance to believe that the Chinese would take on U.S. forces; and to some degree the reluctance of U.S. policy and military leaders to accept intelligence which might have required a change in policy, and of the intelligence services to tell them so. (The U.S. had a major command and control problem. The awe in which General MacArthur was held and his unwillingness to listen to guidance from Washington were clearly major reasons that the intelligence which was available failed to have an impact on policy.)

Recency of a Major Crisis or Intelligence Failure

There is nothing that elevates the status of warning intelligence or the receptiveness of higher authority to indications analysis as much as a major crisis that intelligence failed to predict or in which the indications were inadequately assessed. Almost invariably, postmortems are initiated to ascertain where we went wrong, special committees are appointed to reexamine the evidence, and indications intelligence becomes the method of the hour. Even when the indications were not very good, or highly contradictory, or the adversary's course of action was truly illogical, investigations or other critiques usually manage to make much of the various fragments of information which were given inadequate attention when they came in or which pointed to the possibility that the adversary would take the course of action which he actually did. In these circumstances, indications are not necessarily judged on their individual merits or in relation to the total picture, but by the criterion that they were received at all. The warning analyst, particularly if he had predicted the event in advance or had compiled an impressive list of indications which was ignored, basks in his new-found prestige. People come to see him who had ignored him before; his think pieces suddenly are in demand; he is asked to contribute to postmortems or other studies. The indicator list is hauled out and revised. More consumers want it. The management is assured that the intelligence process is leaving no stone unturned to insure that such a warning "failure" will not occur again, and that every indication will be meticulously examined. We are going to take a "worst case" look at everything from now on.

It is all very heady while it lasts. And it will probably be short-lived. In the meantime, however, an extraordinary change may be manifest in the intelligence process. The climate of opinion has altered. There is real apprehension that the perpetrator of the recent surprise may be plotting more evil deeds. Not only is each indication likely to receive far more attention than before, but indications considered too low-grade before to warrant consideration now receive attention. More collection is initiated to insure that we have not missed anything. Other countries, suddenly awakened to the crisis, flood us with their raw information and analyses. Across the board, the attitude is receptive to warning. Things that would never have been reported to higher authorities now are deemed worthy of their attention, lest something be missed.

This discussion is not meant to suggest that intelligence goes off its rocker in these situations, but only that the changed atmosphere does indeed engender an entirely new perception of the values of indications analysis. Much of this new perception may come from higher level policy officials. Sometimes, warning analysts themselves have been astonished by the changed atmosphere and have found themselves playing the role of trying to dampen down flaps. One such occurrence was the revolution in opinion concerning the intentions of the Soviet Union following the invasion of Czechoslovakia. Many who had been the most surprised by that action—that is, who had been the least receptive to indications of it—suddenly became the most concerned that the USSR might now invade Romania as well. One senior intelligence official observed that we had been in error in not taking the "worst case" view of Czechoslovakia, and we must now do so for Romania. Yet, curiously, there was almost no evidence of any Soviet troop buildup along the border with Romania, and no indications that the USSR was moving more forces into Hungary or any troops whatever into Bulgaria. The military situation thus was almost diametrically opposite to the massive buildup of combat forces that had preceded the invasion of Czechoslovakia and in no way warranted anything like the degree of concern accorded the Czechoslovak situation—a fact, however, that did not preclude prolonged concern over Soviet military intentions toward Romania. Had the same atmosphere prevailed prior to the invasion of Czechoslovakia, there would seem little doubt that much firmer judgments of Soviet intentions would have been forthcoming.

This phenomenon is characteristic of crises. At the peak of the Cuban missile crisis, fragmentary information which would never in normal circumstances have been reported to higher authorities was surfaced for direct reporting to the White House. Even when analysts were at a loss to interpret the significance of these tidbits and would normally have deferred comment for further information, supervisors were encouraging the reporting of all information of even tenuous potential significance.

It is obviously unlikely in these circumstances that any indications are going to be overlooked. The tendency rather will be the opposite—to impart undue significance to relatively unimportant or unconfirmed information, and to issue warning of possible ominous developments on the basis of less evidence than would be the case in normal times. Conclusions in these circumstances may adopt phrases like: "Although we have no evidence (or firm indications) that X will attack Y, it could do so with little warning."

The Attitude of Intelligence Chiefs and Policymakers

The attitudes and demands of higher authorities obviously carry heavy weight in the determination of what intelligence is reported and how it is reported. Policy officials, if they have sufficient rank, are in position to request almost any type of study, on any subject, within reason, from the Intelligence Community, and they usually are promptly and competently served. Many such studies of course are of a long-term in-depth nature, particularly those intended to assist in the determination of military policies. Many other requests are fulfilled by special briefings or analytic papers. Requests requiring interagency assessments of an analytic nature usually are fulfilled through special national estimates. The special interests of policy officials on a continuing basis may also be reflected, to some degree, in the content of daily intelligence publications. In the specific field of warning, intelligence chiefs and policy officials always can request special meetings of watch committees or similar analytic groups, or ask that they give consideration to specific problems or areas in their regular reports; this can be without regard to what the operative charter nominally calls for.

One of the most important things that policy officials can do to obtain the intelligence they need is simply to ask the right questions. No amount of diligence or initiative at the working level can do as much to generate interest or reporting on a subject as a few judicious questions or requests for specific lines of research from the top. Many an analyst has sought in vain to get some thesis or analysis moved upward through the system, until some policy official expressed an interest in the same subject or advanced the same thesis. There is little question also that the senior officials in both intelligence and policy who do the greatest amount of in-depth reading ("homework") are usually in the best position to ask the most penetrating questions. Those who suffer from an inherent distrust of their own intelligence services (for example, Winston Churchill) have sometimes done the most to prod those services to their most productive and imaginative performance. Officials who are responsive to imaginative and perceptive analyses, and who do not reject such work when it is presented to them, are the most likely to obtain meaningful warning judgments. The official who demands an inordinate degree of proof or is contemptuous of anything but established "facts" will probably discourage the type of analysis or reasoning that is usually essential for meaningful warning. Even if the policy official does not himself generate requests or ask many questions, his general attitude and willingness or unwillingness to listen to new ideas or interpretations can do much to determine the kinds and quality of intelligence reported to him.

The Extent of Public Knowledge or Press Discussion

Any discussion of this subject would be incomplete without some recognition of the impact on intelligence reporting and policymakers of what is appearing in the newspapers or other media, and the extent to which the general public is aware of, or concerned about, the situation. In some degree, this is a misleading argument, since the press in large part reflects the information available to, and the concern of, the government on any particular subject. Thus, if the Department of State or the President's advisors are preoccupied with the possibility of an outbreak of hostilities in the Middle East, the chances are good that reporters will be briefed on the subject, even if the cause for alarm is classified data to which the press would not normally have access on its own. Inspired articles and deliberate leaks, as well as the inquiries and research of reporters themselves, constitute a considerable part of what appears in the press in the field of foreign affairs. It is only when the government makes a strong effort to prevent leaks so as not to tip its hand—as in the week preceding President Kennedy's announcement of the discovery of the missiles in Cuba—that revelations to the press normally can be contained at all in this country. Therefore, if the press is surprised by some unforeseen international development, including war, the chances are good that the U.S. government also was surprised, the Intelligence Community included. Over the years, there has been a trend toward the release (or leaking) of greater and greater amounts of nominally classified intelligence to the press, some of it at considerable jeopardy to intelligence sources. In large measure, press reporting does not constitute independent corroboration of government-held data, but only mirrors it.

Nonetheless, the press often does have independent sources in foreign countries, or undertakes special analyses of critical international problems which contribute substantially to knowledge and interpretation of the subject. It is also, of course, the primary channel for dissemination of official and unofficial announcements, documents and the like, as well as current events in general—which constitute a substantial portion of the information with which intelligence deals. Prominent front-page coverage of some international development will attract more attention from far more people than any intelligence write-up, and will probably engender requests from policy officials for comments or further analysis. Sustained press attention to a critical situation is almost certain to raise the level of concern and to influence intelligence reporting on the subject. It is probably true that if the responsible press is forecasting war, it is almost unnecessary for intelligence to alert the policy official. For example, it is doubtful that classified information added much, other than more specific military details and some private opinions of statesmen, to the overwhelming warning conveyed in the world press of the coming of World War II.

GENERAL WARNING PRINCIPLES

Most observers have a vastly oversimplified view of warning intelligence and tend to view it as a compilation of facts which should lead to an either-or conclusion, or as something which we either do or do not have. Warning on the contrary is a highly complex judgmental process in which the collection and compiling of the available evidence is only a portion of the problem, and in which our preconceptions, together with the enemy's efforts to deceive and mislead us, are equally if not more important.

So-called warning failures usually result primarily from inaccurate or incomplete analysis of the available information, rather than from deficiencies in collection, although good collection obviously is essential to warning. The best judgments do not necessarily result from bringing more people into the assessment process, and particularly those who are not familiar with all the available information. The most accurate warning judgments often are made by a minority of individuals. The coming of most conflicts is much longer term than most people believe, and the first indications of the approaching crisis are often received (if not discerned) months before the conflict erupts. As a research problem, warning involves an in-depth, cumulative compiling and analysis of these trends and developments rather than an excessive concentration on the latest or most current information, which can be highly misleading. The most difficult determination often is the timing of attacks, which is flexible and subject to change and is more easily concealed than the buildup of the military capability.

Both new analysts and more experienced ones, as well as their supervisors and policy officials, should have an understanding of warning and where our real problems are likely to lie. There is need for a continuous process of education in this field. But there is no assurance that any educational program or techniques will ensure us warning in the future. We will all remain vulnerable and fallible in varying degrees in each new warning crisis. There is no guarantee that we shall "have warning" the next time. We can never hope to solve our warning problems but only to make some progress in understanding what they are so that perhaps we will be less likely to make the same errors another time.

Each new warning failure, complete or partial, brings forth its rash of postmortem studies and recommendations for changes that will improve our "warning capabilities." Rarely, if ever, is there anything new in these recommendations, other than slight variations in the proposals for a revamping of the organizational structure. The suggestions for improving our warning almost invariably include some of the points repeatedly made in this book. Just as the mistakes made in each warning failure are old ones, so are the proposals for doing something about it.

Nothing is going to remove the uncertainties of the warning problem. There is no way, short of being able to read the adversary's mind, that we can be confident that our warning judgments, or even many of our "facts," are going to be correct. Even the finest collection and analysis cannot insure that we will have accurate insight into the enemy's intentions, particularly if he is using sophisticated security and deception measures to conceal them. Moreover, it is a virtual certainty that individuals will continue, as they always have, to come to different conclusions, even diametrically different conclusions, as to what the evidence means. As we have been surprised in the past, we shall be surprised again in the future.

MOST FREQUENT IMPEDIMENTS TO WARNING

The tendencies discussed in each of the following sections frequently inhibit coming to judgments of another country's intentions or lead to incorrect assessments. But as indicated, we can make some intellectual or behavioral response to each area of concern. The result can be a more professional approach to the intelligence warning responsibility.

Inadequate Examination of the Evidence

It is almost impossible to give too much stress to the importance of the most meticulous and exhaustive examination of all available information prior to reaching warning judgments. It is erroneous to presume that all research will automatically be accomplished in crisis or budding crisis situations, or that the organization and distribution of work within the office or offices involved is necessarily adequate for the purpose. Much good research or imaginative thinking on indications and warning problems may not be published or receive much hearing unless positive steps are taken to insure that such ideas are surfaced or examined. The inadequate examination of available evidence has been a contributing cause to nearly every warning failure, and in some cases should probably be considered the major cause of failure. It is essential to warning that enough people, and the right people, be assigned to the research effort; that management at all levels encourage this effort; and that judgments be reached in the light of a thorough examination of all relevant information and hypotheses.

Inadequate Understanding of Evidence or Precedent

It is possible to examine all available information and still not to understand its significance in relation to intentions. This may be because the information is fragmentary, conflicting, ambiguous, or of uncertain reliability or significance—in which case, of course, it may not be possible to understand it, at least pending further information. But it may also be that there are people who understand it or can interpret it, or who are knowledgeable about some obscure details of the enemy's doctrine or procedures, or terminology, or how he has behaved before. Some relevant information is likely to be from highly classified sources—such as covertly acquired military documents—and therefore has been extremely restricted in distribution. Some developments are likely to be highly technical and understood by very few persons, but their interpretation and integration with other information can be critical to an understanding of what is really happening.

The recognition and interpretation of true indications—those activities that are bona fide preparations for hostilities rather than exercises or other peacetime activities—can be heavily dependent on this type of detailed knowledge and expertise. So can a recognition that the adversary is engaging in a military deception effort, a perception which may be absolutely vital to warning. It is essential not to lose this kind of expertise when it is most needed. In warning episodes, the need of the community for expert assistance in a whole range of military subjects—and to a lesser extent, political—skyrockets.

Excessive Preoccupation with Current Intelligence

It is possible that the single most prevalent misconception about warning is that the latest information is necessarily the most important, or that warning will be insured (or at least made much more likely) if only collection can be speeded up and information communicated more rapidly to more alert centers. The effects of this type of preoccupation with the currency of information are likely to be twofold: long-term, basic intelligence and in-depth analysis tend to suffer both in the allocation of personnel and in prestige; and the cumulative analysis of indications tends to be forgotten in favor of portraying the latest information on charts or display boards in situation rooms. From this, it is but a step to accepting the view that what the adversary is doing this minute is the most important indication of his intentions, or that information which is more than 24 hours old is valueless or at least of minor value to warning.

But this is not strategic warning—and excessive attention to current information tends to obscure the significance of strategic, long-term actions by a potential adversary. The whole pattern of what the adversary has been doing to get ready for major military operations over a period of weeks and months and the political and diplomatic preparations that he has taken to support the military plans are overshadowed by the seeming lull in activity which so often precedes a dramatic action. In this atmosphere, it is easy to believe that the adversary has changed his mind and called it all off. "The situation is quiet."

Warning is cumulative, not merely current. Intelligence reporting at all times must take care to insure that the consumer knows the cumulative background and understands that the latest indication is but one of many which in their totality give us insight into what may occur.

Predominance of Preconceptions over Facts

It is now widely recognized by professionals that this is one of the most serious obstacles to the issuance of warning. Studies by social scientists have confirmed what indications analysts have learned from experience—that judgments are often reached on the basis of prior concepts as much or even more than on an objective examination of the factual evidence. This is particularly true if there is a widespread prevailing climate of opinion that dictates a different conclusion from the available facts. As a general rule, the more widespread and firmly held an opinion is, the more facts will be required to demonstrate the inaccuracy of the widely held premise. In warning, we are often pressed for time and we are short on dependable facts. Thus, both time and the nature of our evidence will tend to work against the analytical acceptance of new courses of behavior by our adversaries, particularly if that course appears to be radically different from what we had come to expect.

Failure to Come to Clear Judgments

This is one of the common inadequacies in the warning process and may involve at least two types of mistakes. The first is the failure to follow through from the evidence to some logical conclusion as to what it means in factual terms. The second is to fail to come to any judgment as to the significance of the development in terms of the adversary's likely course of actions; that is, to come to no judgment as to intent. A warning judgment is a culmination of a series of lesser judgments, each one of which may be important to the final conclusion as to intent. The first judgment to be made, after the evidence is collected, is that the facts being reported have some potential relevance—either positive or negative—to the adversary's ultimate course of action. The failure to come to judgments of enemy intentions at all, and to limit the comments to a statement of capabilities, may arise from just carelessness or inadequate consideration of the impact of the text on the reader. But it may be used also to cover up real differences of opinion as to the intentions of the adversary.

Misjudgments of Timing

One of the greatest hazards in warning is the attempt to predict when military operations or other hostile action may be initiated. Numerous historical examples demonstrate that, even when predictions of forthcoming action have been quite accurate, estimates of timing have often been wide of the mark. This situation can result in false alarms (the "cry wolf" syndrome) and an ensuing relaxation of alertness by the time the attack occurs. Less frequent, perhaps, is the apparent initiation of the attack before it was expected; this misperception may result from deliberate deception from the adversary.

The Reluctance to Believe: the Search for "Other Explanations"

Those who have never worked on indications problems might be amazed at the seeming inability of some people to cope with apparently obvious facts, and their reluctance to believe what appears to be staring them in the face. These individuals have an aptitude for finding possible explanations for the facts at hand other than the obvious one. Indeed, this is the favored method of undermining a warning judgment when there are just too many facts to push them aside altogether. The technique is simple. It involves offering any other explanation, no matter how implausible, to account for each and every indication—other than an ominous one that the adversary might be planning some hostile act.

The proclivity for offering other explanations for potentially ominous developments can be most damaging when a roundup of indications is involved, including a number of developments and reports from sources of varying reliability and whose significance or purpose has often not been firmly established. Very often, these cumulative roundups of indications have proved to be authentic barometers of impending action, even though they may have been inaccurate in some particular details. To reject this type of analysis out-of-hand by offering some other reason for every item can defeat the warning process when it may be most important to national security or the security of friendly military forces.

Warning assessments are sometimes obvious and offered us on a platter which all can perceive, but not often. They are usually subtle, elusive, and dependent on the most imaginative analysis of available information and perceptive insight into the adversary's state of mind. There are few indications for which some palliative or non-alarming explanation cannot be found, if one searches hard enough. If we are to have warning when we most need it, we must insure that we do not permit those who are the most conservative or most reluctant to believe new information or imaginative interpretations to have the last word, or to destroy the fabric of indications thread by thread.

The Reluctance to Alarm

Not surprisingly, there is a considerable reluctance—which possibly increases the higher one moves in the governmental hierarchy—to bother one's superiors with problems that can be solved at a lower level, or to alarm them unnecessarily. It is much easier for working level analysts, who do not have responsibility for doing anything about potentially nasty situations, to come to conclusions that hostile or other surprise action is impending, or may be, than it is for those higher up who must directly warn the policy official or initiate action themselves. The more serious or dangerous the action the policy official may have to take, the more proof he is likely to want that it is necessary. On the other hand, if there is nothing that can or should be done about the situation, which is sometimes the case, it can be argued that there is no point in alarming senior officials. Thus, the Intelligence Community is restrained in some measure, both when action may be required and when it may not, from issuing warning which it either cannot "prove" or which for some reason may be premature, unnecessary or superfluous. This restraint of course will tend to increase if intelligence has issued one or more false warnings (cried wolf) and the policy official has been critical of this action and has made it clear that he does not want to hear anything more of that nature.

There may be a communications or credibility gap between intelligence and policy in this matter. I have found, in discussing this subject with a number of individuals, mostly outside or new to the intelligence system, that many believe that intelligence tends to be alarmist and to issue unnecessary warnings, in order to be on the safe side. Thus, the "warnee," who is expecting this behavior, tends to discount or to play down the import of what he is being told. He feels that he is being over-warned. Policy officials generally, in this view, distrust intelligence in some measure, not because it is incompetent or lacks imagination, but because it is self-serving and seeks to justify its usefulness and importance by stirring up unnecessary flaps.

Insofar as this opinion prevails among policy officials, it is gravely in error and a potential cause of much misunderstanding. In my considerable experience with this type of problem, it has been evident that the Intelligence Community tends to be extremely cautious in reaching alarming conclusions and to pick its words with great care so as not to appear to be nervous or unprofessional. The generally prevailing view is that the sophisticated intelligence analyst should never get excited, never lose his cool, and never use colorful adjectives or other strong phrases to convey his meaning. Rather, he should play down the situation, appear calm and detached. The greatest sin of all is to be alarmist, or to rock the boat.

Thus, the true professional will under-warn, even to the point that the recipient will have to read between the lines or ask for further information to realize that he is being warned at all. I do not believe that this exaggerates the case. Any review of "warnings" issued to policy officials over a period of years will show that they have tended to be most conservative and restrained in wording, to avoid forthright predictions of impending disaster, and in some cases to warn indirectly by ambiguity, omission or subtleties—some of which may be lost on the consumer. It is a precept of warning that the policymaker must know that he has been warned, and he may have an honest difference with the intelligence writer who considers that his moderate and qualified warning should have been adequate to get the point across.

Although intelligence personnel would probably be reluctant to admit it, they probably are inclined to withhold firm warning when they either believe that the policymaker will not take action on the issue, or in their view should not. The limited and restrained warnings of possible North Korean attack on South Korea in the spring of 1950 almost certainly were occasioned in part by opinions in intelligence that the U.S. would not do anything about such an attack. Intelligence tends to respond strongly and in volume on matters which it knows the policy official is interested in and plans to take action on, while it will give less attention to subjects which it believes, rightly or wrongly, will not require policy action. The degree of alarm over developments is directly related to whether we may become involved or not.

Where the Intelligence Community considers that U.S. action would be risky or undesirable it also tends to greater restraint in its warning judgments. The rationale for this is that no action on our part is called for and therefore it is unnecessary, or undesirable, to alert the policy official unduly. The conclusion appears almost inescapable that this attitude lay behind some of the reluctance to issue firm warning of a Soviet invasion of Czechoslovakia, in which a U.S. or NATO military alert might have been counterproductive.

The Fear of Being Wrong

A primary *reason* for the reluctance to warn appears to be the fear of being wrong. This tendency may also be termed "the need to appear to have been right." This is a product of natural human inclination (who wants to appear wrong?) and the types of pressures put on intelligence personnel to be accurate and not to mislead their superiors. It is bad enough to make a mistake on some minor factual matter; even these can reflect adversely on the agency's performance, particularly if some publicity is given the error. It is obviously much worse to be wrong on matters which could have a grave impact on national policy decisions, the security of military forces, or other important issues. There are few intelligence questions on which it is probably more important to be right, both for the community and the individual agencies, than warning. We think: better to be ambiguous, or to phrase warning in terms of capabilities (which we tend to think we do have a firm handle on), or to project the idea that the adversary has not yet come to a decision as to what he is going to do. This way we will be able to appear right, or at least we will not be demonstrably wrong, no matter which way it goes.

I can attest that this is an extremely compelling factor in influencing the wording of warning judgments and probably the principal contributing factor to excessive caution. It afflicts even those who tend toward a firm positive judgment. What they are willing to say in private informal conversations and off-the-record statements is often considerably tempered when they have to put it in writing as formal intelligence opinion. After all, there is a lot we are not sure about, and the adversary always could change his mind. Let's hedge our bets a little and insert a few "possibly's" into the judgment. I recall a discussion with a very competent intelligence officer who held an important supervisory position during the Czechoslovak crisis in 1968. After the invasion, I asked him why it was, with all the evidence at hand, the Intelligence Community could not come to a firm, positive judgment that a Soviet invasion was probable (not inevitable, just probable). His reply was that it was the fear of being wrong. I agree.

The intelligence analyst is also influenced by the fact that errors of commission almost always are considered more reprehensible than errors of omission. It is usually safer to fail to predict something which does happen than to make a positive prediction that something will happen and it does not. In the first case, it can always be maintained that there was insufficient evidence to come to a positive judgment. Who can "prove" that that was wrong? Most professional warning analysts, however, take the position that it is better to have alerted policy officials and the military command several times in error than to fail to do so when the hostile action actually occurs. They argue that it would have been better to have forecast the Chinese intervention in Korea erroneously than to contribute even indirectly to the disaster which resulted at least in part from the failure to warn. Evidence of the value of overcoming the fear of being wrong is rare, however, and tends to be forgotten in the long intervals between crises. The next time, caution may again prevail and those who fail to issue firm warning will likely suffer no setbacks to their careers. After all, they just did not have enough evidence.

✿✿✿✿✿✿✿✿✿✿✿✿✿

As intelligence collection becomes more sophisticated, voluminous and expensive, and devices multiply for the rapid reporting and community-wide exchange and display of the latest information, we must take care that we do not lose sight of what warning really is: the considered judgment of the finest analytic minds available, based on an exhaustive and objective review of all available indications, which is conveyed to the policy official in sufficiently convincing language that he is persuaded of its validity and takes appropriate action to protect the national interest.

Index

I

M

Medical Preparations 67-68
Middle East/Arab-Israeli Conflicts 89-90, 95, 101, 114-115
Military Indications and Warning 51-76
    Capabilities17-24
    Combat Preparations/Deployments 69-76
    Nature & Importance of 51-53
    Order of Battle (see separate heading)
    Understanding How a Nation Goes to War 53-55
Mobilization 60-61, 64

O

Order of Battle (OB) 43-46, 55-60, 61-62, 152
    Conventional Methodology 55-58
    Indications Analysis of 58-60
    Needed: A Voice for Warning 61-62

P

Pearl Harbor Attack 89, 121-122, 123, 132
Poland: Soviet Forces in 59-60
Policy/Policymakers
    Intelligence in Support of 140-145
    Requirements of 136-140
Political Factors in Warning 77-94
    Ambiguity of 77-79
    Critical Role of 79-81
    Diplomacy and Foreign Policy 89-90
    Importance of Particular Issues 85-87
    Likelihood of Conflict 84
    Perception Fundamental 81-83, 84-89
Press Coverage of Intelligence 161
Probabilities 12-13, 20
    Analytic Procedures 151-154
    Assessing 145-146
    Low Probabilities and Critical Dangers 154-155
    Probabilistic Information Processing 146-151
Propaganda 90-92, 95

R

Ridgeway, General Matthew 88
Romania 159

31888530R00106

Made in the USA
Lexington, KY
29 April 2014